WOMADIC WANDERS

Stories of a compulsive traveller

GERDETTE ROONEY

www.gerdetterooney.com
Rooney, Gerdette (author)
Womadic Wanders: Stories of a compulsive traveller
ISBN: 978-0-6489906-3-5 Travel Memoirs
Some names have been changed to protect the privacy of
certain individuals.
All photos and cover design by Gerdette Rooney

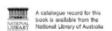 A catalogue record for this
book is available from the
National Library of Australia

GERDETTE ROONEY was born in Monaghan, Ireland. She has worked as a radiographer in many places including Soweto, Baghdad, Saudi Arabia and Australia and taught English in Japan. When not working, she travelled solo with her rucksack and camera, has been known as 'The Lady in the Van', hiked mountains with a tent and squashed into many shared taxis in Africa. She currently lives in Sydney, Australia and is still plotting new adventures.

For my much-loved nieces and
nephews, Hannah, Dara, Matthew,
Andrew, Ciaran and Cathal

Maybe it will be said when I'm gone,
'She didn't write the book!
Didn't stop!
Just took off again'.

Gerdette Rooney 2010

A Good Motto to Live By
Life should not be a journey to the grave with the intention
of arriving safely in an attractive and well-preserved body,
but rather to skid in sideways,
Champagne in one hand —
Strawberries in the other —
Body thoroughly used up, totally worn out and screaming
WOO HOO — WHAT A RIDE
Anon

CONTENTS

FOREWORD

Some people are simply destined to travel, wanderlust is hard-wired into their nervous system. That certainly applies to Gerdette, starting from her childhood smuggling expeditions back and forth across the Ireland-Northern Ireland border, as it was back in those pre-EU days. I'm married to a 'belle of Belfast city' so I'm reasonably familiar with that contentious border and, like people on both sides, wonder what's going to happen when Brexit finally arrives at some conclusion … or other.

Then – after a teenage waitressing spell in Switzerland – she becomes a radiographer. She may have to explain to people exactly what that means, but it's certainly a travelling occupation which can find her work from Baghdad, back in the Saddam Hussein era, to Soweto in South Africa and later in Sydney. But how many excursions have there been along the way? A circuit of the 1070-kilometre Ulster Way around Northern Ireland may have been close to home, but it certainly took her both sides of the religious divide. There's some house-building in post-earthquake Haiti or navigating the economic confusion of post-Soviet Cuba.

She follows Shackleton's footsteps amongst the penguin hordes of the wonderful island of South Georgia, hangs out with twitchers (over-enthusiastic bird watchers) in Guyana, makes the hard slog to the Everest Base Camp on the Tibetan side, inevitably runs into a border where they won't recognize her visa (Somaliland to Ethiopia) and tracks down Irish connections in the most unlikely places. Everywhere she finds that most predictable by-product of travel; when you travel with the right attitude that is, the 'kindness of strangers'. Gerdette brings a real exuberance into her writing; this is clearly somebody who likes to be on the road and doesn't let the odd setback slow her down. And she's also terrifically good at finding something else very important when you're travelling: a cold beer.

Tony Wheeler
Melbourne, Australia

PREFACE

My adventures began early as an avid reader of Enid Blyton books. Aged ten, I had my very own Famous Five Club in our neighbourhood. The Irish countryside of my childhood provided the perfect breeding ground for a ripe imagination. The Ulster Canal ran behind our house, and its overgrown banks led to the woods bordering the Blackwater River.

As a child with two brothers, I was a tomboy. Our father played his role, building us treehouses, rafts and sledges from whatever lay about the house. We children lived an idyllic life over the fields and only came home reluctantly when my mother rang the green bell for tea.

My favourite book was *The Secret Island,* where the children ran away to have wild adventures. Perhaps this is where the escapist seed was sown in me, a trend that was to continue for life.

On leaving school, my favourite hate words were 'a permanent pensionable job'. It felt like a prison sentence for life, always doing the same thing. In my twenties, another question I disliked was 'When are you going to settle down?' I could never answer that one adequately. One of the advantages of choosing radiography as a career is that it allowed me to work in exciting countries and ultimately emigrate to Australia.

I believe that some people are restless souls — destined to wander — and I like to think of travel as the best education in life's skills one can get. The joy of meeting new people and experiencing other cultures has made me realise that there is no right way — it's just different and yet humankind the world over is the same, fundamentally good.

The self-coined word *womad* (a woman nomad) is a name I like, as I've always felt an affinity with the nomadic and the unsettled, forever curiously seeking fresh pastures.

The world is a significantly changed place since I began my travels nearly fifty years ago before the advent of mass tourism and cheap flights. Back then, each country followed its unique traditions and customs, and the era was more colourful pre-denim and western T-shirts. Locals welcomed strangers into their homes, and there was endless time for rich interaction, frequently without a common language.

I miss those days of no planning and unpredictability. To be cut off from the regular life of 'our way' meant severing connection with friends and family other than writing letters and sending postcards from exotic places. This lack of contact with home created freedom to clear the head to embrace the new and be in the moment.

It has always been essential for me to travel alone to pursue my own journey freely, perhaps suddenly taking a different path, not knowing where it might lead or whom I might meet that day. And always the possibility of a small adventure en route.

My mother once asked why I had to go to Tibet to bond with a granny in a mountain village when there were many older women yearning for companionship in Bragan, the bogland district we went to for turf. I couldn't answer her, except to say — 'It's a change and away from the humdrum. I don't want to see my kind everywhere, and I want to hear a different story.'

Some seek comfort in the known and others yearn for the mystery.

In my twenties, I found myself a guru in Dervla Murphy, Ireland's renowned travel writer and I anxiously awaited each new publication of her intrepid travels. This fearless, modest woman, who shuns the limelight, motorised transport and social media is deserving of travel's greatest accolades.

Often when being interviewed, Dervla is asked if she ever felt afraid on her travels. She always pauses, looks puzzled and responds — 'What is the point in fearing what might happen?' A woman after my own heart! I am also frequently asked this question. Once, when hiking in the Himalayas, I did have my trusty Swiss army knife poised to attack when I knew someone was following me and my heart thumped. Fortunately, two young Sikh walkers appeared from the opposite direction, and I latched onto them for safety. So the 'might' never happened.

Dervla also never allowed relationships to get in the way of going places, and I too can relate to this. Travel has always been my primary passion, with careers, men and everything else fitting in around it — it has been my impulsive, compulsive, outward and inward journey in life.

This collection of travel stories stem from fifty years of diary keeping. In the many hostels and doss houses I stayed in, if there was no one to talk to there was little else to do except read a book and keep a record of that day's happenings. This battered collection of notebooks, tatty school copybooks and bound journals has moved house with me many times, but I've never reread the contents. I was usually too busy hitting the road with my trusty rucksack to new destinations.

2020 for me will be the year I was compulsorily grounded in one place, in my beautiful Sydney. During the COVID-19 pandemic, I started writing, transporting myself into the past and reliving the memories of the exciting life I've been privileged to lead. Whilst researching the stories, I've cringed at my foolish young self, laughed at the predicaments I found myself in and ultimately realised life is a solo inward journey towards the unknown but to be lived well along the way.

I'm a very different person now, but there are essential ingredients that have remained steadfast. I've always been curious, taken risks, been loved and robbed, have laughed and cried with many the world over. Some of the people I've met on the journey are now dear friends — part of my tribe.

My nieces and nephews have heard many of these stories over the years, and it is for them I started writing them down. When babysitting years ago, we used to play a game 'find the country', where they had to search for weird places in their school atlas. It obviously fired their imaginations, and I relish seeing them globe-trot now in my footsteps, seeking out Nature's wild places with a tent.

The stories in this book will transplant you to the far corners of our amazing planet: the lush rainforest of Rwanda, the undulating dunes of the Sahara desert and the arid wastes of the Silk Road. There are tales of hammock life on the Amazon, the injustices of apartheid South Africa and the setting for many is my favourite continent, Africa.

I love and admire Africa's colourful, diverse peoples — joyous, heart-warming and stoic in often very harrowing situations. It is the continent where I enjoyed the journey in many shared taxis on long winding roads through changing landscapes, the miles in between when usually very little happened but during which I made friends, stayed unassumingly in strange places and had adventures on a day-to-day basis.

The world will be a different place post-COVID and the future of travel uncertain. My shabby rucksack and hiking boots may rest for a good while, but it has been a remarkable virtual round-the-world tour writing this book.

I hope you all enjoy the journey with me.

Gerdette Rooney
Sydney 2020

A History of Backpacking

The first backpack was discovered in the Otztal Italian Alps in 1991, belonging to Otzi the Iceman and dating back to about 3400BC. It was made of cloth and animal skin. Sadly, the poor fella was murdered on his hike and mummified by being frozen inside a layer of thick ice. Travel insurance was of little use to him.

My own 50 years of travel pales in comparison, and my first journey was not quite so adventurous. Aged 15, my younger brother Padraig and I hit the road for Dublin, 80 miles from our home in Monaghan, on the Irish border with Northern Ireland. We were headed for the big smoke to attend a folk concert and visit a few art galleries. Of course, we told our parents a different story that we would be staying in a youth hostel with a midnight curfew. Before the concert, we mooched around Dublin, and I purchased my first khaki canvas rucksack in the Army Surplus store for a quid. It was more suited to military manoeuvres in a war zone, but it matched the daggy secondhand army surplus jacket I already owned. When the concert ended in the early hours of the morning, we walked to the outer suburbs of the city and curled up in a bus shelter to await daylight, then hitched home.

A basic tent was another essential piece of equipment, which I purchased the following year with the proceeds of my Saturday job in the men's underwear section of Heaton's department store. Now, I was all set to take off, and hitched to Achill Island on Ireland's west coast, embracing my first solo adventure into the unknown. It would set a precedent for life.

I was a bit wary at first, with a lone male driver, but I usually relaxed if he started talking about family and kept his eyes directed on the road. My last ride over the bridge from the mainland was with a friendly farmer, who invited me to stay on his farm, with the proviso that I help his lazy daughter chase a few sheep around the mountain, as his arthritic legs were 'at him'. I readily agreed — working for one's keep or *woofing* as it is now known. It was a fun few days witnessing the hard work and hard play of the islanders at that time. I went to the local dance on the back of a tractor and walked the wild cliffs by moonlight at 2 am with the farmer's good-looking son.

Like many restless young ones from a small town, I was soon raring for the bright lights of London and further afield. Aged 18, this trip was a more complicated undertaking. My father dropped me at the border customs post near my home and hung about until I'd chatted up a lorry driver travelling on the ferry to Scotland, and further south to London. It never took long to get a ride and with a quick farewell of 'See ya, and God Bless' — I was gone!

The driver would turf me off the lorry before boarding the ferry as he wasn't legally allowed to take passengers, and I'd join him on the Scottish shore at Stranraer. As we drove through the night, there was no such thing as dozing off; the driver expecting you would blather away about anything, to keep him awake and amused. The payment deal was usually a packet of fags, or if he didn't smoke — a big fry up at one of the motorway transport caffs. And if you were going to continental Europe, you could strike lucky and be handed over to another lorry driver crossing the Channel on the Dover ferry. I later found out that the Yorkshire Ripper drove from northern England to London frequently in his lorry christened 'Wee Willie', and I realised how lucky I was to escape harm during those reckless years.

The first Round the World Trip was made by Magellan in 1519. In the 19th century, *Le Grand Tour* of continental Europe was a rite of passage for the privileged classes in Britain, with an entourage and collection of portmanteaux in tow. However, it was the Hippy Trail in the early 1960s that let loose a wave of unwashed youth, toting rucksacks, en route from London to India to consult with their gurus. This trend continued until Iran became off-limits to foreigners during the revolution in 1978, and Russian forces invaded Afghanistan in 1979. By then, the intrepid horde had discovered East Asia, helped by the birth of Lonely Planet, founded by Tony and Maureen Wheeler in 1972. Little did the Wheelers suspect that their first guidebook, *Across Asia on the Cheap* would be the beginning of a multi-million dollar travel empire.

Soon, there was a guide for nearly every country. Finding accommodation was very haphazard, and you just ended up where you ended up — often believing a rickshaw *wallah* or *tuk-tuk* driver, who insisted that their crony's guesthouse was the cheapest and closest to the sights and wasn't infested by cockroaches or bedbugs. Yet, it could turn out to be a secret gem run by a lovely family. It was often handier, if arriving late at night at a strange airport, to stretch out on the seats there until dawn and catch the first local bus into town. This tactic was an authentic introduction to a new place and its people.

I was born a bit late for the Hippy Trail, but for Irish teenagers in the 1970s, hitching on the continent was common, and many would pick grapes in France during the school holidays, or skivvy in a hotel, waitressing for low pay. It was experiencing the freedom of life away from parental control that mattered most. A few went to a kibbutz in Israel and others with wealthy parents just bummed about with cash in their pockets.

In the summer of 1974, I hitched to Sweden with Padraig, departing Ireland on the usual lorry route, with a tenner each in our pockets and carrying bread, cheese and the bare essentials in the trusty rucksack. Crossing northern Europe was easy and fun. Several drivers took us to their homes for a feed or clean up, and I recall that one family worried about our safety, insisting we send them a postcard on arrival. It rained heavily on the stretch to Copenhagen, and we got soaked between rides. Drying off in our first sauna at a hostel there, where all were nude, was a mind-boggling experience for our prudish Catholic eyes. However, we soon adopted loose Scandinavian habits and skinny-dipped that hot summer whilst working at a Swedish hotel.

We sometimes slept rough under a bridge or in an old barn if we could find one. In Germany at that time, communes welcomed stray travellers. Genuine hospitality was the norm, and young people were discovering how to have an adventure on a shoestring, as well as getting to know other cultures. Playing the guitar and singing pop songs was the main pastime, and there was always a trendy look — greasy, unkempt hair, faded denim, cheesecloth tops and beads galore. By now, my rucksack was very mod — bright orange nylon on a light aluminium frame, and I thought myself totally 'with it'.

Once on the road, contact with family was non-existent as any mail usually arrived home shortly before the sender. Letters were the order of the day, and the mammies of Ireland wrote regularly and delved into school atlases to make sure they spelt the foreign country correctly. Travellers collected their mail at the Post Restante section of post offices, and these letters were treasured.

More often than not, my parents hadn't a clue where I was and didn't worry either. It was a kind of blissful ignorance. Once you left home, you were on your own, and receiving a telegram, or a phone call meant an emergency, such as a death in the immediate family or final exam results you didn't want to know! Parents also dreaded receiving a telegram with bad news. I'm sure my wad of letters from those times will be a museum item one day. At that time too, collecting postcards, stamps and coins were popular hobbies.

In the 1970s, Interrail Passes replaced hitchhiking and were valid for cheap train travel from Morocco to Norway and east to the hedonistic Greek islands where many headed to burn their bare butts off on nude beaches. You just hopped on and off the trains as you liked, dossing down at railway stations to save bed money with the rucksack making a comfy pillow, or catching an overnight train to free up daylight hours travelling. The gourmet tour on a diet of bread, cheese, grapes and cheap wine was always ample, and by now a Swiss army knife was my best friend, slicing the cheese, opening the wine and doubling up as a weapon in an emergency.

In more bureaucratic countries like India, it could take a day to purchase a train ticket, and you might wait two days for the train to arrive. Carrying iodine tablets or chlorine pills helped stave off the Delhi belly. You had to learn quickly to be savvy and streetwise. I was robbed several times, which was never fun, and even though travellers' cheques were regarded as a safe way to carry money, it was a hassle changing them.

When hitchhiking alone, I had to overcome feeling scared or condition myself not to feel fear in the first place. I learned how to 'read' a stranger, and of course, got it wrong sometimes. There were a few dodgy occasions when a driver 'chanced his arm' as we say in Ireland, stretching the hand across or staring too long at my boobs. I always kept my rucksack on my lap, wary until I felt comfortable with the driver and I did once jump out at traffic lights and fled — the precious jewels intact for another while.

Probably most backpackers grow out of these budget habits sooner or later, and progress to more comfortable and more relaxed means of travel, but for whatever reason, it has remained my *modus operandi* for a lifetime. My well-tested methods brought me closest to the people of a country and their everyday lives. After all, this was the primary purpose of my travel.

I've been lucky to experience many memorable nights interacting with local people. Still, one of the strangest impromptu encounters occurred in a jungle village on the east coast of Borneo in the early 1980s. I was looking for a family I'd heard of, who owned a pet crocodile. I found the house late in the day, and the family invited me to stay as strangers were rare in the area, a solo white woman, especially so. The grandfather, busy welding pots, spoke rudimentary English from serving in some war and explained that his son had rescued the baby croc after its mother was shot in the river nearby. The children raised it as a pet, calling her Bella. The now eight-year-old crocodile had pride of place in the front room of the house where she resided in a big tank.

The exterior wall had been replaced by perspex to facilitate sightseers, and Bella was a curiosity far and wide. My bed for the night was floor space in the children's room behind Bella's, and I lay awake all night listening to her restless thrashing about, worrying that she might sense a stranger next door and break through the thin partition.

On another journey, I curled up in a pile of skins by the fire in a smoky Tibetan household, and we all spent a lively night in song and dance. The family played local handmade instruments, and I demonstrated rock and roll dancing, which had them in peals of laughter. Such events are precious memories of how different cultures can interact without a common language.

In various societies, the sexes played very different roles, and I was often treated as an honorary male and allowed to witness or partake in men's affairs. I found this frequently more interesting than female domestic matters and goo-ing over babies, never my forte, but of course, I had to be sensitive to cultural norms.

One time, this was the case in Sarawak, where I spent a few days with the Penan tribe, still practising a hunter-gatherer lifestyle which was seriously threatened by the logging industry. The elders and young men allowed me to tag along on a wild pig hunt, and I was fascinated with their blowpipe skills and intrigued by the different plants they used as a poison.

In the same region, more settled tribes lived in longhouses by the river, and it was the custom to introduce yourself to the headman on arrival, as you would be a guest of his family for the night. On one occasion, I thought I had found a remote longhouse with no electricity and was enjoying the rusticity and tranquillity. I washed in the river at sunset with the women and was quietly relishing the rainforest sunset symphony when two young people my age insisted I join them for a walkabout.

After ten minutes, we came to a clearing where a group of villagers were hanging around the windows of a crowded hut. My grinning companions steered me through the crowd and sat me down inside, awaiting my reaction to their treat for me. In the centre of the room, perched on a rickety table was a small TV, showing a very snowy picture of JR Ewing in his big Stetson hat. It was the community television, and everyone watched my expression, thinking I would be delighted to watch *Dallas* and hear my own language. It was with great difficulty that I played the part of the thrilled spectator in order not to offend.

The old Hippy Trail left a legacy of destinations associated with travellers looking to find themselves, taking drugs, and chilling on beaches for months on end. Whether sleeping on the white sands of Goa, under the stars on a Moroccan rooftop, or in Kathmandu alleyways, the whiff of wacky baccy was widespread. As an ardent non-smoker, when the joint passed around, I would be content with another slug of my beer, and when the conversation got too nonsensical, I went to bed.

However, it didn't prevent my experimenting while travelling in the Golden Triangle of Northern Thailand, where smoking an opium pipe was something to try when trekking amongst the hill tribes. I gave it a shot one night with a group of fellow backpackers, and just when I thought I was getting to some hallucinogenic highpoint, someone warned us of a police raid on the village. I quickly sputtered to a stop mid-trip, and the experimental evening was aborted abruptly.

The full moon parties of the day took place on Koh Samui Island in the south of Thailand, and there was the allure of magic mushroom omelettes and dope cookies. Curiosity got the better of me one time, and I succumbed to eating a slice of a mushroom omelette. When it did not affect me, I scoffed a second slice which was not a good idea. I was fortunate to be in the company of good friends who looked after me as I wiped out 24 hours of my life in a strange trance, where I thought the palm trees were policemen out to get me and put me in prison. I was in a heightened state of paranoia, where there was no coming down, and as a novice, I was terrified. After that, I decided to remain a boring square in such situations and not take any risks.

Over the years as I travelled to exotic places, my rucksacks increased in size as I purchased weird and unusual souvenirs like soapstone heads, wooden bowls and scary animist masks. It was a relief when luggage restraints were brought in with the advent of budget airlines, and now I travel with a large daypack only, which is very liberating and easy on an ageing back.

In recent decades, travel has changed enormously, and many cultures have homogenised to western models with the effects of globalisation apparent everywhere. Worldwide, people are on the move to better their lives elsewhere, assuming elsewhere is better or the ideal model. In the adaptation to new lifestyles, old ways and invaluable skills and traditions are forgotten and lost. Oil companies and loggers have penetrated pristine areas, ravaging natural food habitats. Everything and everyone suddenly has a price tag, rendering genuine kindness and offers of hospitality cause for suspicion. In too many lands, tourist income has become the primary means of survival.

In current times, the term backpacker can denote different things, and not all good; cheap seasonal labour, wet T-shirt competitions in party bars and hostels, and reliance on parental funding and bailouts with the credit card. Many travellers move as a herd to the next adrenalin kick, whether it be skydiving, bungee jumping or white water rafting, and mix with their kind instead of embracing the wider local community.

Even the humble rucksack has been replaced by massive suitcases full of party clothes, and Uber taxis transport backpackers to the comfortable Airbnb with the welcome bottle of chilled chardonnay. Guidebooks and maps are becoming defunct as trips are organised with precision on social media, leaving nothing to chance. Who is local anymore as the Polish person pulls the pint in Dublin and the Irish serve the latte in Australia?

As I write this in the time of COVID-19, the skies are empty, and travellers are grounded for the foreseeable future. Ethical questions on carbon footprint are being asked as the planet takes a rest from us, and the negative impact of mass tourism on a fragile environment is widely debated. The time has come perhaps to consider the staycation or — who knows? We might eventually hop into our time capsules with nutrient pills for the five-minute whisk to fresh pastures on another planet!

A HARD BORDER

B rexit has been dominating the airwaves for the past three years and talk of hard and soft borders bandied about in a willy-nilly fashion. Few understand what the terms mean and what effect it will have on people's daily lives on the new UK/EU border on the island of Ireland. The following account relates how it was for my family growing up in Monaghan during the 1960s and 1970s with a 'Hard Border'.

I was eight years old in the early sixties when my smuggling training commenced. My mother was an expert at it, and her excitement at evading the customs officers and saving some housekeeping shillings was contagious. For my brothers and I, it was our weekly adventure driving to the North and meant treats of milky ice lollies and Opal Fruits — 'made to make your mouth water'! This was our payment for helping her out in illegal operations, doubling her butter quota, and keeping our mouths shut.

We lived in the Republic three miles from the border with Northern Ireland and were headed for the small village of Middletown two miles further on. The border consisted of two small wooden huts by the roadside manned by uniformed officers. The first we arrived at was the Republic's customs, where my father went in as a formality but was sometimes waved on in wet weather when the officer didn't want to get soaked or was reading the newspaper. A placard in the middle of the road had 'STOP CUSTOMS' written in both Irish and English in bold lettering. It was only on the way back the officers would be interested in what we had bought in the North.

A half-mile further on we stopped at the English customs post with the stop sign of 'Her Majesty's Custom and Excise' service. This was more of an ordeal as my father had to go inside and have his driver's licence and car registration checked. Until 1965 a triangular *triptyque*, or bond, had to be stamped allowing the temporary importation of the vehicle.

He might re-emerge with a uniformed customs man in a black peaked cap who would study us carefully. Then the boot would be searched, but we seldom had to get out of the car. There were few products from the Republic that were worth smuggling North, and the officers weren't too bothered with ordinary shoppers. If you were lucky, a few lorries with commercial loads would be passing through at the same time and distracting them.

The landscape didn't change at all on the journey to Middletown — poor boggy farmland and drumlin hills on both sides of the border. However, the Irish language disappeared from the road signs in the North, and the main street of the village sported a brightly painted red post office and post box with Her Majesty's emblem. Next door was the one grocery store and off-license, into which my father disappeared to compare prices of Bushmills whiskey with Jameson from the South. That was his baby while we children hovered over the greater variety of sweets, bars and chewing gum from England that looked and tasted so different. We would squabble over who was getting what.

My mother shopped carefully because of the currency difference between the Irish punt and the English pound sterling. She kept a special brown purse in her dressing table drawer for her cross-border shopping trips. If any northern aunties or uncles came visiting, complicated exchange transactions took place over tea and apple tart. Kerrygold butter is a high-quality butter brand from the cream of grass-fed Irish cows, and its popularity was increasing in the UK and Europe. The butter, wrapped in its distinctive golden foil with a green logo, travelled from Cork in the very south only to be sold for 20d cheaper in Northern Ireland. It was nearly considered the 'cocaine' of the 1960s.

Across the road were Hughes' pub and petrol pumps where it was no coincidence that we needed a complete fill of cheaper petrol. This too was a significant saving. We were related to the Hughes brothers, and often a quick drink was had in the bar on a cold day, my parents keen to hear family gossip on the Northern side. My father would have a wee Bush chased by a glass of Guinness, my mother a hot port, and we children were given non-alcoholic ginger wine. At that time, Coca-Cola was out of the question.

Whether a warm spring day or a rare sweltering Irish summer's day, our winter coats were donned for these excursions, and on leaving the village, we pulled into a layby and pounds of Kerrygold butter were carefully inserted under our oxters, a colloquialism for the armpit. At the English customs hut, the car registration was noted, and we were waved on. Tension tightened in the packed Beetle Volkswagen. Mammy had us under orders of best behaviour and Daddy, impassive, drove straight ahead towards the stop sign entering the Republic.

The officer inspected the boot, and we all had to step out of the car — it being well known children acted as 'mules'. My baby brother Cathal served as a good distraction, and his squalling or a smelly nappy often did the trick, and we got waved on without searches. It was important not to be delayed as that butter was melting rapidly under our armpits!

I remember so well one occasion when on stepping out, my mother just couldn't keep a firm grip on her pound of butter and it dropped to the ground. There was dead quiet. 'You've dropped something Madam,' the officer said as he gazed at the splat of butter on the tarmac and my poor blushing mother was highly embarrassed as she scooped it up in front of him. Under no circumstances was she going to let it go. Most officers overlooked small-scale personal smuggling, but you could sometimes get one who was rigid with the law, and either confiscated goods or threatened imposing fines.

Smuggling of all sorts was the norm for people of the Borderlands. Baby prams could have a false bottom or coffins filled with contraband — there was no end to the ingenuity employed to smuggle tobacco, cigarettes or alcohol, as well as butter. Livestock prices constantly fluctuated between North and South, and farmers did deals on both sides. Having farmers in the family, we would hear some hilarious tales of cattle swimming across rivers in the dead of night and pigs sedated with Guinness to cross lakes by boat. Bureaucracy and identity tags were a thing of the future.

My mother told us how it was in the 1940s during wartime when the Republic of Ireland was neutral with no food scarcities, yet in Northern Ireland, people were on strict rations. At that time the trains running between small towns on each side of the border were called the butter and sugar express. Women from Belfast travelled south to buy tea, and the rough brown bread native to the South filled northern bellies more quickly than white English loaves.

By the time I was ten, our smuggling exploits had grown more daring. My brother and I were getting our first bikes and a research drive to Armagh, a bigger town 17 miles from the border, indicated significant savings could be made buying them there. After some quick lessons on cousins' bikes, we were deemed proficient enough in our riding skills not to get knocked down and end up in the ditch.

Bikes purchased and strapped to the boot of the car; we took a different route home via an unapproved road. There were many of these straddling the border, often only narrow boreens with humpback stone bridges and badly potholed as the council didn't repair them. Vehicles were not allowed to use them, having to detour to an approved road with custom posts. They were generally used by local farmers to transport cattle and other livestock from one area of their farms to fresh pastures that just happened to be in the other jurisdiction, and they needed special permits to do so.

With random patrols and hefty fines, if caught, my father dropped us off near the border, and my mother led our inexperienced legs home the remaining miles. If stopped by random patrols, we were just 'out for a spin'.

The next rite of passage was getting our first record player, mainly to play my parents' collection of old 1950s crooner LP records purchased at an auction house. Such stuff as Jim Reeves and John McCormack, the Irish tenor. I had won my first single at the school hop — Kenny Rogers' *Ruby don't take your Love to Town* — and with the LP *Top of the Pops 1969* on my Christmas list, I was very excited we were getting a player. Not conducive to the bars of a bicycle, this smuggling operation involved my father's combined skills of a heavy foot on the fuel pedal and the art of skirting potholes on the unapproved road.

The 1970s arrived and with it 'The Troubles'. Sectarian violence erupted in the city of Derry in August 1969, and British troops were sent into Ulster to restore order and protect civilians. They didn't leave until 2007, the longest campaign in British military history. Barbed-wire army camps and watchtowers were constructed along the 310-mile border, and armed soldiers appeared on Belfast street corners. Armoured cars and tanks patrolled Catholic and Protestant ghettoes.

The smuggling continued in 'bandit territory' as South Armagh was known, but now it was guns and ammunition transported by paramilitaries on both sides, Republican and Loyalist. Crossing the border had the added hassle of army checkpoints and searches as well as dealing with customs. A large concrete barracks was built in Middletown, and on entering the village, you had to halt at barricades. As armed soldiers searched the Volkswagen, you could sense the rifle trained on you from the watchtower above. Clean-shaven squaddies hardly out of nappies asked questions, and you could see the fear in their young eyes.

After the first car bomb in 1970 which killed two police officers in South Armagh, the UK government decided to close over a hundred unapproved roads, hoping to put a stop to the gelignite trail across the border. Craters were dug and large concrete blocks or spikes put in place, making the roads impassable, and bridges were blown up where a stream or river marked the boundary. As quickly as they were closed, locals banded together at night with heavy machinery to remove the blocks and fill in the craters with gravel. It was a pointless strategy as all farmers knew the fields well, but anger and resentment were rising.

Meanwhile, ordinary life went on, and times were more affluent for those living on the border. My family was now regularly shopping big time in Armagh city as business declined in Middletown due to the army presence. Each to their own, my mother and I went in search of fashion, she in Lennox's department store browsing through rails of crimplene trouser suits and twin sets, and I in the trendy boutiques looking at bellbottom corduroys and fringed jackets. My brother and I made a beeline for the record shop, pleading for extra pocket money to purchase singles and LPs. Bob Dylan was all the rage. Cheap wine arrived in Ireland — or Northern Ireland at least. Two-pound ninety-nine bottles of Bulgarian Cabernet Sauvignon were available, so my father gave up making his unpalatable homebrew.

My hormones were in full swing in the early 1970s. Rock bands played in my hometown of Monaghan as 'The Troubles' brought entertainment to a standstill in the North. People held their weddings and functions in the South for safety, and the four local hotels were booming. I went out with a scruffy guitarist from an Armagh band playing at our teenage disco, but he got beaten up by the local mob — protective of their home patch and girls. Soon bomb scares regularly interrupted the vibrant nightclub scene when all were requested to vacate the hall and stand outside in the cold while the venue was searched for explosives. The reality of the guerrilla war on our doorstep was starting to hit home to us young ones. I questioned why I wasn't allowed to date Protestants. Neighbours were becoming wary and social tensions rising.

Sex was seeping across the border: 'dirty books' such as Ian Fleming's James Bond paperbacks which my father hid behind his trigonometry books in the bookcase; the *Sun* tabloid with its busty Page 3 girls; and worst of all, johnnies emptied from the dispensers in Armagh toilets or legally bought across the counter in the North but illegal in the South. Licentiousness was the order of the day, and it had the bishop ranting from the pulpit at Sunday Mass. Catholicism was in crisis.

The 'Contraceptive Train' from Belfast to Dublin held 47 members of the newly founded Irish Women's Liberation Movement in 1971, and the triumphant feminists arrived in Dublin waving condoms to taunt the blushing Gardai (police), and customs officials were expected to arrest them. 'Let them through!' the crowd roared. The women were condemned by church and state and deemed to have ideas above their station. The train inspired a musical made in 2015.

At that time, I was having my wild rebellion at age seventeen, deliberately choosing boyfriends my parents disapproved of. The Traenors were strong republican sympathisers and rumoured to run a safe house which harboured IRA activists on the run. I just thought Jim was a good looker with sex appeal, and I didn't understand the politics of what was going on.

1972 was the deadliest year of The Troubles with 500 people, over half of them civilians, losing their lives. The tragedy of Derry's Bloody Sunday in January of that year was portrayed on TV screens around the globe. Sectarian barricades were going up in Belfast and Derry, and people moved house to a Protestant or Catholic area in fear of being burnt out in a mixed neighbourhood. The British Army patrolled the streets with rifles and searched bags at the entrance to stores. They befriended kids with sweets who later stoned them.

Along the winding roads of South Armagh, the Irish tricolour blew in the wind and 'Brits Out' or the 'Sniper at Work' signs on telegraph poles became Republican icons of The Troubles. Army helicopters patrolled the border continuously in search of suspicious paramilitary activity. Tit-for-tat massacres on both sides of the religious divide were on the increase. Ordinary shoppers from Dublin and further South became too fearful of crossing the border, preferring to pay higher prices for goods locally. My father now minded the car with its southern registration number while we shopped on Armagh streets. The bag searches were tedious but necessary.

Leaving the Borderlands behind in 1973 for the safe, pristine beauty of Switzerland, I relished the fact that nobody cared who or what you were. While living in Basel, I dated and nearly married a Bulgarian communist but the border education of sticking to your kind and recognising cultural difference prevailed.

Thursday, the 17th of May 1974 is forever etched in my memory. My boss Herr Dr Nidecker informed me that a car bomb had gone off in Monaghan with seven fatal casualties and many were injured. With telephone lines blocked, it was impossible to phone home and get details. On Thursday evenings, my father usually drove into town to buy the local newspaper, and I was beside myself with worry until I learned they were safe. However, being a small town, I knew some of the victims and one was a relative having a quiet pint in the pub when the bomb exploded outside.

The Dublin government decided to build an army barracks in Monaghan, and it opened in December 1976. It was located a few hundred yards from our bungalow on the outskirts of town, in an old flax field belonging to the psychiatric hospital. Its presence brought a buzz of excitement and new business to Monaghan. However, rumours were rife that the unwanted pregnancy rate rose in the region that Christmas season with young soldiers in civvies fresh prey for bold local lassies. Even I sometimes donned my shortest mini skirt as I strolled past the wire when the lads were playing football. My younger siblings loved to watch the helicopters taking off for border patrols.

That summer I brought a Finnish friend Tina home to Ireland for a holiday. Her family was anxious about the political situation and security issues, but I convinced them the media exaggerated the risks. Our first evening, we were in the pub having a drink with my parents when a bomb threat was announced. Tina went white and was ready to take to her heels instantly in her clogs.

'Steady yerself there girl!' my father said, 'and finish your pint. Sure, it'll just be a false alarm.'

Such was the complacency of those times when people attempted to maintain the normality of everyday lives.

Life changed along the border. A new divisive language was heard on the streets — Prods and Taigs, Orange and Green, us and them. Surnames designated which foot you kicked with, Protestant or Catholic. Short ceasefires came and went, and people disappeared.

Then, with Ireland and the United Kingdom joining the European Economic Community in 1973, there was no need for customs control and the huts were dismantled. The Rooney family could stop wearing winter overcoats on a hot summer's day. The price of Kerrygold butter became irrelevant. All appreciated free trade and both sides of the border prospered.

With the signing of the Good Friday Peace agreement in 1998, the violence of 30 years came to an end and peace prevailed. Crossing the border is simple and hardly discernible nowadays, except for speed signs changing from kilometres to miles. One road crosses the border four times back and forth in ten minutes, but you can't spot where the crossings are.

Who would want to return to the painful previous experiences of a Hard Border?

IN THE SHADOW OF THE EIGER

How to re-capture the magic of being 17 again — that first adventure away from home and my first time flying? My experience was extraordinary. Switzerland wasn't just any old destination. It was and is one of the most picturesque countries in the world and back in 1972, two girlfriends, Ann, Deidre and I, were bubbling with teenage excitement at the prospect of spending the summer in the Swiss Alps. I had a blissful vision in my head of Alpine meadows with languid cows, *The Sound of Music,* and Swiss chocolate galore.

Hailing from a small Irish town, we initially hoped for summer jobs in the glitzy city of Zurich, wanting to party free of parental discipline. When USIT, the Irish Student Union, found us waitressing jobs in Kleine Scheidegg, Berner Oberland, it was perturbing to not locate the place in our school atlas, even with a magnifying glass. We settled for the mystery tour, telling parents that it would improve our school German in preparation for the Leaving Certificate, meanwhile harbouring notions of a fun time in 'foreign parts' where everything would be different.

I was really excited but also extremely nervous on the three-hour flight from Dublin to Zurich, not knowing what to expect. It was a relief when thick clouds hid the Irish Sea far below, and the novelty of an Aer Lingus lunch and a free drink distracted me from scary thoughts of altitude. The time moved forward two hours, and it was comforting to see the vast cityscape of Zurich appear through the clouds.

All set to practise our *wenig Deutsch,* we were rather disappointed that the Swiss spoke excellent English and were very helpful. The queer guttural tones of Schweizerdeutsch baffled us as it bore no resemblance to the proper German taught by Miss Cassidy at our convent school. Switzerland has four official languages, and we would quickly learn a smattering of greetings — and expletives — in Schweizerdeutsch, French and Italian. After expertly exchanging our travellers' cheques, we scrutinised our wads of strange Swiss francs and somehow got ourselves safely onto the express train for Interlaken.

I'd heard of Swiss precision, and sure enough, the slick train departed on the dot of 7 pm, and we settled into our plush compartment. The light was fading over the pretty countryside we passed through. Everything looked spick-and-span and in its place, no litter anywhere. The houses had neat piles of firewood stacked creatively outside, charming gardens and wooden balconies ablaze with colourful flower boxes. It was pure chocolate box cover.

As the train skirted the shores of Lake Interlaken lights twinkled on the water, and a few yachts were out for a night sail. The three of us were tired but kept our wits about us, transferring to a small cogwheel train that snaked slowly up the mountainside, creaking and clanking at steeper sections. We were too late for the last train to Kleine Scheidegg and would overnight at a youth hostel in Wengen, the nearest village.

It was nearly 10 pm when we reached Wengen, the streets deathly quiet and dark. We discovered that there was no road to the village which explained the lack of traffic. A lone man outside a *Gaststube* pointed us in the direction of the *Jugendherberge,* and a kind woman greeted us warmly with *Gruezi mittenand* showing us to our dorm.

Exhilarated to be in a strange place, we returned to the warm and cosy atmosphere of the *Gaststube* where locals and tourists chatted in groups. We promptly ordered scrumptious hot chocolate that tasted much better than that available in Ireland, and I thought — *let the adventure begin*!

I still recall the magic I felt next morning waking to the staggering view from our balcony; forested slopes swooping into sunny meadows and a ridge of snowy peaks etched on the distant skyline. Although early June, there was a crisp freshness to the air and cowbells jingled somewhere near. Our *hausfrau* appeared to make us a jug of milky coffee accompanied by a basket of warm crusty bread, fancy whorls of butter and strawberry jam to die for.

We caught the cogwheel train again and moved from window to window in awe as it chugged upwards through a Santa wonderland. *Where on earth are we ending up*, we all wondered? And were in shock disembarking at Kleine Scheidegg, effectively a mountain pass at an elevation of 2060 metres and to us 'the back of beyond'. There was snow on the ground — in summer!

Aside from the train station, we could only see two other buildings — an elegant chalet-style hotel straight out of a movie set, with the backdrop of a sheer mountain face towering behind — and what appeared to be a restaurant further up the opposite slope. It had Swiss flags flying gaily outside, red squares with a white cross in the centre. 'Is this it?' we all exclaimed in horror. It was.

We trudged through the snow to Hotel Bellevue, and a waiter fetched the owner, Frau Von Almen, our employer for the coming months. She was a tall, stern-looking woman — welcoming, but had a 'no-nonsense' look about her. After settling into our room under the eaves and removing sodden footwear, we were given a tour of the plush hotel that would be our home for the summer. We met Stefan, the head waiter, forever immortalised in the thriller movie *The Eiger Sanction* which was later filmed at Kleine Scheidegg and starred Clint Eastwood. Frau von Almen told us that the impressive mountain face hovering over us was the famous Eiger North Face that had witnessed numerous mountaineering feats and tragedies. Our world education was expanding as we were only familiar with small drumlin hills that we avoided climbing!

The Swiss are a fastidious nation, and it took days to smarten up the slovenly habits of three young Irish girls. I soon mastered the straight-backed posture fit for the catwalk, managing to balance a tea-tray of expensive china and wobbly cakes or crystal cruets of Chateauneuf-du-Pape and fine glassware. The knack of carrying three dinner plates in one hand, with a turn of the wrist, and a precise angle of the thumb, has lasted a lifetime. The three of us scrubbed up well in our black skirts, starched blouses and aprons, and long hair scooped back prudishly.

The meals arrived up in a lift shaft from the kitchen below, and my notorious *faux pas* the first week was to send the *petit pois* flying all over the dining room carpet! Most of the guests had a sense of humour and were forgiving of our clumsy antics, regularly enquiring of our strange accents and funny German.

The typical daily greeting *Gruezi* is an elongated form replacing the formal *Guten Morgen. Danke Schon* and *Bitte Schon* were uttered many times a day. Bernhard, a young Swiss waiter, and Albi, the Italian chef took us under their wing, teaching us colloquial swear words and *scheisse* was how we described some of our working conditions. We laboured long hours and I soon tired of eating *wienerschnitzel* and *goulash,* which often featured on the staff menu. No fancy Swiss fondue or rare steak for the workers! Sometimes, I secretly scoffed a creme caramel dessert or two from a guest tray if left untouched. We devoured a lot of smelly mountain cheese with rough farmer's bread and of course when the chocolate fetish started within days of arrival — I was a lost cause!

The Japanese were the wealthy tourists of the day, arriving in groups, wearing name badges and herded about by a guide carrying a little flag. We were appalled at their table manners — eating with mouths wide open and when finished eating, rooting about with wooden toothpicks. It was far from toothpicks we were reared, and we considered such public displays the height of rudeness. But wasn't that the reason to travel, to experience different habits and discover toothpicks? We met many mountaineers and hikers, who mostly stayed at the bunkhouse over the train station. A gregarious lot, with sunburnt faces and decked out in all the right gear, Patagonia jackets and Dexter boots, they collapsed on the sunny hotel terrace to drink cold beers and pore over trekking maps of the region.

We met one interesting character called Norman Croucher, a young British climber who was a double amputee, with artificial aluminium legs and plastic feet. He successfully scaled the west flank of the Eiger that summer and laughed with us in the bar on his safe return — commenting how lucky he was not to have to worry about getting frostbite in his feet! He also regaled us with stories of his marathon 900-mile walk from John o' Groats to Land's End in the UK the previous year and was a courageous, positive person to brighten up our working week.

From time to time, there would be dancing at the hotel, an opportunity for the three of us to glam up a bit and pretend we were guests rather than waitresses. But most of those attending were 'old fogeys' to us young girls, and we usually ended up knocking back cheap schnapps with Bernhard and Albi and shaking our youthful hips unsuitably to the conservative Swiss folk music.

There was little to do in our free time between working shifts. When the snow melted, and the summer heat dried the meadows, we donned bikinis and sunbathed on the grassy slopes among the buttercups and tinkling cows, determined to return to Ireland with a tan. I have a colour photograph of myself squatting happily beside a big white and chocolate-coloured bovine, with a large bell around its neck, and I look incredibly content and happy with my lot. The dreams of city parties long-buried, I developed a love and appreciation for the beauty of nature.

Unfortunately, I was rapidly gaining weight on creamy milk coffees, delectable cakes and Swiss chocolate. My favourite chocolate was Ragusa bars, exquisite melt-in-your-mouth praline with crunchy hazelnuts, topped by a thin layer of dark chocolate. At breaks, we would rush to the station kiosk, buy chocolate, and lounge on our attic beds munching and writing letters to boyfriends back home. It was rather sad that there was no fanciable local talent to lead us astray in our Swiss paradise.

The waiter at the rustic Stockli restaurant up the hill soon got to know our regular orders for hot chocolate and a slice of delicious black forest cake with its alcohol-drenched cherries. If not working, we would head there in the evening as deep pinks and purples highlighted the mountain ridges, and a scene reminiscent of the book *Heidi* was re-enacted. A dirndled woman would yodel high shrill notes enough to scare the cows, or a man in lederhosen played the alphorn, a wooden instrument over three metres long, used in olden days to communicate news throughout the valleys. Its deep reverberating echo around the hillsides was a joy to hear.

On our first day off, curiosity got the better of us, and we took the train up to Jungfraujoch, the main tourist attraction in Berner Oberland that the guests raved about. We had no idea it was the highest railway station in Europe at 3454 metres and an icy wonderworld. After departing Kleine Scheidegg station, the train shortly disappeared into a long dark tunnel bored through the mountain, and we disembarked briefly at a large opening in the sheer cliff face. I felt dizzy looking down at the vast abyss below, and it gave me a better appreciation of the risky life of the climbers we met.

It was a nine-kilometre trip to Jungfraujoch train station, an astonishing feat of engineering, and from there, an elevator took us higher to the Sphinx Observatory. Its observation deck was like a throne in the clouds, with a mind-boggling 360-degree vista of jagged peaks, particularly those of the spectacular Jungfrau and Monch right beside us. A piercing arctic wind was blowing, yet I stood in brilliant sunshine looking down on the glistening sheen of the Aletsch glacier. 'I am in heaven!' I shouted at the others. It was mind-blowing.

We retreated from the gale to visit the Ice Palace; its high vaulted chambers hollowed out of ice and lit up with electric lighting. We slid through the frosty world of incredible ice sculptures exhibited in nooks and crannies; a large bear, an eagle in flight and even a Beetle Volkswagen you could sit in and get a freezing bum. *No wonder so many tourists come here,* I thought. Travelling to Jungfraujoch is one of Europe's most expensive train journeys, and we were so lucky to visit with our discounted staff passes for the region.

On other free days, we hiked down the valley on one side to Grindelwald, a bigger town than Wengen, with road access from Interlaken. However, Wengen remained my favourite for the beautiful walk there, weaving through pine-forested slopes where squirrels scuttled off at our approach, and sunny alpine glades made great picnic spots with a view. The traffic-free tranquillity of the village was unique, and I enjoyed browsing through its small shops for souvenirs to bring home; rustic cowbells, pretty Edelweiss ribbons, schnapps shot glasses and of course, chocolate with pistachios, minty chunks and gooey liqueur.

As the weeks passed, we watched our stash of Swiss francs grow as there was little to spend our meagre salaries on and separately made plans

Kleine Scheidegg and the Eiger North Face

Befriending a local in the Swiss Alps!

for a deserved holiday before returning to school for our final year. I was flying to London to meet an Irish boyfriend and finally see the glitzy city lights — Deidre was hitching to Amsterdam with her hippy bloke, intent on checking out the cool scene there — and Ann was going to Paris. We were a fearless, intrepid trio for the time and fortunately came to no harm.

On my day of departure, I looked about sadly, realising I would never experience a summer like it again — cocooned from the outside world, in a bubble of beauty. I promised myself that I would one day return as a tourist to Kleine Scheidegg, learn to ski and sit on the sunny terrace sipping Chateauneuf-du-Pape as a guest.

And I did.

BLACK AND WHITE IN SOWETO

Baragwanath hospital, or 'Bara' as it is popularly known, is one of the largest hospitals in the world with 3400 beds and nearly 7000 staff. It is in the locality of Diepkloof on the edge of Soweto, South Africa's vast former township twenty kilometres from Johannesburg. Officially, in 1980 when I worked there, a million blacks resided in Soweto, but in reality, the numbers were much higher.

Townships in South Africa were created by the apartheid regime under the Group Areas Act in 1950, segregating non-white race groups into separate residential areas for Coloureds, Indians and black people. To eradicate black ghettos in Johannesburg city and make space for white working-class suburbs, Soweto evolved as the most significant black city in the country. In the 1980s it was a sprawl of concrete block houses with corrugated iron roofs and few had electricity or running water. Extended families of fourteen to twenty people often lived in one dwelling.

However, it did have a millionaire's row in the suburb of Dube where 'nice bungalows' were well guarded and protected against vandalism and theft. Usually, *tsotsis*, the local gangsters, were paid protection money to leave the residents alone. No matter how wealthy a black person was, they could never buy a property or reside in Johannesburg city.

Arriving as a raw immigrant from London in 1980, and used to the niceties of an egalitarian society and health service, my first month in downtown Johannesburg was a shock to the system and a rapid education in how to behave for the following two years. Park benches were segregated, as were toilets, shop entrances, public transport and ambulances. It took just a few weeks of hailing the wrong bus or absent-mindedly waiting at the wrong stop, for my brain to segregate too and kick into apartheid mode.

Choosing which park bench to sit on became a spontaneous eye to brain reflex. Deciding to test it out at the beginning, I sat next to a black lady and passed some pleasantries, but she looked strangely at me as if I was on her patch and quickly moved off. If a black person had an accident on the city streets of Jo'burg, they waited a long time on a black ambulance to take them to Accident and Emergency at Baragwanath hospital, a lengthy drive in atrocious traffic.

Domestic servants were allowed to reside in Johannesburg with special permits to do so and lived in garden quarters, often sheds, where husbands and wives were not allowed to visit. Thousands of workers commuted daily at first light from Soweto, hanging perilously on the outside of overcrowded buses and trains to descend on the city and perform the low-paid jobs.

Shortly after arrival in the country, I visited Johannesburg General 'Blanc' or 'White only' Hospital seeking work as a radiographer, but the x-ray department was too quiet for my liking. A Welsh friend Christine, who was a surgeon at Baragwanath, assured me I would benefit greatly from the extraordinary expertise I would witness there. How right she was! As a major teaching hospital, all manner of unusual diseases were investigated and treated, and the violence and crime knew no bounds. Most males over the age of thirteen bore the scars of multiple stab wounds, and I witnessed a stabbed heart patient survive when most wouldn't. With the patient in cardiac arrest and no time to go to a sterile theatre, a doctor rapidly opened the chest with scissors after splashing the area with antiseptic and massaged the heart while an assistant controlled the bleeding. This emergency procedure is called 'cracking the chest' and was performed in a crowded corridor.

I'd found my niche, realising that Baragwanath was 'more me' as an ardent anti-colonialist, and I would be working with Africans; otherwise, why be in Africa? Also, from a professional perspective, I would gain invaluable medical experience in extreme trauma, something I wouldn't witness in a quiet white hospital in Johannesburg. And my skills would be put to better use where they were most needed.

I commenced work the following week, driving a commute of 30 kilometres from an exclusive white suburb of Johannesburg. I was one of only seven white radiographers among a staff of seventy-seven blacks who were mostly ex-nurses. We privileged seven shared a staffroom with three white doctors. In 1980, only 2% of doctors in South Africa were black or coloured, most in the Cape Province. It takes a while living in South Africa to understand the unique racial divisions, where 'coloured' is a person of mixed race, and being Indian is a separate category again. There was also a big social divide between English speaking South Africans and the Afrikaaners, descended from the first Boer settlers.

The administration of the hospital and my boss were Afrikaans, as most public servants were. During my time employed at Bara, I was a pig in the middle as an Irish person, working with two groups of colleagues. It was different in that I got invited to both the English and Afrikaaner homes, and I diplomatically steered clear of discussing politics. I was quickly initiated into the ritual of the *braaivleis,* the traditional BBQ with quality steaks and *boerewors,* (spicy sausage), often served with *mielie pap,* a type of corn mush. My boss, Agatha, showed me how to bake trays of calorific *koeksisters,* a sticky mess of syrup-drenched doughnut. At the same time, I went to poolside Sunday brunches in affluent British homes.

The hospital had been a military barracks during the Second World War for convalescing British Commonwealth soldiers and was still a sprawling campus of single-ward pavilions linked by open corridors where patients spilt outside to catch the breeze. Everywhere was teeming with the sick and injured, corridors and wards overflowing capacity, patients in pyjamas wandering in the dust and sunshine with drip bags on their heads and urine bags in their hands. A vibrant chatter never ceased and everywhere was awash with colour; women in *kikois* (sarongs), *doek* (headscarves) and blanketed children carried piggy-back.

My first week's work was with Reggie, a delightful old great-grandmother in her 70s, still working because she couldn't afford not to. She lived in a shack with no electricity, and numerous grandchildren lived with her studying by candlelight. Even though she was a senior radiographer, the white doctors made a beeline for my white face to make enquiries and request x-rays. Any directing them to Reggie was a source of puzzlement or annoyance at my non-compliance.

There was no time to catch breath, it was so busy. The chest x-ray room was a production line alternating male and female patients, all stripping to the waist at once, no gowns available, and then being shown how to breathe in and hold their breath. I quickly learned how to demonstrate this in the three common Bantu languages of Zulu, Xhosa and Sesotho. Young babies arrived down from the wards in open cages as an easier mode of mass transport and were always playing with each other, laughing happily and seldom crying. I noticed immediately how stoic and long-suffering Africans are when in pain and their remarkable patience and resilience never ceased to astonish me.

Bara's maternity hospital was the busiest in the world at the time, and I witnessed my first birth there — trolleys lined up to deliver the mothers and not a doting father in sight. Sometimes newborns with abnormalities, and twins, went missing as they were deemed 'evil' children by some tribes, and would be killed in ritual practices. Sangomas, or traditional healers, practised in the community, and frequently patients only sought help with conventional medicine as a last resort.

As the only white working 'on the floor', I was a novelty to my black colleagues who interrogated me on why I came to their country knowing of apartheid and then chose to work at Baragwanath, the black hospital. Whites asked me the same question. I would explain that I didn't support the system but working at Bara would be some recompense and I'd always wanted to visit Africa.

The hospital was a bed of anti-apartheid activism, and a few of my black colleagues came from ANC (African National Congress) families and had fathers or brothers interned on Robben Island, or under house arrest. Several treated me with hostility as a white and others were friendly and gave me a thorough induction course on apartheid. Conversations were brief during work time as it was so busy and staff rooms segregated. However, I was keen to hear about their lives and understand the unjust system. There were many unspoken rules of behaviour, and before long, I was warned to stop asking questions and keep my mouth shut or risk deportation. Liberal political views were not tolerated or discussed, according to the Afrikaans management.

My black colleagues loved fashion and bought beautiful clothes on hire purchase — to be proudly paraded in when paid off. It was quite a sight to behold. The nursing sister, Constance, belonged to a famous tribal family and attended royal weddings all over the African continent in designer shoes purchased in Kenya. Zodwa's father was a sangoma, and he would show up adorned in shells, animal skins and bits of bone that made it impossible to x-ray him. Young Beauty was a fond tippler and frequently disappeared for a very long lunch across the bridge over the highway to the shebeen on the other side.

It made me sad that I couldn't be friends with them as our daily lives were so different, and it was dangerous for whites to wander around Soweto and socialise there. It had only been four years since the Soweto riots of the 16th of June 1976 when 575 people died, mostly resulting from heavy-handed police action. On the anniversary every year, white staff risked their cars getting stoned, and it was always deemed too dangerous for me to do night duty at the hospital.

At the end of my two years working there, a representative group of the girls in their best finery bade me fond farewell with swaying Zulu dances and chanting. I was very touched. As a consequence of witnessing extreme trauma and pathology, I had collected an exceptional portfolio of rare x-rays which later raised eyebrows in the more sanitised hospitals of the western world. One patient had a flick knife sticking out of the side of his eye whilst getting x-rayed, and I had a prized abdominal film with a tapeworm a few metres long visible in the intestines. The Aids pandemic was widespread at the time, but the first case wasn't diagnosed in South Africa until 1987, several years after I left.

Apartheid finally came to an end with the formation of a democratic government in 1994 after Nelson Mandela's release. Seven years later, in the new millennium, I returned for a visit to South Africa, keen to witness the transformation in my old workplace. It was very emotional seeing the multiple changes in the country. As in other former African colonies, it didn't happen for everyone overnight, and the crime rate was still too high. Public transport had deteriorated as many whites in government service and management roles fled the country. Their black replacements lacked experience and training because they were never treated as equals. There was still anger on the streets, and I had to be careful. It takes a long time to dismantle an oppressive regime and switch leadership roles.

At Baragwanath, one of my former students was now the boss in x-ray, and we had a fond reminisce on old times and discussed changes in the hospital. My former white colleagues had all left. Miriam, the staunch ANC activist who had been hostile to me before, invited me to lunch with her in the now communal canteen for all races. Her journalist husband had been released from prison with Mandela and was now a minister in the new government. They had been invited to Ireland to lecture on the evils of apartheid.

The casualty corridors were much quieter than during apartheid times as blacks could now present at any hospital for treatment. Waves of black radiographers started travelling to the UK and Ireland to work, and a few young students asked me if I could get them jobs when they qualified. Finally, they could reach for new horizons.

And I ran into an older Constance, still dancing in designer Kenyan shoes.

THE CRAIC IN BAGHDAD

I'm probably one of the few people in the world indebted and grateful to Saddam Hussein, the former Iraqi dictator. My bonus for working in a war zone during the Iran/Iraq war got me on the property ladder in Sydney, and I call my apartment 'Saddam's Pad'. I could never have imagined that this two-year contract between 1983 and 1985 in Baghdad would be great fun as well as an excellent career move. However, I do feel sad that circumstances at the time sheltered us significantly from the pain and suffering of the Iraqi people.

Desperate to escape the economic recession of the 1980s in Ireland, I applied for a job as a radiographer and couldn't believe my luck when I got it! I was euphoric at the prospect of exploring new horizons in the Middle East and a tax-free salary. The fact of it being an active war zone didn't even cross my mind at 28 years of age. I'd been working in Soweto, South Africa for the previous two years and the trauma I'd witnessed there had been horrendous. *Baghdad couldn't be much worse*, I reckoned.

The war had been ongoing since 1980, and as a consequence, Iraqis weren't allowed to travel to the UK or US for medical treatment. Saddam decided to bring the expertise to Iraq, and an Irish company PARC won the contract to establish Ibn-al-Bitar hospital in Baghdad. It would specialise in kidney transplants and cardiac surgery and bring the first CT scanner to the country.

During an initiation course in Dublin, we were briefed on the mores of the Islamic faith. At the time, 80% of Iraq was Sunni Muslim, 10% Shia, with the rest a mixture of Christian and Orthodox sects. However, Iraq under Saddam Hussein, was a secular state unlike a few other Middle Eastern countries, and women were not required to cover up, they could drive, and alcohol was not forbidden. Without these freedoms, PARC might have had more difficulty recruiting 400 Irish people to work there! We were advised to be discreet in our behaviour and warned against fraternising with Iraqis because of security issues. 'Don't mention the war,' they told us, as the Iraqi Ministry of Health would be scrutinising us carefully.

I was among the first 50 staff to arrive in Baghdad in May 1985, just in time for the official opening of the hospital by the President. After the ceremonial sacrifice of the sheep in the parking lot, Saddam toured the various departments and my boss James, and I got to shake his hand as he passed through x-ray. A dark, handsome man in his smart army uniform, I do recall a cold glint in his eyes as he inquired when the new scanner would be operational. My hand was sweaty with the heat, and I shivered with nerves meeting the dictator. I was very politically naive at the time, utterly ignorant of his iron hold on the general populace and it was only later that his genocidal treatment of the Kurds came to light.

The imminent arrival of the Irish nurses, as we were all labelled, was eagerly awaited for months in advance. There were many ex-pat camps of male engineers, builders and other workers situated in desert regions, who looked forward to English-speaking female company.

On a somewhat derogatory note, I did hear the term 'fresh meat' mentioned, and the rubber dollies of the desert got deflated!

The Islamic weekend commenced at midday on Thursday, and Friday was the equivalent of the Christian Sunday. The first weekend after arrival, a group of us were invited to the 'security conference' at the British Embassy and in our naivety, thought it was instruction on evacuation procedures in the event of an emergency. After passing security, we walked across the well-watered cricket pitch, which was the greenest spot in all of Iraq and entered the elegant villa. Welcomed by the Embassy staff, we were then handed a Harvey Wallbanger cocktail and directed to the balcony overlooking the Tigris River. It felt surreal gazing across to the opposite bank where a communications centre had been bombed by the Iranians the previous week. And yet the 'bubble' of the cocktail party continued unabated.

The war front at the time was in the east, but stray missiles did make their way to Baghdad, and at times our revelry would be interrupted by an explosion somewhere in the city, and everyone would rush to windows to see where the missile hit. Some new arrivals, fresh off the plane from Dublin, would often freak out and a few took the next flight home. One time, when the war escalated, we were evacuated out of the city centre and were always advised to have a bag packed ready to flee to the Jordanian border.

Walking, or driving around the streets of the city, there was no escaping Saddam. His face was portrayed on billboards everywhere, and he featured daily on the television screen. An English speaking channel on Radio Baghdad played an excellent selection of Western pop tunes interspersed with broadcasts of Saddam's *communiques*. One minute, Lionel Richie was crooning *Stuck on You*, then was followed by *Communique No 3201*: *Today the Iraqi Armed Forces pushed forward and succeeded in a great battle inflicting 1000 enemy casualties*. In current times, they could be compared to Trump's tweets, and there was undoubtedly a lot of fake news!

As our accommodation blocks weren't yet complete, we spent many months billeted in the famous Al-Rasheed, a luxury hotel well known later as the haven for Western journalists reporting on the Gulf War. The nuclear bunker in the basement was always reassuring. I was more impressed with my plush en suite with the marble-floored bathroom and bidet. The fluffy towels with the Al-Rasheed logo were to be found in homes throughout rural Ireland for years afterwards.

A rumour circulated that the bidet was bugged as well as the lighting in the corridors, however as a race unfamiliar with bidets, the Irish most often used them as beer coolers. We were also highly unlikely to be accused of seditious plots, and those listening in must have struggled to understand the boisterous conversations of raucous room parties.

The Scheherazade bar on the ground floor poured premium Johnnie Walker whisky and the 1001 Nights Disco on the rooftop sported glammed-up Asian call girls and the wealthy Iraqi elite until the rowdy Irish took over the joint. Sometimes Uday, Saddam's playboy son would turn up, and our minders would keep a close watch on which Irish girl he was eyeing up and endeavour to get her off the premises before an awkward situation arose. At the time, we were unaware of his reputation for getting exactly what he wanted, and that when out cruising the streets, if he spotted a woman he fancied, his bodyguards were ordered to drag her into the car. The abducted would be dumped later when he'd finished with her.

I learned after reading a book titled *I Was Saddam's Son*, that both Saddam and Uday had many 'lookalikes' trained to 'be' them, adopting all their physical characteristics and personality traits. These doubles would appear in public, and no one knew if it was the real Saddam or Uday present. This strategy was a security measure in the event of kidnapping or assassination.

As the staff numbers increased with the workload of the hospital, life in Baghdad took on a particular routine. All kinds of sports clubs were established, and quite a few Irish joined the Hash House Harriers — an international ex-pat running club. The Hash was an excellent opportunity to explore the city suburbs and witness everyday life among the date groves, but the poverty in some areas was confronting. Many shanty houses hooked up to electricity pylons with dodgy wiring, and there were litter-strewn open sewers adjacent to where children played in the dust. We were a novel sight for the neighbourhood to behold, unused to seeing females in shorts — and the residents cheered us on.

I did struggle with the expatriate lifestyle, unused to its particular restraints in a war zone like Iraq, where people disappeared, and were jailed or deported. I was used to freedom and independence when visiting a new country and usually would bond with local people at a deeper level. I did befriend the family of one of the Iraqi telephonists at work, and she invited me to her home. Her brother was an English teacher in Babylon and asked me out a few times, but I always ensured Salma, his sister, accompanied us. He quickly got fed up with that, not understanding platonic friendships, and sadly, the contact ceased.

I also met a wealthy Iraqi, Tarek, who socialised in the high echelons of the military elite. He invited me for a picnic to an island on the Tigris River with a few of his army friends, and I took some girlfriends along. After a while, we were none too amused when a macho, competitive streak took over, and the 'trigger happy' army guys started a shooting game with their rifles. Tarek also took me to the cinema one time which I thought might be enlightening, but it was just more glorification of Saddam's Baath Party. The small audience of snogging couples were probably only escaping strict Islamic homes.

Despite the partying, serious work was achieved and the reputation of Ibn-al-Bitar was growing, as word of first-class surgery performed in a war zone spread in medical circles. Cardiac and renal teams would fly out from Dublin or London for a week to perform the operations once the patients were prepped. We called them 'seagulls' who flew in, dropped shit, and flew out again. In Ireland, there's always been a medical hierarchy of consultants who usually don't fraternise socially with the lower medical ranks; however, on the well-paid junkets to Iraq, they let their hair down. There was a saying — 'What goes on in Baghdad, stays in Baghdad!' President Hussein rewarded well a number of these consultants with gifts of diamond-studded Cartier watches, the only drawback being, his mugshot was on the watch face!

My daily work in x-ray was very satisfying as we had state-of-the-art equipment, and there was always some improvisation required due to the war. I learnt basic Arabic, enough for everyday pleasantries and the x-ray phrases essential to communicate with the patients. From time to time, interesting high-profile persons arrived for examinations, and the new CT scanner was much in demand by the top military echelons.

I performed a scan once on a close member of Saddam's family with the security entourage standing guard in the background. Sadly, I didn't receive the infamous gold watch! Once, a wizened old Kurdish chief, who was certainly over 80, accompanied his latest young wife in her 20s, who was undergoing fertility tests. It was usually deemed to be the woman who had problems conceiving, and we struggled to hold our amusement in check.

Noor was our young receptionist, whose brothers were away at the battlefront and came home for a few days' leave from time to time. As we continued living our very different lives, it was distressing to see the anguish on her face some mornings when she'd said goodbye to one of her siblings returning to the fighting. I became increasingly aware of the vast chasm between our ex-pat lives and those of Iraqi families suffering the horrors of war and Saddam's dictatorship.

In the cool of the evening, groups of us wandered downtown to the souks, a labyrinth of arcades which were a step back in time, all manner of intricate craftsmanship going on. The constant din of copper being beaten into ornate plates or ordinary household utensils echoed in the alleyways. The artisans were welcoming and proud of their work. Men in white *dishdasha* and *keffiyeh* on their heads, chatted over mint tea served in tiny ornate glasses, and the aroma of strong Arabic coffee filled the air. On the sidewalks, others inhaled from their hookahs while watching the passing parade. After dark, families strolled by the river Tigris and ate the tasty local fish *masgouf*, which was cooked in foil on charcoal burners.

The main roads were always busy with military vehicles going to and fro, and taxis with a coffin on the roof were a regular sight. There were rumours that Saddam stockpiled war casualties in a warehouse on the outskirts of Baghdad and that he deliberately underestimated the death numbers. Strategic points in the city were heavily barricaded, and there were anti-aircraft guns on rooftops. It was surprising how quickly it all became normal for us.

Shortly after arrival, while out exploring, I unknowingly took a photo of one of Saddam's palaces and was quickly surrounded by pointed guns and bundled into an army patrol vehicle. At the police station, I was quizzed and shouted at in Arabic for three hours and the film torn from my camera. It was frightening, and I was close to tears until a hospital translator arrived to rescue me. This man was reputed to be a spy in our ranks, but on this occasion, I was relieved to see him and knew I was lucky to be released with a warning.

Saddam loved his grand monuments glorifying war and the Arabic revolution, the most famous being the Monument of Liberty stretching across Liberation Square and the newly built Martyrs Monument dedicated to the sacrifice of soldiers in the current war. A massive onion-shaped dome in turquoise tiles illuminated the night sky, with the national flag flying; a tricolour of red, white and black, with 'God is greatest' written in Kufic script. His other fetish was constructing scenes from the popular folktales in *A Thousand and One Nights*, and a favourite of mine was at Ali Baba roundabout where a golden Murjana was perched atop the forty large jars pouring his boiling oil on the thieves within.

The short Islamic weekends were precious to us, and everyone was keen to escape the city and explore the cultural or scenic sights in the countryside. On Thursday evenings, a convoy of British Land Rovers would drive to Lake Thathar, in the middle of the stony desert, which was an exciting 4WD off-road trip for the last section. We would camp by the lakeshore, some people sleeping on mattresses on the roofs of vehicles for protection against crawly sand creatures, and others braving it out on the ground by the campfires. I learned to windsurf there, and the lake was a major recreational area for Iraqis before the war. We would often see the odd group of local men out hunting with their hooded falcons.

Modern-day Iraq is ancient Mesopotamia, the area between the Tigris and Euphrates rivers, and frequently referred to as the 'cradle of civilisation' because it was the first place where sophisticated urban centres evolved. It was hard to imagine the Baghdad we knew as a model of city planning when constructed in 762 AD, and ironically called 'The City of Peace'. It boasted palaces, mosques, baths, and most importantly, old schools of learning. We visited the Mustansiriya Madrassah, the world's first free university providing food, lodging and a monthly stipend to students of astronomy, mathematics, medicine and theology. Its extensive ornamental arched galleries were still striking.

Apart from the culture, we were curious to explore the restaurants of the city, and a favourite was The Rathouse on Rasheed St. It was called this for obvious reasons, and I found it best not to let my eyes stray into dim corners. Friendly waiters greeted us and brought large skewers of succulent meat, often aflame, to the immaculately white-clothed tables. On my first visit there, there was much laughter as I licked my lips in appreciation, only to discover that the soft melting texture and irresistible flavour I'd been enjoying was lambs testicles and an Arabic delicacy! I nearly threw up and never ordered them again, but generally, the food was delicious.

As a contrast, I celebrated my 30th birthday with a few friends at the majestic Khan Murjan, which had a stunning vaulted ceiling and soft light falling from the apertures above. It had been a major trading centre and caravanserai in the era of the Silk Road. Melodic classical Arabic music resonated which originated in Iraq as sung poetry and stories. The echo of the flute and oud soared heavenward, and I was happy to be embracing a new decade in such a place. We tucked into platters of rich, spicy biryani and skewered meats dripping in fat — accompanied by dishes of tabbouleh, hummus, dolmas, olives and warm lavash bread — all washed down by bottles of the local Ferida beer. And there was no wildlife lurking nearby for the leftovers!

The hospital management organised bus trips for us on Fridays to various archaeological sites or Islamic shrines. Of course, high on everyone's list was visiting Babylon and its legendary Hanging Gardens; conjuring an image of lush greenery falling over exotic waterfalls and figurines of sensuous maidens reclining amongst it all. It was nothing like that in reality and very disappointing after a sweltering journey in 40C temperatures to arrive at a pile of crumbling mud walls. The Germans, who excavated the site, brought the original magnificent Ishtar Gate with the Lions of Babylon to Berlin, and left a poor facade, fast deteriorating in the desert conditions. There were no guides at any of the cultural sites as understandably, all men were at the war front, and no tourist information was available at that time — pre-internet.

I was very disappointed to not visit the marshes on the border with Iran, as I had read Wilfred Thesiger's fascinating book detailing the extraordinary life of the Marsh Arabs. Living on islands of reeds, burning animal dung as fuel, they were fishermen renowned for their hospitality in big reed houses called *mudhif.* Some of the staff stayed in this remarkable region in the early days, but as the war worsened the marshes became a scene of horrific slaughter and were off-limits.

Another time, a group of us travelled to the far north into Iraqi Kurdistan, a beautifully green and scenic mountainous area and a welcome break from the hot plains. We visited the ancient city of Hatra, renowned for its marble statues and old cuneiform clay tablets; the world's oldest form of writing dating to 3000 BC. If stone could utter words, it would be a rich tale. We overnighted in the capital Erbil, which has featured so much in news broadcasts. The dark kohled faces of Kurdish women were stunning, and they looked colourful and stylish in puffed pants and sequined gowns with jangling jewellery. They sat on the kerbside, surrounded by a cluster of children and sold an array of spices and the juiciest apricots I've ever tasted.

One of the craziest ventures was flying from Baghdad to Cardiff in Wales for an international rugby match at Cardiff Arms Park! On a Friday morning, we flew into London Heathrow on Iraqi Airways, travelled by coach to Cardiff, and immediately got into the spirit of the occasion — Ireland v Wales. We girls hit the high street to buy multiples of everything in a short few hours, cosmetics, lingerie and the latest fashion trend — in my case, three jumpsuits in various colours. These splurges happen when living a sheltered ex-pat life! Pints of Brains Dark beer got drunk on the afternoon of the match, and more when Ireland won 21-9. The six-hour flight returning to Baghdad early Sunday morning was riotous; however, the atmosphere became immediately subdued as we landed in darkness due to impending missile strikes. It had been a brief reprieve from war.

The two years of my contract passed quickly, and although I could have extended, I was keen to move to fresh pastures and was considering emigrating to Australia and an ordinary world.

My farewell party was in the infamous Rathouse, where a Welsh friend compered a *This is Your Life* sketch that was highly embarrassing but very funny and clever. It incorporated all those stories you tell and mad moments that you hope get forgotten! I was sad saying goodbyes to great friends, but one of the most precious rewards of ex-pat life is the friendships lasting a lifetime. And I nibbled a skewer of lamb's testicles 'for old times' sake'!

The war had escalated again, and no international flights were departing Baghdad, so I travelled overland to Jordan across the desert. This journey was an adventure in itself as it was during Ramadan, and I had to cover up and keep a low profile accompanying a single man who wasn't my husband.

Baghdad and Iraq changed utterly after my departure in May 1985. The Iran/Iraq war ended with a truce on the 20th of July 1988, and there was a brief period of normality until the Gulf War started after Saddam invaded Kuwait on the 2nd of August 1990. The Irish staff fled then as it was too dangerous to remain and Ibn-al-Bitar closed its doors as the 'Irish hospital'.

The infrastructure and daily life in Iraq have been destroyed since, following the country's invasion by a coalition of foreign powers and eventually Saddam's downfall and capture in 2003. In his wake, Iraq suffered a civil war, widespread corruption and political turmoil with occupation by US troops lasting until 2011. It was left a devastated country after the constant bombing, with sanitation and health services in havoc. When I witnessed the horrific street scenes frequently on TV, I would think of Noor and our other Iraqi colleagues whose lives were persistently ruined by warfare.

And as we all now know — the weapons of mass destruction were never found.

THE SNAKEBITE

September 1985 on the slopes of Mt Merapi, Indonesia

It was 5 am when it happened. There were six of us climbing the mountain to witness dawn from the summit, and we had only two torches between us. The narrow path was overgrown and steep as we walked in an eerie silence, not properly awake yet.

Suddenly Diana screamed behind me and jumped to the edge of the path shouting that something had bitten her. On turning, I saw a snake quickly wriggle away into the undergrowth and looked at Diana's panic-stricken face. The snake got her on the ankle through her socks, and there was a small mark, but no immediate swelling or unbearable pain. We looked at each other in ignorance of what to do, and someone suggested a quick scout of the immediate area to see if we could sight the culprit for identification purposes, but we saw nothing.

To be on the safe side, Richard, who knew the area well, volunteered to return with Diana to the guesthouse and ask advice from the locals who must surely know the procedure.

As it wasn't far to the summit, the rest of us continued, but it put a dampener on our little expedition, and I felt guilty. Being a fast walker, I was first in line, and they say that person disturbs the snake and it bites the second in line — a chance of place. It could have been me. Also, I had befriended Diana in recent days and perhaps should have accompanied her down the mountain.

Mt Merapi, the 'Fire Mountain' is one of Indonesia's most destructive active volcanoes and frequently the caldera rim is off-limits because of dangerous sulphurous fumes. However, we were in luck and breaking through the cloud at 2911 metres were just in time to see the fireball of a new day emerging over the opposite edge. I stood in awe at the glowering hell below in the crater. Dawn broke in a splash of pinks at 5.40 am, and after snapping a few photos, we weren't keen to hang around, wanting to descend quickly and check on Diana.

Back at Vogels losmen, the news wasn't good. Her leg had swollen, and the pain was increasing. She'd visited the local clinic, but there was no doctor present, and a nurse advised she seek treatment at Jogyakarta hospital. More worrying, Christian the guesthouse owner told us that a deadly black and white snake was endemic to the region, and if bitten by it, death can occur within hours. It was now 7.30 am, and I assured the terrified Diana I hadn't seen such distinct marking, and I offered to accompany her to Jogya.

She and I had met there a few days before and clicked immediately as two solo female backpackers but heading in opposite directions. Swopping travel notes, she raved on about the beauty of Tahiti where I was going, and I warned her of the dangers of Khaosan Rd in Bangkok, famous for shopping but also a warren of pickpockets and scammers. We shared an interest in the old Sanskrit epic Ramayana and sought out the best dance performance that evening while bargaining for batik at the market en route.

She looked no different from other travellers I'd met. It was the era of colourful sarongs and baggy cotton pants purchased for a few dollars at roadside stalls. Everyone scraped by on a shoestring budget gorging on seasonal fruit during the day and cheap spicy street food at night. Pre-internet, Lonely Planet guides were the bible, and new friendships were forged easily in the popular rock-bottom guesthouses they recommended.

It didn't feel right to abandon Diana, and I'd been moving quite quickly anyway, so I could afford to rest up for a few days and lend support. A crowded bemo, the local minivan, was leaving the village at 9 am and the locals found a hobbling Diana and myself very amusing as we squashed in next to live chickens and produce for market in hessian sacks on the floor. The driver refused to take us directly to the hospital in Jogyka, leaving us to balance in an unwieldy rickshaw for the last leg of the journey.

The hospital was operated by nuns and looked somewhat run down. We were hours waiting for the doctor, and I tried to keep Diana distracted from her pain with humorous travel tales and my childhood history of smuggling on the Irish border. At one point a Catholic faith healer arrived with holy water for her to drink and proceeded to massage a little into her swollen leg. At the same time, the nuns mumbled a few prayers in Bahasa Indonesian. When he eventually arrived, the doctor looked perturbed and didn't appear very knowledgeable on the matter. He injected a dose of serum, administered a pain killer and packed us off in an ambulance to the zoo to consult Alex, the snake expert there.

By now, it was early afternoon, and Diana was going ballistic, crying with pain and frustration. I felt so helpless. Alex took over in a very professional manner, immediately producing a book on snakes written by himself and asking us to identify one if possible. He stated that it was most likely a common snake in the Merapi area, which was poisonous but not lethal.

Looking very confident, he made some pinholes in Diana's ankle, sucked on the area for a time until the poison started draining out itself under slight pressure. Her foot was now like a balloon, so he made more pricks near the toes and alternated sucking at the two places for the next few hours while Diana yelled in agony. Finding it all too harrowing, I took myself off to wander around the zoo.

The sucking process would be the treatment for the next few days until the swelling went down, and Alex invited us to his home so that he could keep a close eye on progress. The family appeared well-off, owning a beautiful tropical villa where Diana and I shared an ornate four-poster bed overlooking the lush backyard. Caged enclosures housed a fascinating menagerie of animals Alex was training at home. Three Sumatran tigers groomed each other regularly, an orangutan cowered shyly in the corner, and an exotic mix of birds would chirp and screech us awake in the early dawn.

That first evening while Diana was miserable, uncommunicative and sorry for herself, I enjoyed the company of Alex's wife and daughter who fattened me on delightful spicy foods. With the help of my invaluable Lonely Planet dictionary, I reciprocated with ad hoc English classes.

The following few days were a fun time for me. However, I couldn't stay around as I had a flight to catch to Bali. Diana had decided to abort the remainder of her travels and fly to Thailand to stay with an aunt. Alex would work on her daily until well enough to travel, and I knew she was in good hands.

It was emotional saying goodbyes. Diana and I had bonded during our time together under challenging circumstances. We swopped addresses promising to meet up the following year. After my trip, I would be working in London for a time, and she invited me to visit her Scottish home when I settled.

The Scottish Highlands August 1986

After some hours hugging the wild sweeping cliffs, the bus trundled into the sleepy town of Dooncrief where Diana was to collect me. I recognised her immediately, waving from a nifty little sports car and looking more glamourous than the previous year. Bear hugs exchanged, we retreated from the driving rain to a nearby coffee shop to catch up. Although I'd received a letter from Thailand filling me in on her recovery,

I wanted to hear the nitty-gritty of her last days in Indonesia with Alex. She informed me that her foot returned to normal after a few days, but the whole incident had shaken her travel confidence, and she didn't remain long in Thailand.

She changed the subject then, enquiring what I'd seen at the Edinburgh Festival which had just finished. I raved on about panpipe music from the Andes, and an Irish play called *The Intimate Memoirs of an Irish Taxidermist* before Diana told me her father's family were musicians and frequently performed at it. 'What a shame I didn't know', I said.

We didn't linger chatting as other guests were arriving for the weekend and she had groceries to pick up. She said that 'the season' had started, which mystified me. However, I soon got the gist of her family wealth as we collected an 18 kilo T-bone steak fillet-joint and a large box of prawns which was all put on the estate's account. She didn't carry any money. And we left a few fresh salmon in to be smoked.

It was a beautiful drive up into the hills above the village of Kilconell, over which she revealed her father Andy MacDonald was the laird. Arriving at a grand stately home called Kinloch with a couple of Saabs parked in the driveway, I was ushered into a big farmhouse kitchen, and Diana went off to find her mother. The two cordon bleu cooks employed for the summer seemed busy with platters and pies but took time to make me a welcome cuppa and chitchat. The gamekeeper wandered through with his brace of fowl.

Mrs MacDonald was young and jean-clad in a horsey fashion. Not over friendly or curious, she was nonetheless welcoming and thanked me for being Diana's saviour in Indonesia. She whisked me off for a tour of the house and instructed a maid to prepare the blue suite for me. The mansion had 15 bedrooms, seven bathrooms and six large reception rooms, all elegantly furnished in polished antiques yet with a homely atmosphere. There were no less than five staircases due to a great-grandfather's paranoia about a fire, and the route to my room passed a gallery of forbidding looking ancestors and priceless artworks.

Diana's mother explained she was a fine art consultant and her husband Andy dabbled in property. He and his sister were famous in the US and toured the world as talented folk musicians, but Andy then settled to run the clan's estate. She quizzed me on who I knew in Ireland, quickly realising that I wasn't related to anyone of importance among the Anglo-Irish gentry of the day and therefore didn't mix in her circles. I was a nobody.

Later that evening, I was to learn that Diana's mother before marriage was Countess Claudia Bergman von Hofmannsthal, a branch of the

Hapsburg Empire and whose family owned 100 castles in Austria until they had to flee the Nazi invasion.

Unpacking my well-worn rucksack in my grand suite, I quickly realised that I didn't have any suitable attire for the evening ahead and went in search of Diana to borrow a little black number for dinner. We were to meet for drinks in the library at five. I'd never thought to ask Diana what her job was and curious now, I enquired. She said she worked for an antique business in London and lived in the family's London residence in Hampstead but planned to travel shortly to Mali for a while. I would later realise that travelling incognito in the ordinary world was a rite of passage for the offspring of wealthy families before conforming to family class expectations.

Scrubbed up and reasonably presentable, I heard the bell tinkle at five and wandered into the well-stocked library to be served French champagne by the butler, and I met Diana's father. I asked about his folk music days in the US learning that the MacDonald duo was part of the Greenwich Village scene and they hung out with Pete Seeger and a young Bob Dylan who played support for them on a few occasions. Diana dragged me off to meet her younger set of cousins and introduced me again as her snake rescuer. I was beginning to feel like a genuine heroine from a wild jungle story. When asked about my job, no one knew what a radiographer was — they thought I repaired radios!

The cross-generational talk was arty and educated, where I felt out of my depth at times. After a delicious dinner of prawns with homemade mayonnaise and fresh salmon to follow, we adjourned to the drawing-room for board games that got rather too heady after a few glasses of exquisite Bordeaux. Retiring to my boudoir at 3 am, I reflected on my extraordinary evening that was so alien to my everyday bohemian lifestyle. I realised it is all just a chance of birth as every society has its social strata and often when travelling in Africa, I've been perceived as the privileged one and provided entertainment for the locals with my strange habits.

Next morning, breakfast was a running buffet served by maids in starched uniforms, and I felt slightly uncomfortable deferred to as being important. Surely they had seen my battered rucksack on arrival? Afterwards, the family were preoccupied organising a banquet that evening for guests from London, so I took off over the moors for a stroll. Kinloch was a smallish estate of a mere 1200 acres compared to its previous size of 4500.

I met the shepherdess on my rambles, moving sheep to a new area. She told me she had never left the valley to even go to Edinburgh a few hours away. She pointed to an old farmhouse in a lonely glen which was the writing studio of Diana's younger brother Harry who had invited me to call in. Glad of a distraction from writer's block, he made me a hot chocolate and explained the plot of his first novel.

Shortly after my return at noon, the bell rang for a pre-lunch cocktail; the MacDonald clan version of Bloody Mary's, before a sumptuous lunch of smoked turkey, prawn loaf, an array of salads, and a whole cheese with gingerbread. I dug in with gusto after my dose of moorland air. Afterwards, an impromptu jazz/blues session started up in the music room led by Andy and his nephew who played the sax well. An elegant French woman, Madeleine, was a gifted pianist.

Mid-afternoon, the whirr of helicopters landing on the pad on the lawn halted the revelry and heralded the arrival of new guests. The line of sports cars was growing in the driveway, and Diana's parents disappeared to allocate rooms and supervise servants scurrying about with luggage and tea trays.

A Scottish mist was creeping in over the hills, and soon heavy rain was pelting the high Georgian windows. The bad weather delayed a few guests. Backgammon boards and cards filled the gap until it was time to dress for dinner again. With a storm brewing outside and darkening skies, a game of Cluedo would have aptly fitted the scene. *Who killed Colonel Mustard in the library with the spanner?*

Borrowing another dress off Diana, I wallowed in an old cast iron bath from the last century wondering how I'd gotten myself into this situation. At drinks before dinner, the guest numbers had swelled to near twenty, and I was struggling to memorise the aristocratic names — mixing up the Ruperts, Ronalds, Alexandras and Victorias.

A few spoke with positively plummy accents; they were called 'Hooray Henry' types in London at the time. Diana's father, brothers and male cousins were attired in the MacDonald tartan and sporrans. Even the two maids serving dinner wore the clan kilts and starched blouses. Between courses of borscht soup, rollmops from Sweden and hides of roast meats and venison, sorbet layered with pressed edible flowers and leaves was served in magnificent iced bowls to cleanse the palate.

A merchant banker to my left rapidly tired of my normality and started casting the eye lecherously at the young girls with short skirts and endless legs. An amusing woman, who introduced herself as Margarita, soon occupied the vacant seat to my right. Her ancestral home wasn't far from my Irish hometown, and she launched into friendly banter.

Knocking back the good Bordeaux at rather an unladylike pace, she was soon offloading some of the torrid details of her marital problems and contentious divorce. I was a fascinated audience. Only later when the butler called her to the telephone as Lady Devereux did I suddenly realise that she was the wife of Lord Devereux, a relative of the Queen. I felt enveloped in the drama of a Barbara Cartland romantic novel, and it was positively surreal.

After dinner, the young men were shepherded off by the older males for port, cigars and gentlemen's talk in the library. Countess Claudia gathered her peer group to gossip on the scandals of the day and Fergie's antics trying to hook Prince Andrew was a favourite topic. A silver tray with shots of schnapps, Poire Williams and Grand Marnier was laid on the sideboard, and I circulated among the 'Sloane Ranger' younger set, wondering how long my stamina could keep going. A stylish woman called Arabella cornered me for a conversation and seemed genuinely intrigued by my nomadic lifestyle and strange career. Around 2 am and pleasantly intoxicated, I sneaked quietly off to my suite and left the gentry still in full swing.

Sunday dawned bright and clear after the heavy rain and thunder during the night, and it was a perfect day for the hunt. The men assembled on the lawn in kilts again, and the groomed horses were brought from the stables. I was very sorry to be leaving, but the day's activities were not my scene, and I probably would have disgraced myself on a horse. Before departure, I signed the visitor book as a snake rescuer and radio operator and glanced through the many titled entries of past seasons. Before the tally ho-ing commenced, I thanked Diana's parents for their generous hospitality and kindness, ensuring them I had had a fantastic time.

As Diana hared along the scenic route to Dooncrief to drop me at the bus, I wondered whether we would see each other again in London and despite exchanging addresses, somehow doubted it.

On the old bus to Edinburgh, I could feel my body relax into the worn seat and become itself again, all thought of correct Ps and Qs forgotten.

A HIKE INTO EVEREST

My Tibetan granny has kept me company for 30 years now, on the wall above my desk. I am probably older than she was then in 1987, and she has long gone to the carrion sky god in the heavens. I do hope her family received the photos I posted afterwards — a fond reminder of the evening we all danced the night away.

In that year, the border post at Khasa on the Nepalese/ Tibetan border opened to foreigners for a time, and as I was hiking in Nepal, it was an opportunity too good to miss. Since the Chinese occupation in 1960, Tibet had been mainly off bounds to outsiders.

After a hassle-free border crossing, public bus transport was erratic and rough, so I hitched onwards on the main road to Lhasa on a Chinese lorry with three other foreigners and a mixed group of Nepalese and Tibetans. The route crossed several passes over 3000 metres, increasing the risk of altitude sickness and hypothermia and we were very exposed in the back of the open truck. When an icy wind got up, I huddled down in my sleeping bag and peered out at the barren plateau called the 'rooftop of the world'. It was absolutely freezing, and I sipped my bottle of homemade Baileys for solace. I had concocted it in a monk's kitchen in Kathmandu where I'd hung out with a Canadian fisherwoman, who made liqueurs for a living during her harsh winters.

I planned to disembark at Xegar in a few hours, the closest village to the turnoff to Everest Base Camp. It had long been my desire to see Chomolungma, the Tibetan name for the mountain — the *Abode of the Mother Goddess* at 8848 metres. I'd been forewarned that a strong heart, even stronger will, a devious mind and a heavy dose of recklessness were required for the trek, and I was unsure if I possessed anything other than recklessness.

Despite being crammed in with many warm bodies and glad of them, I was chilled to the bone. The landscape was arid, but in places people were tilling potato fields in traditional clothes, the thick woollen robes called *chuba* worn by both sexes, tied at the waist with a broad belt. Before each Chinese checkpoint, we few foreigners descended and skirted around, as it was forbidden for Chinese drivers to give us lifts.

The truckstop hotel near Xegar was a gloomy soldier's barracks that made spare cash from passing trekkers. Four of us shared a basic room, and the classic stone-platform toilet with a view stood outside the back door and was open to the elements. It was dire, best not witnessed in daylight, and we couldn't find a cold tap to wash.

The usual Chinese flasks for tea held lukewarm water sufficient to make packet noodles palatable for the desperate. My three companions suffered various symptoms of altitude sickness; difficulty breathing, headaches and nausea, but I was lucky to be symptomless. I wandered out before dark to see what the small shop down the road had to offer, washing my face in an icy stream on the way, gasping with the cold. Chinese stores held little at the time, and I dined on glucose biscuits and a tin of spam; packed the bare minimum for my trek by the light of a dim bulb and crawled into my warm sleeping bag.

Tibetans get up late because of the cold, and the next morning I could have easily remained in a state of lethargy in my sleeping bag all day. But I had to return to the turnoff ten kilometres back and needed to hike over the Pang La pass in daylight, with no idea where I'd spend the night. The effect of altitude on me and weather conditions would be unknown factors. The Chinese constructed a rough road the 100 kilometres or so to Base Camp, and I hoped to find accommodation in the small villages en route. Ancient tractors with trailers, used as transport by the locals, would be the only traffic I'd encounter. Spotting no life in the kitchen, or water in flasks for a last hot cuppa, I headed out into the streaky dawn, dressed in all my clothes for extra warmth. It was silent and beautiful as I trudged back along the road; not a bird sang anywhere, and a lorry soon stopped to give me a ride to the turnoff.

I made speedy progress with a spring in my step, and it was a good feeling travelling light, with just a sleeping bag, camera, water and nibbles in a daypack. As a glary ultra-violet-laden sun rose in the sky, I draped my towel around my head for sun protection. I loved hiking alone at my own pace, finding it therapeutic and spiritually enriching to think of nothing, just observing raw Nature around me.

An hour after the turnoff I reached Che village, little more than a few whitewashed houses, the roofs weighted down with boulders. Tibetans are a dark race, further darkened by sooty interiors and harsh weather. One such lady seated on a low stool outside a small store beckoned me over for yak butter tea called *suja* from an old black kettle beside her. This oily tea is an acquired taste and best drunk hot before the rancid globules of congealed fat cool and cause stomach problems, but I was glad of the warmth and she of the few yuan.

The hot drink fortified me for the nearly four-hour hard slog to the pass above, an ascent of almost a thousand metres. Due to the altitude, I struggled breathlessly at times to maintain a steady pace and frequently halted for rests on the steep incline. The sparse sedge grass and wind-resistant lichens and mosses softened the grey slopes, and wild goats grazed in the distance. Finally, I reached the summit at 5200 metres, where gaudy prayer flags flew in the wind and shrines of coloured stones sat in piles. Collapsing to the ground, I reaped my reward. The view beyond was stunning — the entire canvas of some of the world's highest peaks spread out before me — Makalu, Lhotse, Everest, Nuptse and Cho Oyu. It was hard to distinguish the triangular-shaped Everest among the snowy summits. It was one of those moments that make travel worthwhile, and I lingered looking at the impressive view for as long as I could spare.

The descent was slow on the slippery shale slopes and patches of snow, and I decided to cut across country to shorten the zig-zagging track. It was peaceful, and I watched a bird of prey, perhaps a griffon vulture hover over an unsuspecting target. There were rabbit burrows in the patches of tufty grass below. I reached the outskirts of Perriche village after two hours, and my weary feet yearned to rest. It was late afternoon, and I got strange looks from villagers working in the spud fields. I must have looked like Lawrence of Arabia gone astray from the desert, with my turbaned towel!

A group of men drinking *chang* called me over, and I gratefully downed a few slugs. This fermented barley hooch has a tangy taste and sour smell, but I tired of drinking sterilised water tasting of iodine drops. The men were delighted when I said *shapta*, meaning 'cheers' and a young guy wanted to see my phrasebook. I squatted happily among the dug potatoes and reflected on my father digging at home in Ireland. I feel very much at home with spuds and stony grey soil! One man sitting near murmured 'Chomolungma' in a respectful tone, pointing towards the mountains, and I nodded.

Only in recent times were intrepid young travellers wandering into their valley, in search of food and lodging. The villagers had cleverly mastered the sign language necessary for barter and business to take place. After some time, an older man made the sleeping sign, indicating an offer of a bed for the night with his family, and I happily accepted. He packed his rough spade and simple cloth sack, bade *kal-leh phe* to his companions and I accompanied him into Perriche.

The small hamlet was empty of people; only dogs barked, agitated by our passing. The flat-roofed stone buildings looked battened down permanently against harsh winds and bad winters; small windows soot-darkened and most shuttered. We entered a two-storey dwelling in a back alleyway, where three donkeys brayed downstairs, and a few scrawny hens pecked the dirt around them. Ascending to the living quarters above, Jampa then introduced his wife Dorjee and extended family. *'Toshi Dili,'* I greeted them. Granny at the fireside responded with a toothless grin and continued kneading *choo* bread with weathered floury hands. Tibetan greetings are deeply rooted in Tibetan Buddhism, and any efforts by foreigners are much appreciated.

It was the standard Tibetan living space; dark, with a beaten earth floor and the low roof supported with heavy logs and wooden pillars. Two beds were in the corners and brushwood piled by the hearth. Dorjee rekindled the fire for *suja,* and a picture of Mao Tse Tung on the wall nearby stared grimly at me. Three dirty curious children watched my every move, fascinated.

Just before dark, Jampa's son, who had remained in the field, arrived with a young American, Pete, thinking I would be glad of English-speaking company. However, it was the opposite — I was quite happy with the game of cultural sign language and comfortable silence. But Pete was a friendly type and was only travelling as far as the next village for a festival. In a while, two well-used candles were lit as we ate a feed of potatoes and eggs, and my head torch amused the children. Grandpa brought out some old batteries to test them and on seeing they worked, promptly sold them to me for a few yuan. The canny dealer later produced a box of oxo cubes for the same purpose and I happily humoured him — his big smile was sufficient reward.

The family kept late hours, and after dinner, the son Jungney played the *droma*, the Tibetan guitar, accompanied by Grandpa on a goatskin drum. Jungney's five-year-old son took this as a cue and had no inhibitions beginning to dance, joined quickly by his older sisters. Pete and I shortly got the message that it was our turn, and we both jived to rock and roll, then Pete started swinging to the jitterbug, which caused much hilarity. Granny couldn't rest and stood up, grabbed his arm and imitated his gestures. This funny scene raised the roof. Her feet stomped rapidly under grimy worsted woollen layers, and her parchment face took on a wistful look of lost youth. It was a joy to behold. Teacups were filled often and tsampa handed about, roasted barley grains that proved teeth-busting.

The merriment continued until midnight when brushwood and a few animal skins were placed by the fire for Pete and me to lie down on.

The children watched and sniggered as I removed my partial denture and brushed my teeth. Granny opened wide to show her toothless mouth and retired to the dark corner, looking very happy. I was soon completely out of it on my rough bed.

I woke early, keen to breathe the fresh mountain air and escape the stuffy room. The slumbering bodies about me might not wake for some time yet. As I crept downstairs, Granny was below in the dim dawn feeding the donkeys and clucking at her hens. I pressed some notes into her hand and gave her a picture of the Dalai Lama, which transformed her old eyes. I carried a few with me for special people who would show kindness. We hugged an awkward goodbye — the Tibetans as emotionally undemonstrative as the Irish at the time, and I hit the road. Sad goodbyes after random meetings are never easy.

The village of Passum was only an hour away, and a few hikers breakfasted outside a lodge there, munching on muesli bars, crackers and hard yak cheese. The Tibetan tsampa porridge wasn't very popular with Westerners. I didn't dally long as I had a six-hour walk to Chessong and I'd noticed my pace decreasing as I struggled to breathe. A few of the travellers complained of altitude sickness symptoms, and were getting worried; but I was still lucky in this respect, the only headaches experienced from drinking rough *chang*!

I plodded on in a semi-mesmerised state, the track flattish and monotonous until midday. A bitter wind rose then which soon changed to icy sleet, and I pulled a rain poncho close about me. As I neared Chessong, the fast-flowing Dzakar Chu from Everest meltwater involved dangerous stone-hopping in a boulder-strewn plain of tributaries. Coming to a rough plank bridge over one icy rivulet, I glanced up from my feet and got a shock to see three teenage boys wielding stick-like guns at me. I felt fearful but forced myself to smile, but they got quite aggressive as I proceeded, and I wasn't sure if it was a game or genuine hostility to a stranger! I couldn't see the 'weapons' clearly in the driving sleet and was never to find out, as a young woman approached to scare them off.

After filling her bucket at the river, Dawa brought me home with her, and I calmed down and warmed up over a bowl of thick *thukpa*, noodles that would glue your insides. She kindly heated hot water for me to wash. Western washing habits amused the Tibetans, many not seeing their naked bodies for months on end! Dawa lived with her brother and mother in a small house, warmed by the usual livestock below; this time a pair of yaks and a family of kittens mingling with the chickens. She was only in her late teens, had beautiful facial bone structure, and I admired an amulet that encased her slender neck. It was crafted in metal resembling old silver, and the intricate 'tree of life' symbol featured small turquoise and coral stones. Her brother was quite a spiff too, with his Tibetan bowler hat and a dangling turquoise earring in one ear. Seemingly, ancient superstition states that a man without an earring would be reincarnated as a donkey.

There was a lot to learn about Tibetan customs, and I had fun interacting with hand gestures and my basic phrasebook. Somehow I understood that their grandfather was a craftsman and there were gemstones in the surrounding hills. Tibetans believe that turquoise brings good fortune and happiness to its owner, and I later purchased a small string of rough greenish stones from Dawa hoping for luck on my travels. We conversed quietly around the fire, the newborn kittens frolicking around us. I was glad of a quiet early night after the energetic antics of the previous one. This family had a picture of His Holiness the Dalai Lama on the wall, and Dawa's mother insisted I sleep with my head towards him, reminding me of our reverence for holy pictures in Irish kitchens.

I was excited the following day to be reaching Rongbuk Gompa, or monastery, where I would spend the night and do a day hike to Everest Base Camp. The gompa didn't have a good reputation among travellers. The few monks were mercenary and unfriendly, and thefts reported, so I was warned to be extra vigilant with my stuff. It was a five-hour slow ascent into a freezing wind from Chessong, and I could feel my energy sagging quickly. A tractor with a crowded trailer stopped at one point, but I waved it on, being a stubborn hiker and not wanting to ruin my walking record.

It began to snow, and when I sighted buildings, the thickening white carpet made the monastery stupa and prayer flags a welcome sight. I could see nothing of the mountains behind. Rongbuk, at 5000 metres, is the world's highest monastery and its brightly painted buildings would have been a romantic sight for pilgrims who had walked thousands of miles. It has a sad recent history though — destroyed by villagers during the Cultural Revolution after they were indoctrinated to think the monks exploited and oppressed them. Now in 1987, the gompa was only partially restored, and it was upsetting later seeing beautiful old frescoes deteriorating among the ruins.

Two grinning young monks greeted me at the door, garbed in maroon robes and with shaved heads. This cheeky pair seemed to run the guest house and showed me to my spartan room where you had to rent blankets. I retreated to the kitchen in search of *suja* to warm up. A crotchety woman reluctantly made me some and didn't respond to friendly greetings.

Before dark, I ventured out into the snowy Rongbuk valley and was disappointed the usually spectacular view of majestic peaks eluded me in the whiteout. Having come so far, I prayed for clear blue skies in the morning. The valley is named the 'Sanctuary of the Birds' because no animal was ever killed there, or plant or geological specimen taken, out of respect for the Buddhist philosophy. The red monastery building where the monks resided stood out among the ruins and a cluster of humble stone dwellings. I shivered watching a few scantily clad children play in the snow and retreated for my usual sleeping bag hibernation from the cold.

There was no food or hot water available, and I ate my muesli rations for dinner, feeling resentful of the asceticism imposed on me. It was a shame my first experience of a Tibetan monastery was a negative one. In Lhasa and other towns later, I would find the monks welcoming and hospitable, and the atmosphere of the monasteries spiritually uplifting and contemplative. Perhaps, the remoteness and hardship of the Everest region left its legacy on the monks' daily lives at Rongbuk.

My temporary blues disappeared the next morning waking to a magical white wonderland and clear blue sky. Chomolungma dominated the skyline behind the monastery stupa, and I gazed reverently around me. A favourite book from my father's collection suddenly came to mind — James Hilton's *Lost Horizon*. In 1933, the setting was based on a pass in this same area called Changri La. The book's 'Shangri La' was an imaginary paradise on earth, an idyllic hideaway utopia and I felt my spirits soar happily looking at the magnificence surrounding me.

The hike to Base Camp would take me two hours and the thin air was exhausting. I envied the yaks on the hillside their thick coats as I proceeded slowly trying to follow in someone else's deep footprints. I was tired after a freezing sleepless night but exhilarated now my goal was in sight. A few Swedes passed me with loaded yaks, re-supplying their expedition and invited me to tea at their camp.

The tented Base Camp sat snugly in the shadow of imposing peaks, surrounded by stunning ice formations and a frozen lake in the vicinity. The Swedish setup was very impressive, with a full medical team including a neurologist and a well-equipped radio tent with the latest computers. Their friendly chef fed me delicious pancakes while I chatted with the support team. Their mountaineering colleagues were camped higher up intending to summit the following day. I was thrilled when they presented me with an autographed postcard of Everest. Enquiring about a lone Canadian flag flying in the wind further up, I learned that a well-known solo climber Roger Marshall was aiming for the summit too.

We talked about the calamitous history of Everest, regarded by the British as the 'Third Pole'. After their failed attempts being first to reach the North and South Poles, they wanted to restore national prestige in the 1920s, and with Nepal closed to foreigners, attempted the northern approach in Tibet. Climbers Mallory and Irving tragically disappeared in their 1924 attempt to summit and their bodies were never found, claimed by the goddesses of the peak. A significant handicap on the Tibetan side is the tight weather window for climbers. After the tragedy, most expeditions undertook the climb on the Nepalese side when that country opened, and the Chinese were the first to summit in Tibet in 1960.

Bidding the friendly Swedes farewell, I climbed a further 500 metres to reach the junction of two impressive glaciers above and the mere drizzle of the Dzakar Chu torrent from yesterday emerging from the ice. I could have trekked further on the world's highest trail to Advanced Base Camp at 6500 metres, but I'd risked enough on my own. With a last glance at the icy majesty that overwhelmed me, I turned back humbled into the wind.

I spent another night at Rongbuk reading about the yeti — the elusive, big-footed monster of the snows from children's storybooks. At the monastery, it was called *Mugyi* and rumoured to carry off women for supper. Unfortunately, the only thing to disappear that night, in an unguarded moment, was my treasured Swiss army knife, an essential travel companion.

I was offered a lift out next morning on tractor transport heading to the festival at Passam. It was *Saka Dawa*, celebrating the anniversary of the Buddha's birth, enlightenment and death. A group of locals also hopped into the trailer, scrubbed up and wearing cleaner robes than usual for the festive occasion. One sat next to me clutching two trussed chickens and a young pup. Our driver was a lunatic speeder on the stony track, and I clung on desperately as we bumped along. Some sacks of dried dung for firewood spilt over the trailer floor, and we picked up other passengers en route, many wrapped in colourful blankets and everyone was in a holiday mood. Passing through Chessong, an audience of children cheered the foreigner amongst the happy mix, recognising me from my overnight there.

The driver stopped many times for *chang* breaks, arriving back with brighter eyes each time and driving even more erratically, obviously happily pissed. It began to snow, and a few young lads next to me started singing. An old woman worried that I would freeze and shared her thick blanket. Then the pup shitted in anxiety, and all laughed. The tractor was spewing up mud on the track, and the stops became longer. It was all an indescribable scene of comedic farce.

Tibetan Granny in the Everest region

We eventually reached Passam at 4 pm, and I stretched my cramped limbs in relief. There was a vibrant atmosphere in the village as groups of men, dressed in yellow and orange robes rode about on festooned horses. Young girls in colourful shawls strutted about confidently with heads held high. Their braided tresses glittered with ornate combs studded with gemstones. Older women wore clean aprons with geometric patterns, and their necks heavily hung with talismans and multiple strings of amber, turquoise and coral.

I watched a group of musicians set up in the dusk light and listened spellbound as the soft tones of bamboo flutes and the gentle drumming quickened. Suddenly the deep, haunting wail of the Tibetan horn filled the night air, and people stopped what they were doing to listen respectfully.

I felt a tap on my shoulder and turned. It was Granny, beaming from ear to ear and wearing a soft fur hat. Her watery eyes gleamed as she reached out to hold me close, and I just knew she was ready to dance.

FIRST ENCOUNTERS

As a native of Ireland, I first moved to the Inner West of Sydney in January 1988, just in time for the Bicentenary Celebrations. A long panoramic photograph of the First Fleet re-enactment in Sydney Cove on the 26th of January of that year, showing a multitude of craft on the harbour, is mounted on my living room wall as I write this.

Thirty-two years on, I would like to imagine I am more informed on the contentious events of the day the British First Fleet arrived here and what they represent. But back in 1988, a conflict of conscience had me with a foot in two camps.

Mary Wickham from Nowra was a friend of mine from London, and it is thanks to her, I ended up sharing a house with her and other Australians in Birchgrove. At the time, the two-storeyed house with wrought-iron balcony struggled to be described as 'shabby chic', but it retained the faded grandeur of former days. Its occupants disguised well the flaking walls and damp patches with swathes of Indonesian batik and cheap sarongs from Thailand, as well as political posters. Six legal tenants were residing there during the week, but the numbers swelled at weekends when bodies crashed anywhere.

As one of the few workers in the house, I had the most expensive room with a water view, although the balcony was for communal use. The one bathroom on the landing nearby consisted of an old gas shower with an antique sink, and the dunny, out the back at the bottom of the garden, contained an assortment of left-wing newspapers in a wicker basket, whether for reading material or other emergency use, I could never work out.

The cheapest rental was the shed extension at the rear of the house, occupied by Jill who worked for Telecom Australia, and whose Aboriginal boyfriend, lived next door. Patrick and his mate Charlie had moved to

Sydney from Dubbo and shared their house with a motley crew of mostly stray Kiwis and our friendly gatherings were very multicultural.

As our garden sported the most shade, the barbies and impromptu corroborees happened more on our side of the common wall, and a patch of sand with a fire pit served well as a dance floor. One of the guys next door owned a few guitars and a 'didge', which Charlie played. Clapping sticks could always be found among the firewood, and I sometimes contributed with two spoons from the kitchen. The music and yarning sessions were good fun, and there was no doubting which side of the political spectrum my housemates adhered to, so the animated debates proved a rapid education for my new life in Oz. I learned to keep my mouth shut and listen as plans were being made to boycott Australia Day, which was approaching.

It was decided to fly Aboriginal flags from my balcony and blast out Radio Redfern for the day, as a form of protest against the perceived hypocrisy of celebrating the founding of the colony in 1788 on the presumption of it being *terra nullius,* when in fact Australia was inhabited for more than 60,000 years. Charlie and Patrick explained that busloads of Kooris were arriving from all over Australia, including elders from remote communities to march against the injustices and suffering caused by colonisation. Many were angry that the Hawke Labor government had excluded any involvement of indigenous peoples in planned events. The protest march would attract world attention, and our two households were going to join it in solidarity as it weaved from Redfern to Hyde Park.

I had a dilemma. I didn't know what to do. On arrival in December, I had spent Christmas with some old English friends on the North Shore who had given me a great introduction to Sydney and generously welcomed me into their circle. I was invited to spend the afternoon of Australia Day with them on their catamaran to enjoy the festivities and fireworks happening on the water. Having looked at this iconic harbour on television for years from afar, I was excited at the opportunity to see the tall ships and other events at close hand. In those days, my weak political conscience swayed towards youthful Irish craic instead of serious moral issues.

Each morning as I fixed my healthy grains for breakfast, I often shared the kitchen table with Patrick, who rose early for his morning 'bong'. He claimed it was a great start to the day to get his creative brain working on composing radical poetry. I, who was rushing out the door for a frazzled commute to Bankstown and a busy workday ahead in a medical centre, didn't have much empathy for Patrick's creative life on the dole and I frequently challenged his ideas.

He had the surname Duffy as he'd had an Irish great-grandfather. And I would question why he disowned his Irish heritage and knew little about Irish culture while concentrating solely on his Aboriginal background. With little patience for drugs of any sort, as his eyes got more glazed over, my furious little righteous madam within would rear up. I had a lot to learn.

The landlord, a wealthy barrister, arrived to collect the rent at random times, hoping the element of surprise might line his pockets better. One morning, he caught me coming out the door in my smart radiographer's uniform and nearly fell backwards off the step. 'Do you live here?' he inquired. 'Yes,' I replied. 'And you're working,' he exclaimed! With a grin, as I could sense his pleasure at the social status of his tenants improving, I scuttled off quickly before he expected me to foot the shortfall in that week's rent.

As the 26th approached, my devious Irish brain got to work plotting how to have the best of both worlds. I devised a plan. Often, I was on call for medical centres at Lakemba and Marrickville at weekends and public holidays, and I told my housemates that I might have to carry the 'bleep' on Australia Day. This was often the case as I was the only foreigner in the practice who had no family in Australia to celebrate with. I gave the same excuse to my friends on the North Shore, whom I knew had some reservations about my bohemian lifestyle in the Inner West. The seed of deception sown, I relaxed and arranged to meet them at Rushcutters Bay in the late afternoon.

On Australia Day morning, my housemates and I draped my balcony with a string of Aboriginal flags — the bi-colour of black and red with a yellow disc in the centre. Declan, who lived downstairs, rigged up an amp to broadcast Radio Redfern out to the street below. Patrick and Charlie were drawing up placards for the march at the kitchen table amidst a strong whiff of the 'wacky baccy', with Yothu Yindi blasting from the cassette player. 'Don't celebrate 1988, White Australia has a Black History', the slogans read. Jill had printed a bunch of flyers for handing out in local bars and to passersby on the way into the city.

It was an impressive spectacle of thousands of people making their way to Hyde Park where speeches, dance and ceremonies were scheduled. The crowd, which comprised many non-indigenous supporters were chanting for land rights and other important issues like healthcare and protesting against the injustice of incarcerated youth.

Arriving in Hyde Park, I learned that on Gadigal and Bidjigal Country, it was the custom to pay respect to the custodians of the land with a smoking ceremony. Aboriginal Australians believe the smoke from smouldering native flowers and leaves has cleansing properties and wards off evil spirits. There were speeches by the activist Uncle Gary Foley and others. The park was a sea of painted faces proudly representing mobs from all states, and as a newcomer to Australia, I felt swept along on the emotional tide.

I guess as an Irish person belonging to a nation that had experienced its rebellions and conflict with the British, I'd always had empathy for the underdog. Despite this, the tourist in me resurrected itself mid-afternoon, and the harbour beckoned. It was easy to slip away from my companions in the crowd but not so easy to quell the pang of guilt I felt. I would just tell them that my 'bleep' went off, and I'd had to rush off for an emergency.

Sydney Harbour was at its best and awash with the pageantry of eleven Tall Ships that had sailed across the world for the event; elegant yachts, and the usual ferries and tugboats adorned with lights and flags. Local watercraft with revellers on board moored in all the small bays, and I learned later that nearly two million spectators lined the shoreline. I had missed most of the air displays and Navy gun salutes that had happened earlier in the day, but the atmosphere was still electric.

At Rushcutters Bay yacht club, my friends and other members were glammed up for the occasion. Pimms and champagne were flowing, and trays of seafood were waitered about. Most people had been there since early morning, and the yarns were getting maudlin and a bit repetitive. I added my tale of deception on being queried about my morning's work and was delighted when John Williamson's *True Blue* drowned out the scant details as a group nearby belted out the chorus. My housemate friend Mary was a big fan of the singer, and she was taking me to the Tamworth Country Music Festival a few weeks later as my initiation to rural Australia. The mood changed with the music as Redgum, and Paul Kelly livened the crowd and young children and grannies danced on the decks. Everyone was waiting for the skies to darken for the firework display over Sydney Harbour Bridge.

At 9 pm the pyrotechnic extravaganza was everything I thought it would be, as fireworks exploded off the arches of the bridge and illuminated the scallops of the Opera House and nearby cityscape. Yet somehow, as the performance fizzled to a close, I experienced another twinge of guilt and regret.

I was with the wrong mob.

THE CUBAN MISSION

It was the summer of 1996, and Cuba wasn't yet on the regular tourist circuit. Growing up with the attractive image of the rebel Che Guevara and intrigued to see Castro's communist system in action, was enough of a lure to this Caribbean island. At the time, Aeroflot flew from Moscow to the capital Havana and made a stopover to refuel at Shannon airport, on the Irish west coast. The logistics of getting there were easy.

There were few travel guides available back then, and I contacted the pretty much defunct Irish Communist Party, hoping for practical travel information. At that time, they dispatched small groups of socialist-minded young people to work on collective farms or building projects throughout Cuba. Sean was a cheerful young guy who didn't give me the hard sell and recognised my independent spirit. He asked if I would deliver a letter to one Alvaro Gonzales O'Callaghan in Santiago de Cuba, as I was intending going to this region to see Fidel's former guerilla *campos* in the hills nearby.

Sean then gave me a brief history lesson on the Irish diaspora in Cuba. When Britain was advocating the abolishment of slavery in the 19th century, the Irish provided cheap indentured white labour for the Spanish to build the first railroad and work cotton and sugar plantations. Alvaro was of Irish descent from that time and an academic who wished to deepen cultural connections between Ireland and Cuba. He sounded like an interesting character worth meeting.

Sean also explained the impact of the Helm-Burton Act imposed by the Americans on Cuba. The strict embargo caused lots of shortages and rationing, which created extreme hardship for Cuban citizens. He advised on what useful gifts to take with me, such as toiletries, medicines, and any western wares.

True to form, the Aeroflot flight took off in a steamy haze from the air-conditioning system with no safety drill whatsoever. I had hoped a quick shot of Russian vodka would be served to calm my nerves. The pasty-faced hostesses were a stocky, humourless lot rationing out the soft drink and bean mush that was dinner. The nine-hour flight was monotonous, but the time passed quickly chatting to Maria seated beside me — part of a Cuban sports team allowed to compete in Moscow. In broken English, she explained that only certain people could travel abroad, and the regime strictly monitored them.

Arriving at Jose Marti airport, I shared a local taxi into Havana with Maria and a few other team members and eagerly looked at my new surrounds. As we approached the city, a deep red polluted sun was setting behind the towering high-rises, reminiscent of all Eastern Europe. The girls made sure I got dropped at my homestay on Calle 23, a busy street sporting a giant billboard of Che Guevara.

Elena showed me to my $US15 room where it was apparent a family member had recently vacated to accommodate me. Clothes were shoved aside in the wardrobe, and a rusty, noisy fridge occupied the corner, overflowing with meat packs, dozens of eggs, and pineapples. I took a cold shower in the rustic bathroom next door, which was devoid of any toiletries other than a cracked, discoloured bar of soap. The family were delighted when I replaced it. Feeling too tired to be sociable with my rudimentary Spanish, I was soon fast asleep on the hard bed, despite the incessant traffic outside.

Waking refreshed, I had more energy for interacting with the family in sign language and grins that had us misunderstanding each other. Comprehending little but fortified with strong Cuban coffee, I set out to explore Havana and find the tourist office. The street was a mixture of grandiose three-storied buildings in a dilapidated state and ramshackle stores with youths sitting in doorways with ghetto blasters. It was comforting to learn I was not yet beyond the odd cat-call that put a spring in my step. I had a penchant for that bronzed Latino look in my reckless twenties, but I was now well past quickly succumbing to dark strangers.

I was soon lured into a small store to change my $US to local pesos at the lucrative black market rate. Pesos were needed to pay for street food and local buses, but tourists had to pay for official accommodation, souvenirs, and official taxis in $US. With only those working in the tourist industry having access to dollars, the black market was rife. My homestay was registered and taxed by the authorities, but whispers and subtle waves on the street got you a better bargain and helped a more impoverished family earn dollars. As in most communist countries, being a member of the party or who you knew in it considerably improved the quality of daily living.

The heart and soul of Havana is the old town, Habana Vieja, which is a Unesco heritage site. I quickly fell in love with its vibrant atmosphere and crumbling old colonial buildings, several restored to their former glory around the Plaza de Armas.

It felt like a step back in time to a 1950s movie set with numerous vintage cars cruising the streets in an array of bright colours, Chevrolets and Ford sedans in polished, pristine condition. Yellow tourist taxis lined up outside hotels, but the locals hailed unlicensed peso taxis to get about.

The waft of exotic smells led me into a warren of narrow cobblestone streets where I feasted on spicy pork balls and yucca fries while de-rusting my basic Spanish. I discovered Cafe O'Reilly nearby, named after Alexander 'Bloody' O'Reilly, one of my kin, and Inspector General of Cuba in the 1760s.

The cafe-bar was a lively little joint with a resident cigar maker in the corner hand-rolling smokes for a dollar. The smell of strong Cubano espressos mingled with the cigar smoke. Many strange rum concoctions were offered to the unwary tourist, but I wanted to sample the traditional mojito, which is white rum with mint leaves and fresh lime juice. The refreshing cocktail washed down the pork balls nicely.

It was exactly my kind of scene, and after a while, I got chatting to Dulce, a friendly lady who spoke excellent English. As one mojito led to another, she shared her history and explained the average Cuban's problems. Her son was a famous jazz musician who travelled overseas, but despite his dollar wages, she still struggled to make ends meet. Dulce ran a *casa particular* or illegal homestay to supplement her income, promptly offering me an attic room for $8 a night. She showed me her ration book for basics, saying the quota of meat and cooking oil was never enough, and she used the black market. Seemingly many Cubans relied on dollar remittances from family members living in Florida, but Dulce had no one living there.

I promised to take up her offer the next day and continued to the tourist office, where I was shocked to learn the reality of the chaotic Cuban public transport system. With petrol in short supply and strictly rationed, few buses operated in the country and crowded cattle trucks called *cameons* replaced them. A train to Santiago de Cuba would take 24 hours at a crawling pace with the likelihood of disruptions and delays. I didn't hesitate and promptly booked a flight few Cubans could afford.

In the fading light, I strolled along the three-kilometre stretch of Malecon — the promenade with a high sea wall protecting the city from the ravages of the wild Atlantic. Resting awhile under a shady tree, I observed the small gems of Cuban life, fishermen on the rocks behind the wall; baseball games played in the shadows, and the Afro-Cuban beat seductively echoing from geranium filled windows. Families were laughing and joking on their evening *paseo*, and souvenir sellers touted their wares.

The Cubans are excellent artists, and I purchased a canvas of swirling dancers in glorious colours, ignoring the flirtatious advances of the teenage seller! High waves swept over the wall at times, and my light sundress was probably see-through at this stage! I noticed a long stretch of grand four-and five-storey buildings in bold pastel shades of green and pink. If adequately restored, they would have been worth a fortune.

The next few days at Dulce's home were lively as many of her family and neighbours were musicians, firing up into song and dance spontaneously. Her son played the sax, and often his young friends came over for a jamming session. It was like having my own private Buena Vista Social Club! I appreciated being able to communicate easily in English and got a valuable insight into how the system worked.

My attic room had a little balcony where I overlooked a cheery woodcarver next door who earned roughly $US300 a month, the equivalent of a doctor. Cuba seemed to train a lot of doctors, many for deployment to needier countries, which was admirable. Yet here in Cuba, I would meet a few driving the *cameons* that ferried people around, and they earned more doing this. *What a loss to the health service*, I thought to myself. Cubans, as in other communist countries, were extremely well-educated, and it was common to see them poring over an array of secondhand books splayed out on the pavement for sale.

I stumbled across the famous Johnson's Pharmacy dating to colonial times, decked out with antique cupboards with brass fittings, a long polished mahogany counter, and its walls lined with shelves of coloured glass potion bottles. There were few customers and little sign of pharmaceutical supplies. I learned later that clinics and hospitals lacked essential medicines and frequently gave patients a shopping list to buy drugs or bandages on the black market. Sean had advised me to donate my stash of medical supplies from Ireland to a rural clinic where the situation was more desperate than the capital.

It was a must to visit the Museum of the Revolution where Che Guevara's black beret was a prized exhibit, as well as the famous Granma boat, sailed by the revolutionaries from Mexico in 1956. I recoiled from some bloodstained items of clothing on display, continuing to the very amusing 'Corner of Cretins' featuring life-size caricatures of Ronald Reagan and George W. Bush. A plaque read, 'Thank you, cretin, for helping us to strengthen the revolution!'

In need of lighter entertainment, I wandered off on a Hemingway crawl to the Floridita bar where the daiquiri was invented and found out that Papa had his special recipe. The writer lived in Havana for twenty years from 1940 onwards and wrote *The Old Man and the Sea* and *For Whom the Bell Tolls* between fishing and bar crawling. A couple were shimmying sexily around the small floor space to a salsa beat, and I had to reluctantly tear myself away to another of Hemingway's haunts — the Bodeguita del Medio, touristy, yet retaining its authentic bohemian atmosphere.

Customers had scribbled on every inch of the walls over the years. Nevertheless, Hemingway's trademark, 'My daiquiri in the Floridita, my mojito in the Bodiguita', was given pride of place. A lover of writer's bars and cafes the world over, I was delighted to find that Graham Greene, Errol Flynn, and Fidel himself were regular customers here too.

By the end of the week, feeling rather sozzled with the rum and in need of a rest from the Afro-Cuban beat of drums and banjo, I flew east to Santiago de Cuba on an old twin-propeller Russian plane. I had heard that Cuba's second city was quieter and more relaxed.

Before settling into a cheap hotel, I decided to get the delivery of Alvaro's package out of the way. It was a fascinating meeting with this academic who was President of the Cuban-Irish Association. However, he was very disappointed with the Irish response in connecting him with an O'Callaghan contact. Alvaro insisted that I stay with his family as a guest and promptly farmed his two children out to granny who lived downstairs so that I could have their room. His wife Maria rustled up a delicious lunch of rice, fish and fried plantain, and I felt embarrassed at the red carpet treatment, suspecting that the family struggled to make ends meet.

The former professor and I settled down for a long chat; he inquired about contemporary Ireland, and I got an education on the politics of Cuba. It was a total contrast to my frivolity in Havana. When Castro toppled the former Batista regime, academics were victimised, and Alvaro lost his lecturer's post at the university. To support his family, he rented a bedroom to sex tourists, foreign men who picked up Cuban girls, grateful for payment with cosmetics, bars of soap, or shampoo. It was so sad to hear his wife was seriously ill with leukaemia, and he had to seek out horse meat and liver on the black market to boost her immune system. Despite all these woes, Alvaro exuded an incredible zest for life and interest in history. His mother called in to meet me, and with her dark hair and pale skin, there was no doubting her Celtic ancestry.

For the next few days, it was too hot to sightsee, but it was also challenging to escape Alvaro's earnest political conversations that only lightened up later in the day when the cheap rum appeared to ease his worries. Many politicos came and went, and one professor invited me to dinner but then cancelled because there was no food to be had on the night! It all highlighted the privileges I held as a tourist.

To express my gratitude and contribute to the family, I went in search of extra bread and other foodstuffs each day, which I could purchase with my foreign passport. I was shocked to discover how meagre the family rations were. I discarded clothes and other things I didn't need, and a doctor in the neighbourhood appreciated the medicines and syringes I'd brought from Ireland. It angered me to hear that international medical donations were sold on the black market.

I often visit local hospitals when travelling to get an indication of the state of the health service, and it was shocking in Santiago. Only one x-ray room was operational as spare parts were required to repair pieces of equipment, and the American embargo made this impossible. The ultrasound service was suspended indefinitely, which was a disaster for pregnant women, and the supply of x-ray film was running very low.

Feeling depressed with the reality of the situation I was witnessing, I needed light relief and used to sneak off to the Hotel Las Americas around the corner for a swim. It was bliss for a few hours to soak up the sun, sip an expensive cold beer, and forget for a while that I was in Cuba. The foreigners I chatted with there had no idea what was going on outside their tourist bubble.

I was keen to visit the Sierra Maestra mountains to the west, famed as the area where Che, Fidel, and his comrades planned the revolution. It is also Cuba's largest national park, rich in wildlife and lush vegetation, and I badly needed a dose of natural beauty to cheer me up. It took many hours getting there on a sardine-packed *cameon* and then the last leg by horse and cart to the village of Uvera. The magnificent coastal scenery of high cliffs and wild stony bays was impressive, and the *campesinos* were a humorous lot.

I was invited home by Carlos, whose wife Isabella would be grateful for dollars and the bars of soap I had with me. Her statement later was touching — *pobre mas sincero* meaning 'poor but sincere'. They lived in a small wooden cabin, with the backyard in shambles, housing a fat pig and her piglets. I was fed a platter of beans and not seeing a toilet, headed for the adjacent hills just as the sun was setting behind Torquino, Cuba's highest peak. The air was balmy and tropical, and I felt relaxed after the turmoil of frenzied cities. A couple of *rancheros* on horseback passed me with curious stares, but on seeing me smile, broke into broad grins themselves. The tidy shacks I passed had lush gardens with bountiful mango and avocado trees, and a kindly man gave me a few juicy mangoes.

That evening, I was embarrassed to be served spaghetti and meat with grandpa and wondered what the family was eating. However, Isabella was delighted with the soap. I shared a bed with her granddaughter Elena who, too excited to sleep, kept saying, '*Mira!, Mira!*' as she demonstrated her few toys.

Wandering in the hills the next day, I came across an old colonial coffee plantation and met Luis, keen to practise his English. He related an interesting story about reaching Guantanamo, the American base, to seek asylum, but they turned him away as they'd exceeded some quota. He planned to make a fresh attempt shortly, by scuba diving there from a boat and paying a professional diver $US1000 to accompany him because of the landmines in the water. Like Alvaro, he was also victimised for holding opposing political views.

When I returned to Santiago de Cuba some days later, I found Alvaro distraught as Maria was hospitalised for blood transfusions. The doctors had told him it was only a matter of months. It was grim news indeed, and I felt so helpless to comfort him. They were married for twenty years, and she was only 41 years old. I thought I should get out of the way of their grief, but he insisted I stay, wanting the distraction of my company.

Alvaro had a friend who worked in a cigar factory and sold me 100 Cohiba cigars for a reasonable price. These were premium cigars typically exported or sold to foreigners. I intended to sell them in Ireland and mail care packages back to Cuba.

When leaving, there was little I could say under the circumstances. I told Alvaro I would contact an O'Callaghan in Ireland for him and promised to stay in touch. It was the least I could do.

It was an icy winter's day when I arrived back at Shannon airport, still clad in shorts sporting a good tan, and luckily I got through customs with my stash of expensive cigars. I had left my car at a friend's house and related my Cuban story over a cup of tea, enquiring if she knew any O'Callaghan's in the region I could call on. I was delighted to find out there was a village thirty miles away called O'Callaghan Mills, with a funeral director named O'Callaghan living at the entrance to this village.

I entered the premises to find the director putting the finishing touches to a corpse, and I soon detected he had little time to waste on a scantily clad Irishwoman, babbling on about his long lost O'Callaghan brother in Cuba who wanted a contact in Ireland. I suspected it was only out of respect for the deceased, that he didn't tell me to f… off! There was no point in even offering him a Cuban cigar to quell the rising annoyance!

In the ensuing weeks, I had no luck finding an O'Callaghan pen pal for Alvaro, but I did a roaring trade selling the Cohibas. Family and

Old Havana, Cuba

Ranchero in the Sierra Maestra, Cuba

friends donated clothing and western goods in short supply in Cuba, and I posted large packages to Alvaro as well as to an orphanage in Santiago. Sadly, they never arrived, most likely stolen by corrupt customs officials. Undaunted, I collected donations once more and was successful on the second attempt.

I also contacted Siemens and Phillips medical engineering companies, who both supply and service x-ray equipment worldwide, and asked if they could donate obsolete medical equipment to Cuba or provide a new probe for the ultrasound scanner in Santiago. Everyone quoted the restraints of the Helm-Burton Act and with hands tied, couldn't assist me.

I stayed in touch with Alvaro for a short time, knowing that I had disappointed him and regretting that I couldn't help him.

The tone of his letters got sadder as his wife's health deteriorated, and then I heard no more.

KICKING WITH
BOTH FEET IN ULSTER

In memory of Clare Rooney (1928-2000)

A friend shouted *'Go n'eirigh an bothar leat!'* as I put my best foot forward. Translated to English, this Gaelic saying means, 'May the road rise to meet you', wishing a traveller good luck on a journey. I would need it as in late summer 2002, I took a mad notion to walk the entire length of the Ulster Way, a mere 665 miles or 1070 kilometres. I'd climbed many peaks and hiked into Everest Base Camp, but it was time to explore my home turf and follow the signposts of the 'yellow man'.

The Ulster Way is the longest waymarked trail in the British Isles and was developed as a walking circuit around Northern Ireland, with a spur going into the Republic in Donegal, and a short detour to the Sliabh Beagh area in my home county Monaghan.

Sadly, Ulster has been synonymous with 'The Troubles' and the political entity of Northern Ireland, instead of being recognised as an ancient province of Ireland.

It was Wilfred Capper, a founder of the Youth Hostel Association, who was the brainchild of the Ulster Way. A local farmer once asked him, 'Are you orange or green?' as politics were never far from daily life. 'Neither,' he replied. 'Black, white, yellow or brown — it's all the same to me! I broke all the rules,' he admitted. 'I told no one where I was going and walked all alone.' I agree with the man wholeheartedly!

I would also walk solo, and wear the bright yellow T-shirt of the organisation Aware, which supports depression. The walk was in memory of my late mother, Clare Rooney. She suffered from this incredibly debilitating condition for many years following the death of my brother Cathal in a car accident. I understood only too well the impact of depression on immediate family, and how helpless one can feel to help and provide adequate support.

Growing up on the border, knowing the subtle psychology of being either Catholic or Protestant, was advantageous in understanding the little innuendoes of many situations I would find myself in. Like Wilfred, I didn't care 'which foot a person kicked with' as they say in Ulster to define your religious persuasion. My unusual name and quasi-Northern Irish accent which became more pronounced as I walked north, made it challenging to suss me out and slot into the usual boxes.

To minimise detours off the main route for a bed, I carried a bivvy bag to sleep in and asked local farmers in the evening if I could camp on their property. It was this decision to leave myself open to hospitality that would bring the greatest joy on the walk. As a woman walking alone, I was unthreatening, and the many quick cuppas proffered en route often evolved into marathon off-loading sessions at kitchen tables, where I sometimes felt like a counsellor. Hearts opened, and minds unburdened, as many commented on the stress and fast pace of modern living, where people have no time to communicate and listen to a friend or family member with problems.

My marathon walk commenced one Saturday in August, from the Sliabh Beagh Centre in Monaghan, with a large group of family, friends and representatives of Aware, all wearing yellow T-shirts, cheering me off. The town newspaper took photos, and the local walking group was accompanying me on the first stretch to link up with the Ulster Way. The rugged terrain across wet bogland and through the conifer plantations of Bragan was an area I knew well.

My parents would take us there for a spin on Sundays, to collect turf and picnic near the windy Mass rock from the Penal Laws era in the eighteenth century. During this time, when Irish Catholics were forbidden by the English to practise their religion, priests said Mass for their congregations in these remote areas, using a flat lonely rock as an altar.

The official Ulster Way signposts of the yellow man soon led us into the dark understory of Mullafad forest, and we passed the Cooneen Ghost house. A popular ghost story from childhood, I remembered scary tales of pots and pans flying about in the night, strange happenings, and an exorcism being performed to cleanse the house. Shaking off the spooky surrounds, we emerged from the woods near the shores of a quiet lake and enjoyed an alfresco lunch with the swans waiting on our sandwich crusts.

I continued on my own on the lonely bog roads of the Clogher Valley, suddenly sensing the freedom of the weeks ahead. In this area, the Ulster

Way darted back and forth across the border, and I never knew if I was in the Republic or Northern Ireland. I savoured the prospect of it all evolving as I walked — the surprise element of not knowing where I would end up each day, or who I would encounter.

To alleviate the monotony of just walking, I visited areas of interest on the route. One such place in Monaghan was Favour Royal Forest, formerly known as Port Clare, which I felt was a good omen being my mother's name. There, I sat like a queen in an ancient stone Druid's chair from pagan times, and fervently wished for good health and luck on my journey, praying that the rain gods would be kind to me. A holy well close by was renowned for its healing properties, with 'clueties' or rags strewn about as offerings. It was all good karma as I fondly remembered my mother.

I carried an official letter from Aware, allowing me to fundraise on their behalf, as well as police permits sanctioning public collections. The plan was to rattle my bucket at events I happened on and to ask for donations at local businesses in the towns and villages I passed through.

I got off to a good start on the third day at a bikers' rally in Glaslough village, where riders in the pit stop and the audience lining the route were generous and supportive. I felt a bit embarrassed at first to be publicly asking for money but as I soon discovered — 'Only the bold and brave fill the bucket'!

The first week was pleasant walking on quiet country lanes amongst gently rolling hills and tranquil lakes frequented by fishermen. Tragically, this region had experienced abductions and murders during the Troubles. Still, past suspicions didn't prevent the Smythe's from inviting me into their picturesque cottage one morning and relating harrowing tales over morning tea. They'd heard of my walk on local radio and caught sight of the lone walker in her yellow T-shirt.

I was in the 'bandit country' of South Armagh, heavily policed by armed British soldiers until the early 1990s and well known to me from my childhood smuggling days, and from visiting our cousins, the Duggans, who owned apple orchards. I sometimes spotted some laden trees near the roadside and, looking carefully about, stole a few red apples to keep me going. Old habits die hard!

Each village I came to had its Orange Hall and churches of the two persuasions; either the Union Jack or the Republican tricolour flying from poles, depending on the majority in the locality. Often, I met nobody for hours on end and sang to myself as I strode along, attracting curious stares from horses and cows in fields, distracted from their grazing.

Most people thought kindly of charity walkers, so when I'd ask if I could camp, I'd often be invited in for a cup of tea. Then the guessing game commenced; figuring out which foot I kicked with, a slow comedy I learned to enjoy. Once they'd gotten the measure of me, I was frequently offered a comfy bed, sometimes under the glaring eyes of Ian Paisley hovering above me on the wall, and on visiting the toilet in one house, a portrait of the Queen watched my every movement! I would often laugh with my hosts about it the following morning.

There was one memorable evening after asking a farmer if I could camp on his land; Leo Hegarty said I could sleep in his garage on my camping mat, as rain was forecast. He apologised for not offering a bed in the house, but his wife a nurse, was on night duty and with his in-laws living opposite it would not look great if a strange woman was seen about the house. Putting a tenner in my bucket, Leo disappeared off to the pub, and I to the garage floor.

I slept well but decided it would be discreet to depart early in the morning. However, when I was a few miles down the road, a woman standing at a farmhouse gate stopped me. It was Leo's mother, and he'd phoned her with an order to cook me breakfast. Sitting down to a good Ulster fry of black and white pudding, rashers and thick sausages, she interrogated me thoroughly on the sleeping arrangements of the night before!

Going astray one time during a torrential downpour, I met a kind 'Born Again Christian' woman, who offered me shelter and a mug of hot chocolate until the weather cleared. We chatted about my walk and discussed the world's troubles. When the rain ceased, she insisted on driving me back to the route, donated a tenner to Aware and gave me an umbrella. It was very touching as she prayed over me before parting, in memory of my mother, and for my safety on the walk.

I was getting fitter by the day and soon averaged twenty miles on most days. To avoid blisters, I wore cushioned trainers on the roads and changed into sturdy boots on rough ground. The terrain varied greatly, ranging from minor lanes to forest tracks, coastal paths, wet bog, muddy fields and the many 'nettle alleys' I had to dart through. Forestry was incredibly confusing where one clearing started to look like the rest. My compass became my best friend, and it required 21 ordnance survey maps to cover the entire walk.

The Mourne mountains were the first taxing wilderness area I had to navigate across, a constant up and down boggy traverse in a howling wind. It rained heavily, and as the mist descended, I felt very exposed and isolated on the barren moorland. I was relieved to reach Batts Wall, which was constructed in the middle of nowhere in famine times using workhouse labour. Not quite the Great Wall of China, it served as an excellent landmark to follow in poor visibility.

I dried out in Downpatrick that night, where I was staying with friends, and earned my keep assisting in the caesarian section of a heifer! *My* duties were to draw up the penicillin and boil the kettle — thankfully not to stuff the intestines back in like the vet was doing!

After two weeks walking, I entered Belfast city, conscious that the Ulster Way ahead passed through dodgy areas renowned for sporadic sectarian violence in the past. One evening in a lonely park, a few young cider heads with glazed eyes approached to ask the time and then just wished me well on my journey. In another neighbourhood with burned-out cars, several gangs of idle youths eyed me suspiciously, and I just beamed and waved. Trusting that humanity is fundamentally good is a premise of mine when travelling alone anywhere, and I was never once afraid during the walk. It was at a time when many Irish southerners wouldn't venture across the border, fearing attacks on their car with a southern number plate.

The yellow man signs took me through the grounds of Stormont Castle, the seat of government for Northern Ireland. As I collected my permit to fundraise, even the security guards contributed to the cause. I was often surprised at sudden instances of unexpected generosity.

One such time was in a small village, where the manager of a local factory hardly listened to me before whipping out his cheque book. A dear friend of his, heavily in debt, had committed suicide the day before. The man was devastated by the tragedy, regretting that he hadn't noticed his friend's troubles and there were tears in his eyes as I was leaving.

After climbing the bleak hills surrounding Belfast, I crossed the Sallagh Braes, detouring around the infamous Sinking Bog, a graveyard of livestock that had met their end there. Before descending to the lovely Glens of Antrim, the views across the Mull of Kintyre to Scotland were breathtaking and the 'ladderfield' method of cultivation intriguing, a touch of Asian terraced rice paddies in Ulster.

I struck lucky that my walk coincided with the Auld Lammas Fair at Ballycastle, Ireland's oldest harvest festival. I bought myself a different 'yellow man', the name given to sticky honeycomb toffee that tasted divine and would boost my energy levels! Another custom is to sample dulse, a reddish seaweed high in calcium that strengthens the bones. Everything a walker needed to quicken the pace! My bucket speedily filled as I mingled with farmers at livestock sales, among crowds gathered to listen to musicians and dancers, and I ventured into the crowded pubs.

The weather turned wild the following day as I neared the halfway point of the Ulster Way route. I trudged head down, struggling against dangerous winds on the north Antrim coast, only the screech of seabirds for company. It was necessary to descend a few times to slippery, bouldered beaches that were difficult to walk along. Rough swells battered chalk stacks in the small bays, and wild Nature was in its element. The sky was awash with pink hues by the time I sighted the organ pipe cliffs and basalt steps of the Giant's Causeway, signifying the end to a crazy day.

This popular tourist place is the most well known of Ireland's world heritage sites, with 40,000 hexagonal columns of basalt paving the bay and rumoured to be the footprints of giants in bygone days. The Bushmills whiskey distillery is equally well known in the village nearby. As my father's favourite drop, I toasted his memory on a wee dram and warmed my jaded bones.

I stayed with the Doaks, a family beset by tragedy when their daughter Tracy, was murdered in 1985 by the IRA. She was a policewoman in the RUC, and the event destroyed their family fabric. Jean and Beatty eventually coped with their grief by doing positive work in uniting a bitterly divided community. These strangers to me, who had good reason to be prejudiced against Catholics, became dear friends — accommodating me in their farmhouse B and B and arming me with sandwiches and snacks when I was leaving.

That evening, over a bottle of wine, we discussed ordinary lives, whether Protestant or Catholic and wondered how it could all go so wrong in a small province like Ulster. Similar to battles in other parts of the world, peace can reign on the surface for a good while, only for the embers of conflict to be reignited suddenly by a minor local event. This brave couple devoted their lives to dialogue despite difference, and I learned years later, that the Queen decorated both of them for their outstanding efforts.

Stopping for a coffee one day, I met an eccentric character dressed in his clan kilt. Liam coincidentally was from my hometown and told me he'd been sailing around Ireland with the Nuclear Free Irish Flotilla protest organised by the pop band U2. It was interesting to learn that the Greenpeace ship, *Rainbow Warrior* was docked in Belfast that same week. Liam owned a hostel in Donegal that was on my route and gave me a note for his staff, allowing me a complimentary stay. You never know who you run into walking the roads of Ireland!

By now, I had walked nearly 400 miles and was pleased with my progress. I looked a lot leaner, was tanned by the wind, and my feet were holding up well. It certainly helped wearing good quality breathable socks and to switch footwear according to the terrain.

The desolate Sperrin mountains were the most solitary section of my entire walk. There were rumours of gold in the remote hills, and I thought this must be true, noticing one or two grandiose Spanish haciendas in the middle of nowhere. I reflected that this was the new face of affluent Ireland as no one was ever at home, the owners hitting the urban sprawl to cover high mortgages. Often, a lonesome dog whimpered when I knocked at a door looking for water. I felt that as a nation, we had lost something valuable in the rat race for wealth and status.

This fact was verified one morning as I struggled to hop forward on a muddy and puddled nettle track! At times, the marked path was difficult to discern through private farmland. The farmer was close by and hearing me swear in frustration he approached for a chat. Sean lived alone and was desperately lonely, a familiar story of the son who cared for an ageing mother, who then died. 'No one wants to stop and talk anymore,' he complained. 'Everyone is too busy.' I felt very sorry for him, at the same time realising he could talk the hind leg off a donkey, and I'd be there all day. But I listened to his woes, realising this was the purpose of my walk after all. It was a valuable lesson.

I had an extraordinary experience stepping back in time in County Donegal. I was shattered this one particular day after walking 30 miles, most through confusing forestry, and I'd strayed off the correct path. As the light diminished, I took note of a wrecked car in case I needed emergency shelter for the night and started jogging down a firebreak, hoping to clear the forest. I was just about to give up, sweating and scratched when I heard a dog bark, and like Little Red Riding Hood, sighted a cottage with a woman standing in the doorway. I must have looked like a scared deer as Mary beckoned me inside. It was only after drinking two pots of tea that I stopped shaking.

An old collie dozed by the turf fire, and in the dim light of an oil lamp, I heard Mary's story. She lived alone with no electricity, running water or toilet, yet appeared fearlessly content with the company of her dog and books. She looked to be in her sixties and said that in her youth, she wanted to train as a nurse in England. Instead, she was dispatched by her parents to help a widowed aunt on her farm and never escaped.

It was a sad story of missed opportunity, and I would have loved to crash on her couch and hear more, but I had to move on to the nearest village for the night. Mary bore all the signs of a woman accustomed to solitude and independence, and after relating her tale lapsed into a comfortable silence, just stroking the dog. She led me by torchlight down a dark lane to the main road and wished me Godspeed for my walk. It was a rich encounter with a welcoming stranger.

The weather turned damp and miserable as I walked north to the coast again, but the excitement at the prospect of meeting the King of Tory Island put a spring in my step. Patsy Dan Rodgers was another of Ireland's eccentrics, not a real king but rumoured to have resurrected some mythical lost royalty after a bet in the pub one night. It was a good ruse to encourage tourism to the island, and the king had become a TV celebrity.

Patsy Dan greeted me warmly in his unique accent that often lapsed into the local Gaelic, and I had a photoshoot with His Royal Highness against the whitewashed wall of his cottage. The island had a neglected air about it with the landscape too rugged for agriculture and an exodus of young people seeking work on the mainland. But it was rich in myth and legend, and a wild cliff walk took me to Balor's old fort, home to a one-eyed giant in pagan times, and now inhabited by nesting gannets.

I had heard the story of 'blessed Tory clay' which is supposed to get rid of rats. Being plagued with them at home in my shed, I was on a mission to score some of it. It must be blessed by a member of the Duggan clan to work. And sure enough, I met the shaman elder himself that night in the pub, and was given my little holy pouch for the price of a pint! However, I confess that the blessed clay didn't succeed and the rats continued to multiply!

September was drawing to a close, and the days were getting shorter in the sixth week of my walk. It is said that solitude, as opposed to loneliness, can benefit the mind, body and soul.

I intended to spend a solitary night on Lough Derg as the spiritual element to my walk. At times labelled the 'Ironman' of pilgrimages, St Patrick's Purgatory is an island in the centre of a lake, where pilgrims walk barefoot for three days in all weathers, praying around stony penitentiary beds. At night they stay awake and continue to pray in a vast basilica, and a meagre diet of black tea and dry oatcakes is all that is allowed. My mother brought me here when I was 17 as a rite of passage in the hope of achieving good results in the Leaving Certificate, but I'm not convinced it influenced my grades!

The pilgrim season had just ended, and I had permission to spend a night alone on the island. It was a spell of quiet contemplation — food for the soul. In the evening, I left the fading light of the basilica to watch a glorious sunset over the surrounding hills and sat by the shore until a crescent moon rose over the dark waters. The feeling was as good as any monastery in the Himalayas, or ashram in India, and I said a quiet prayer

Map of the author's walk

Preparing for the bog!

to my mother as well as thanking my feet for bringing me this far with only a few blisters.

Waking to a pea-soup mist on the lake, my ferryman Martin arrived at 8 am, and I embraced the last leg of my walk spiritually enriched and with renewed vigour in my step.

The Fermanagh region of Northern Ireland is a hidden gem of striking limestone cliffs, peaceful lakes and old wooded estates with historic yew trees. It was magical one day to come across an old Irish sweathouse or sauna, challenging to find in modern times. These earth and stone structures were used for a wide range of ailments, primarily arthritis, but also helped with fertility problems and psychiatric disorders. Stones in the cavity were heated with a wood or turf fire, the ashes raked out and the hot stones covered with bracken. With the entrance sealed, the sweating period could last a couple of hours and how I wished this one was still in use to heal my aching joints! Sweathouses went into decline from 1850 onwards with the advent of modern medicines.

There was exhilaration, yet reluctance, arriving back at my starting point in the early days of October, to a jubilant reception. I experienced a real sadness on completing the Ulster Way. It was time to abandon the tranquillity and peace of Nature for the noise and bustle of real life again and return to work. My walk for Aware raised nearly seven thousand euros, and I requested that the funds go towards dealing with youth suicide and post-natal depression. These were the two issues I came across most often on my journey.

As a hiker, I felt immensely satisfied by completing the long walk, which took seven weeks. However, the real reward was the memory of engaging with the ordinary people of Ulster whose kindness, warmth and hospitality were legendary and would remain with me forever.

THE BEYONDERS

In the footsteps of Ernest Shackleton 2006

London 1915

'Men wanted for hazardous journey. Low wages, bitter cold, long hours of complete darkness. Safe return doubtful'.

Ernest Shackleton is said to have written this advertisement to recruit men for his Endurance Expedition to the Antarctic in 1915. Few know that the famous polar explorer, 'The Boss', as he was known, who served in the British Merchant Navy, was born in Ireland to a Quaker family in County Kildare. The extraordinary tale of leaving his marooned men on Elephant Island while he and a few men sailed to South Georgia to seek help at Stromness whaling station is one of the most remarkable stories of perseverance and survival of all time.

Dublin 2005 — 90 years later

Wanted — 'Ordinary men and women for an extraordinary adventure'.

I'd answered the Irish mountaineer Pat Falvey's advertisement, with the same yen and eagerness for an adventure that Tom Crean and the other unsung heroes accompanying Shackleton felt all those years ago. And I was ecstatic to be chosen for the 'Beyond Endurance Expedition', a re-enactment of the traverse of South Georgia in Shackleton's memory.

There were two groups on the expedition — 32 members of the traverse team, ordinary men and women who'd perfected ice and crevasse skills in Norway for the dangerous venture ahead. Their objective was to follow Shackleton's footsteps across the island of South Georgia, from his landing point at King Haakon Bay, across the Crean Glacier, Trident Tower and Fortuna Glacier, to the now abandoned whaling station Stromness, on the island's northern coast. They hoped to complete the 32-kilometre traverse in three days.

I was part of the 52 person support team that would join them on the final day's walk. While they crossed the island, we would sail north and around, on standby in case of any emergency. A film crew sailed with us, making a documentary for RTE, the Irish TV station. We were chuffed to have Kate Buchanan with us, a descendant of the Boss himself and I mustn't forget our loyal mascot, Freddy Bear, who would accompany the traverse team.

We'd been three days at sea since leaving Tierra del Fuego, southern Argentina — which evoked memories of the 'ends of the earth' and the 'land of the soaring albatross' I'd dreamed about in school days. We had a rough passage on our ship *Ushuaia* through the infamous Drake Passage, where only a few brave, green faces surfaced sporadically for air, took a look at the rollers, and scarpered below deck again.

However, after that rocky start, we were up on deck birdwatching and had seen a few blows from minke whales and orcas. A sense of teamship and camaraderie developed, culminating in this moment and the adventure ahead. I shared a small windowless cabin in the bowels of the ship with Niamh from Cork, who was to become a lifelong friend, despite our contrasting habits. She was the early bird, on deck at sunrise, and I was the night-owl, creeping in in the early hours, a few gins under my belt.

King Haakon Bay 5 am 13 November 2006

We came into view of South Georgia, a crescent-shaped island with a ridge of snow-capped peaks barely visible below the clouds. The deck was bustling with activity as the traverse team made final preparations. I peered up at the low dark sky, wondering how it would have been for Shackleton and his men sighting the same land under very different circumstances. They would have been soaked to the bone in clothes they'd worn for seven months — hands frostbitten, bloodied, and grimy from eating seal and penguin meat. Worn out after their incredible 16-day, 800-mile crossing from Elephant Island, they had no idea what lay ahead. The lives of many men depended on them reaching Stromness whaling station successfully.

Here was I, snug and warm in my layers of polar fleeces, down jacket, socked and gloved to the hilt. Giant petrels and cormorants dive-bombed for breakfast next to the ship, and the screeches of skuas filled the air. There was great joy on spotting our first wandering albatross gliding elegantly in the air currents as if performing for us.

'Is this for real?' I asked myself, remembering the *Rime of the Ancient Mariner* from school days; where the albatross followed the ship for days only to get shot in the end. 'Soar away safely, my friend!' I yelled into the wind. Onboard, we'd all caught the addictive 'Antarctic fever', inundated with lectures on krill and phytoplankton, katabatic winds and converging currents, fragile lichen beds, and the facial characteristics of every penguin known to humanity. In other words, we were all fit contestants for the grand final of *Mastermind* with 'polar regions' being the topic.

At 9.30 am we said emotional farewells with the team who'd spent their days onboard practising crevasse rescue, ropework and erecting tents while the rest of us watched on or relaxed. As they disembarked, their hooded faces were a mix of apprehension, exuberance and relief that the moment had come. Our two Norwegian scouts, Rolf and Bjorn, had gone ahead to check out the ground conditions on the first ascent to Shackleton's Gap and give the okay to the others.

Gale force eight winds were blowing, and it looked unlikely that the rest of us could land, but suddenly the direction changed, and a roar of 'Yahoo!' went up with the great news that we could go ashore for a short time.

It was our first Zodiac landing, but we'd been drilled expertly in Ireland, and it went without mishap. I trained my binoculars on the stony shore where our trusty ship's crew were wielding thick sticks to ward off the giant elephant seals that were lazing on the beach. It was the breeding season when the bulls get aggressive and can often prevent landings. In our briefing, we were warned that their bites are vicious and if attacked, advised not to run but to poke them in the whiskers with our walking poles!

On landing, we skirted around the snarling monsters, and gazed immediately up at the snowy slopes leading to Trident Tower on the ridge, to watch our comrades snaking slowly upwards, in small groups, towing sledges. Everyone mentally wished them well and then concentrated on the wildlife circus at our feet.

Elephant seals have to be amongst the ugliest of creatures with their astonishing proboscis and massive slug-like bodies. Several bulls were bloody-faced from fighting and many sported battle gashes on their bodies. They guarded their harems carefully and roared at our approach. I didn't blame them; perhaps we evoked memories of the mass slaughter of their ancestors that nearly rendered them extinct in the 1930s. In those days, their oil was much in demand and blended with whale oil to make an inferior, more economical mix. Early explorers ate the raw meat which is rich in iron and vitamin C and prevents scurvy. It might be considered the 'steak' of the day!

Snowy sheathbills

Cute baby seals

Traverse team en route to Shackleton Gap

King Haakon Bay was a bleak and lonesome spot, the pebbled beach giving way to scraggy tuft grass with beds of moss and lichen we were warned not to walk on. A little band of king penguins marched determinedly along the foreshore, as if on a critical mission, and ignored us completely.

A few of us wandered to the north end of the bay where Shackleton and his men landed at Peggotty Bluff, and lay on the stony ground, silently contemplating past and present under an icy sky. The Boss was renowned for his leadership skills and mingling with his men, perhaps a product of his Quaker upbringing, and I imagined him keeping his little band positive and optimistic. It was this spot where they made a temporary home under the upturned boat, the *James Caird*. I, on the other hand, found it comforting to see our ship peacefully anchored in the bay and know that I was returning to a warm cabin.

Back on board, we watched the traverse party disappear out of view over Shackleton's Gap and waited for assurance that all was well with them before lifting anchor. Weather conditions improved and we raised faces to a wishy-washy sun, but above on the gap, our friends battled high winds.

We sailed onwards through the Stuart Straits between Willis and Bird Islands and hit rougher seas. Many went up onto the bridge to witness first-hand the up and down swell of the Ushuaia. Our friendly captain Jorge loved to have classical music blaring out, and it was reminiscent of the last orchestra of the Titanic sounding its death knell. Sadly, a scheduled landing at Elsehull Bay to see nesting birds, had to be aborted and we observed the vast site through binoculars; thousands of blue-eyed cormorants, shags, assorted petrel and prion whitening the rocky cliff face. Two beautiful snowy sheathbills landed on the ship's rail to rest, and our cameras clicked continuously.

The ship was quiet without the lively atmosphere of the traverse team training. We could track their progress on Google Earth, and we received news later that they camped for the night after passing Trident Tower. A big roll of the vessel after dinner sent us all flying, and one woman suffered a concussion. The technical term 'katabatic winds' was joked about often during our trip, but these wild gales were no laughing matter in action! That night we berthed at Prince Olaf Harbour in good spirits after our first significant landing.

I awoke the next morning to see Prior Island in the early mist, the world's second-largest nesting site for wandering albatross. We were privileged to be allowed to visit it as there is a quota of 300 people per year. As the Zodiac landed, we looked at each other wriggling our noses in disgust. The pungent smell of penguin shit permeated the air as we beat a pathway through the thick compost mess in our squelching wellingtons, to the tufty hillside beyond.

The albatross nests were well hidden in the grass, and many fluffy grey chicks were flapping impatiently on the nest, waiting on mama to return with lunch. I squatted quietly, enthralled, watching the drama that unfolded. A starving chick stuck its head right into the mother's throat and greedily gulped regurgitated fish. Nearby, a nest of breeding giant petrels sat amongst the albatross like black sheep, and I watched the male pecking sweet nothings in the female's ear, perhaps rendering prenatal support! Scavenging skuas hovered overhead, beady eyes alert for a vulnerable chick or egg. I felt just like David Attenborough wandering about but always kept a ten-metre distance from the nesting birds.

Our second landing of the day was at Salisbury Plain on the Bay of Isles, a rookery home to thousands of Emperor Penguins, dress-suited as if waiting for a concert to commence, huddled in gossiping groups making quite a racket. The smell was atrocious again, and I pinched my scarf to my nose in the wind. However, the beauty of the adult birds compensated for the stink — the egg yolk splash on their white breasts and earpads was so vibrant. The plain was awash mostly with brown, furry babies and several approached us curiously, sniffing at our boots, trying to fathom the strangers in their midst. Near me, a fur seal family rested, and a baby took a shine to me, waddled towards me and began suckling my knee! It was a shock, but I burst out laughing at the cute creature.

That evening we anchored in Fortuna Bay, and just before the light dwindled, it was uplifting to behold our traverse buddies slowly descend the Fortuna Glacier in roped-together groups. Gung-ho Rolf and Bjorn skied ahead to check the dangerous icy slope. On sighting them, the *Ushuaia* repeatedly sounded its horn, and we flew the Irish flag. We'd heard that the group experienced a rough night, losing a few tents in gale force winds, and they cramped in together not getting much sleep. The *Ushuaia* must have been a comforting sight for them as they set up camp on the sandy beach, with the penguins and elephant seals for company.

Later, under a clear starry sky, the entire ship gathered on deck waving torches and sang loudly, *Are You Lonesome Tonight* in solidarity. Many of us were teary with emotion, and we all looked forward to continuing the walk with the traverse team the following day.

Hike from Fortuna Bay to Stromness 15 November 2006

A great huggy reunion took place the following morning on the shores of Fortuna Bay where seals and penguins resented the invasion of their patch. I'd carried a batch of West Cork flapjacks from Ireland for the celebratory occasion, and offered Ger McDonnell the first one. He'd taken my little penguin mascot with him on the traverse, and I would treasure it as a result. Tragically, this Irish mountaineer, along with Rolf, our other dear comrade, would lose their lives on K2 two years later.

After our happy chatting, it was time to bend heads to the wind and climb a steep scree slope at the far end of the bay. When I reached the summit breathless but exhilarated, I gazed back on the stunning view with our little ship home anchored in the cove below. Both teams mingled on this final day's hike as we proceeded through the waterlogged tufty terrain that resembled Irish bogland. I tried to stay towards the front to capture people-less photos of the pristine snowy landscape ahead.

We halted near the frozen Crean Lake, named for our countryman. Back in 1916, the Kerryman had stepped through the icy surface of this tarn. It wasn't long after this point that the Boss and his men heard the hoot of the factory horn that was music to their ears. It heralded the start of the working day at Stromness whaling station.

Our first sighting of Stromness, its rusting roofs and holding tanks hugging the distant shore below, was evocative of a bygone era folded into the pages of history books. I stood a moment in silence, teared up with the emotion of a moment that I too would always remember, as our expedition was making history also. There was no horn hooting for us, and it started snowing, reminding us exactly where we were. Time to keep moving — we weren't there yet!

A mass scramble and tumble ensued down the slopes with many sliding on their arses in the deep snow, roaring in laughter. On reaching the old whaling station, we disturbed a large herd of slumbering elephant seals at siesta amidst old propellers and rusted machinery. This time, something else made us keep our distance. A large warning sign read, *'Approach within 200 metres of Whaling Station Prohibited. Danger — Unsafe Structures and Asbestos'.*

The thickly falling snow added to the atmosphere of the derelict settlement as back-slapping and hearty congratulations for the traverse team took place. They'd made it — just as Shackleton and his men did in 1916! We unfurled the Irish tricolour and gathered as a group to sing our national anthem with pride; many eyes welled up.

Whalers abandoned Stromness in 1931. The era of boned corsetry and oil lamps had long gone, and the whaling industry reached its peak in the early 1900s when the oil was used in making margarine and soap. Factory ships replaced the shore processing after 1920.

I wandered over to a small graveyard where several Norwegian whalers didn't make it home again. It was the most forlorn graveyard I ever witnessed in my life as I mumbled a few words in their memory. Meanwhile, I was getting wetter and starting to shiver in the bitter conditions. Yet I was reluctant to leave this unique place and waited on the last Zodiac returning to the ship. A large elephant seal grunted farewell nearby. 'You can keep your icy patch!' I shouted and departed.

Of course, there was a mighty celebration onboard the *Ushuaia* that night. As the ship sailed for Grytviken, the small capital of South Georgia, different versions of the traverse were related; of blowing gales and tents, snowshoe problems, exhaustion, exhilaration, and melting snow for breakfast.

The British Commissioner came onboard, and the champagne flowed at dinner over joyous speeches. Only 30 people permanently reside in South Georgia, and they rely on the arrival of 50 ships a year to provide a social life. We wild Irish did just that, but a crisis arose when the bar ran dry of gin, not surprising after the vast quantities consumed. The Commissioner saved the day, replenishing from the island's supplies and all was well.

Freddy Bear took pride of place on the bar counter, and the party started. Cormac played the guitar, soon joined by the Commissioner, happy to let his hair down for the occasion. A riotous singsong commenced and Fergus, our Antarctic veteran, aged 74, who'd worked on Deception Island as a young biology graduate, turned out to be a mean pole-dancer. The camera crew captured the hilarity into the early hours. An Irish saying sums it up — *Ni bheidh ar leithead aris ann!* — 'None of us would experience the likes of it again!'

There was still another 20 days of the expedition to go. Shackleton died in South Georgia in 1921 on his next voyage to Antarctica, and it was emotional paying our respects at his graveside. After departing South Georgia, we officially crossed into Antarctic waters at the 60th parallel, and everyone looked forward to seeing huge icebergs.

The next landing on Elephant Island would also be historic. It was here that the marooned men from the ship *Endurance* weathered it out in dire conditions for 497 days, unsure of the Boss' return to rescue them. Further south on the Peninsula itself, we camped on the ice for a night at Camp Dorian and visited a few modern-day research stations, learning more about climate change, penguin behaviour, polar history and those dreaded katabatic winds!

We landed on the remarkable volcanic Deception Island where Fergus reminisced on his youth, and many of us took an icy dip in Antarctic waters followed by a hot-spring bath on the black-sand shore. It was my most memorable and briefest dip ever!

And I fell in love with penguins.

Two years later, in January 2008, Pat Falvey, Clare O'Leary, Jonathan Bradshaw and Shaun Menzies were the first Irish expedition to reach the South Pole, thus completing Shackleton's unfulfilled dream. The Beyond Endurance Expedition of the 21st century was an enormous success.

Zodiac in Antarctic icescape

Definitely a nose job

A severe case of penguinitis!

TIMBUKTU

It was an idyllic evening scene on the banks of the Niger River, where a big bend boomerangs towards Timbuktu, as I waited on the last ferry of the day to cross. Two fishermen were mending their nets nearby in the dusky light in preparation for the night's catch ahead and chatting in the soft Bambara dialect. I was looking forward to some capitaine fish, or Nile perch in the coming days, sick of my recent diet of goat skewers and bananas. Higher up the bank, a few women were throwing wet mud at a new hut in the making, and happy children shrieked as they booted an old ball about.

I was tired and dusty after a harrowing seven-hour journey on the gear stick of an old jalopy of a 4WD that had left Mopti early that morning. I was squashed between a jolly fat lady all dolled up in elaborate cloth and beads and a variety of ever-changing wiry drivers at the wheel. The temperature soared to over 40C midday as we bounced through a spartan landscape dotted with acacia scrub and the odd palm. The last leg reminded me of the corrugated Old Telegraph Track to Cape York in Australia and was better than any Jane Fonda buttock exercise.

The very name Timbuktu held a mysterious allure for me since childhood. It connotes an end-of-the-earth image of dunes and camels, and now in 2009, I was only 12 kilometres away! Many doubt its existence, yet this legendary frontier settlement is real. It has been a strategic trade hub on the edge of the Sahara in Mali, linking West Africa and the Mediterranean since medieval times. Camel caravans carried gold, slaves and ivory to the north, and slabs of salt came south from the mines in the desert.

The ferry appeared just as the reddish-orange globe of the sun slid slowly down the sand horizon, and a few Tuareg nomads were in silhouette prostrating for evening prayer. These 'blue men of the desert' looked mysterious with their exotic blue robes and *taguelmoust* or veil, which serves both as a protection against the desert sand and wind-borne spirits they feared. The ferry was little more than a motorised wooden platform, and as I squatted on my rucksack, an old man with a half-hidden face started conversing in French, asking where I was from. His eyes crinkled when he learned I was Irish, and the words 'James Joyce, Ulysses', emerged from his lips. I was surprised, but I was later to discover that Timbuktu was renowned as a seat of scholarship. His cheeky young grandson clutched a cardboard box and was selling tiny trucks fashioned from old Fanta and Pepsi cans. The young entrepreneur grinned in delight when I purchased a couple as presents.

Darkness descended quickly and disembarking on the other bank at Korioume passengers piled into a beaten-up truck for the last leg to town. It dropped me off at the centrally located Hotel Boctou. It was an old caravanserai with basic but clean rooms on the first floor surrounding an inner courtyard where the camel trains would have unloaded their wares in bygone days. On opening a heavy ornate studded door that creaked, I was pleased to see a mosquito net hanging over the slatted bed with an old mattress that had seen better days.

After a quick splash in the basin and spray of repellent, I wandered out into the muggy night in search of food and came across the Poulet D'Or restaurant, which seemed to be the happening place for travellers. Soon, I was contently swilling that welcome cold beer, and was overjoyed to see chips and chicken tortillas on the menu, ignoring the skewers of camel meat for now! Four boisterous French guys were at the next table and had driven an aid truck overland carrying medical supplies — Jean was celebrating his 47th birthday. A good-looking intrepid bunch, I mourned the fact I wasn't ten years younger!

Rising early with bright light streaming in the arched window, I was delighted at my view of the endless sandy waste of desert stretching to nowhere. Somewhere beyond was Niger, or Algeria or Mauritania. *Timbuktu, I've arrived at long last!* Surprisingly, I slept well and was only woken once by the muezzin calling prayer at 3 am when dogs howled, but I soon drifted off again into a deep slumber.

After a simple *petit dejeuner* in the courtyard below, I wandered down the wide main street where the traffic mostly consisted of donkeys with loaded carts of branches for firewood, or heavy hessian sacks. The labyrinth of back roads and sandy alleyways was much more interesting to explore. The low flat-roofed mud buildings lacked any uniformity, and many were graffitied with drawings of Sufi saints and Arabic script. Children were spinning old bicycle wheels with sticks, and veiled women with heavily kohled eyes and beautiful beaded jewellery sat on doorsteps and smiled timidly. A young boy pounded out flatbread on the strangest looking oven I'd ever seen.

Soon I emerged at the main town roundabout with a big calico sign reading 'Timbuktu, City of 333 Saints'. My curiosity was satisfied at the tourist office nearby, where I learned that the town has Unesco status because many Sufi saints were buried in the cemeteries and mausoleums. Sufism is a mystic branch of Islam, embracing literature and ritual performances at shrines but I expressed surprise at there being 333 Saints in one place!

'We had one of the world's first universities here in the 12th century,' the girl boasted, determined to impress. 'And the desert climate has preserved thousands of precious Islamic manuscripts that are in many private collections. Would you like a Timbuktu stamp in your passport?' she proffered. I was so pleased to get this significant stamp, but unfortunately, that passport was stolen the following year, leaving me only the photos and memories.

The midday heat was scorching when I came out, and I dived into a pleasant shady restaurant to pore over the pamphlets given me. I read that the Europeans always assumed the dark continent of Africa was illiterate, ignorant and with no history, and were surprised to discover on their quest for gold that Timbuktu was a sophisticated seat of learning at a time when Europe was in the Dark Ages. In the middle of my highbrow research, the butcher arrived with a fresh sheep's head, dripping blood and with a cortege of buzzing flies in his wake. I knew this was a local delicacy for some celebration, but it looked and smelled disgusting as he stood near me, haggling over the price with the restaurant owner.

I wandered off to observe the goings-on at the vibrant *Grand Marche*, which was a bustle of traders and choosy shoppers. Kola nuts were piled high by the sandy roadside — the currency of West Africa and given as a symbol of hospitality and friendship, but also an offering at prayers. Shortly after arriving in Mali, I learned the etiquette of being invited to a person's home; that presenting kola nuts is the equivalent of bringing flowers or a bottle of wine to a host. People chew the bitter nuts as a caffeine stimulant, and they aid digestion, but of course, I only knew it as an ingredient in Coca-Cola.

An older man with a weatherworn face sat behind a stack of salt slabs doing his accounting in an old copybook and looked up when I touched the salt. 'Fresh off the camel's back this morning Madame,' he laughed, speaking in English. 'Where is the salt mine?' I asked, and he replied that it was a two-day camel ride away, whilst chipping off a piece as a souvenir for me. 'Thank you,' I said, wondering how long before it would disintegrate in the heat or would it last until my dinnertime? I marvelled at the barbers next door where two scrawny goats lounged in the dust beside a solitary chair where the barber was snoozing, and a painted sign on the wall behind displayed vivid versions of the latest No. 1 or No. 2 gent's cuts.

I felt an urge to reach the edge of town and get a sense of the frontier between Timbuktu and the vast Sahara — a hazy view stretching endlessly into the distance. On the way, I passed through an impoverished Bella settlement of squatter tents in dire condition and an open sewer adjacent. The Bella, traditionally slaves, are the bottom caste of Tuareg society and still now, they flee cruel masters in remote villages. The ragged children looked malnourished but captivated me with their resourcefulness with anything that could be used as a toy. Rusty old carts of metal were raced with the same excitement as a slick Ferrari in the Grand Prix.

As the more miserable mud huts petered off, I came to the *Flamme de la Paix* peace monument where at the end of the Tuareg rebellion against the French in the 1990s, 3000 weapons were ceremonially burnt. I climbed up a precarious tower to gaze out on the desert and get a view of Boctou's well nearby, the old woman the town was named after. From the top, the flat scrub stretched to an infinity of low dunes, and I wondered where a group of orange and red swathed women were going with heads bent low against the sand winds.

Between 1588 and 1853, nearly 50 Europeans tried to reach the fabled city of Timbuktu; only four made it, and three made it back. In the historic Sankore neighbourhood, an elaborate wooden door in a cracked mud wall led into Gordon Laing's house, now a museum. He was the first foreign explorer to reach Timbuktu in 1826. Inside, fragile early manuscripts were on display, centuries-old copies of the Koran and scholarly tomes on law and astronomy. I was in awe looking at a palm-sized book written finely on fish skin and illuminated with droplets of gold leaf. *What a gem compared to the generic paperbacks of the present,* I thought. A degree certificate from years of study at the *madrassa* or university was etched on old wood with ink from charcoal and Arabic gum. On leaving, it seemed too simple to pen my signature in the visitor's book with a biro!

Three of the oldest mosques in West Africa are in Timbuktu, dating back to the 14th century and I was bewildered how such haphazard piles of mud, straw and sticks could have withstood the centuries of sand storms. I was only allowed to enter one as a non-Muslim and sat in the women's section listening to the quiet chatter of a group gossiping. They beckoned me over for a glass of orange juice, and it was an opportunity to satisfy our mutual curiosity.

Mothers in Mali

Djinguereber Mosque, Timbuktu

Ancient manuscripts of Timbuktu

Mending nets by the Niger River

Fun with Bella kids in Timbuktu

On my last evening, I had dinner with a mixed bunch of travellers, and as we chewed on tough camel meat, we remarked how lucky we were to be assured a safe and quick passage home from Timbuktu. Little did we realise what events would unfold in a few short years that would render the town unsafe for tourists to visit for many years.

Al Qaeda jihadist groups invaded the city in 2012 and demolished many Sufi shrines with shovels and pickaxes, and plotted to destroy the valuable manuscripts. However, as happened with precious artworks in Europe during the Nazi invasion, local clans had hidden their collections of manuscripts underground or transported them secretly downriver to the capital Bamako. Many risked their lives to protect their heritage for future generations.

The message resonates loud and clear from Timbuktu — its people are resilient, and this iconic city will endure the sands of time.

THE BIG CATS OF THE SAHARA

'Yahoo!' we cried out, high fiving for yet another Mossad trip. And this time to the Libyan Sahara. I was with my two Portuguese friends, Paulo and Carlos, whom I'd met hiking in Patagonia a few years before, and we remained great buddies. Younger than me, they both had family commitments, and couldn't get away readily. Still, every few years, we organised a 'Mossad Mission', our in-house revolutionary language we invented for our travels together. I was the Irish agent due to the IRA connection.

Libya wasn't an easily accessible destination for independent travellers in 2009. Fortunately, Paulo had a friend working at the Portuguese Embassy in Tripoli, and the embassy took me under its wing, arranging my visa. However, they weren't overly happy at our plans to disappear into the desert wastes of the south in search of ancient rock art.

Whilst in Tripoli, we visited the ruins of Leptis Magna, the once resplendent western frontier of the Roman Empire. We were lucky to have the serenity of its lavish columns and marbled floors mainly to ourselves. The tranquil ruins were a pleasant contrast to the bustle of Tripoli's streets, where the ever-present military patrolled the thoroughfares, and Gaddafi's blatant socialist propaganda was everywhere visible.

There was no escaping the onslaught of billboards at every roundabout featuring Colonel Muammar Gaddafi, the 'Brotherly Leader of the Great Socialist People's Libyan Arab Jamahiriya', and one of the world's longest-serving leaders from 1977-2011. It was quite a mouthful. But I was delighted to have seen his famous blue Beetle Volkswagen from the 1960s in the National Museum, and I'd reflected that my father and the great leader had similar good taste.

I was longing to stretch my legs as it had been a lengthy 800-kilometre drive south from Tripoli through a parched, featureless landscape. We had just arrived in Sabha, our launching pad to the Sahara and a major transit hub for laden lorries coming from Chad, Niger and Algeria. As we drove through a mix of stark modernity and crumbling mud buildings in a warren of covered alleyways, the driver told us the town had been an old salt caravan trading post in the 11th century.

Gaddafi was a desert boy, son of Bedouins, and attended school here in Sabha. We had just passed the green dome of the publishing house of *The Green Book,* Gaddafi's bible, and a mirror of Mao's *Little Red Book.* I had purchased a copy in Tripoli and looked forward to some further insight into the dictator while reading his philosophies under desert skies. Still, I somehow suspected I would abandon it quickly for an easy-read novel.

Arriving at Fezzan Camp, I felt the buzz of a place where long-distance drivers and dusty travellers, fatigued after endless sand vistas, looked forward to a shower, a clean bed and a good feed that wasn't canned goods. I was looking forward to the same!

Over the staple dinner of rice, *ful* beans and salad, we met our guide Mohamed, who spent six years in the UK and had travelled extensively as a steward for Afrique Airlines. We would be in good company with no language difficulties. I'm a lover of maps, but the one we plotted our route on showed the emptiest terrain I'd ever seen on paper.

Our little convoy departed Sabha early the next morning in two 4WD LandCruisers. Salim our cook, and Ahmed, his assistant travelled in the first with all our supplies, camping equipment and carpets on the roof. We would get used to this pair routinely taking off in a whirlwind of dust ahead of us and catching up with them later in the day, often capturing a grinning Salim in the heart of an acacia tree, harvesting firewood for the night. They usually had the camp set up by the time we arrived, and Salim's kitchen was the back of the LandCruiser. Ahmed was our tea maker and expert bread baker.

My two Mossad companions and I rode in the second 4WD, with Mohamed upfront with Hussein, our Tuareg guide and driver. Hussein's knowledge and skill would prove invaluable in terrain where there was no signage and in many places, no roads. It wasn't long before I discovered a unique connection with him.

Until now, as often happens in Arabic societies, Mohamed focused on interaction with Paulo and Carlos, directing his conversation at them. As the only female, I felt a little on the fringe and kept quiet for a change, listening. Therefore, when the question came out of the blue, it flummoxed me completely.

'Do you know Clonsilla?' Hussein asked me with a quick turn of the head. 'Yes,' I replied hesitantly, as this was a suburb of Dublin near the hospital I worked in, and I'd left all that behind in another world.

'I used to live there,' he replied and went on to tell us that he had studied hospital administration in Ireland for two years and rented a house in Clonsilla with his wife. He had recognised my Irish accent during the banter with the lads. I was astonished. 'I can't believe it,' I said, laughing at the coincidence.

'My wife returned to Libya after six months,' Hussein continued. 'She hated your soft Irish rain and the constant cold,' he chuckled. 'I finished my studies and worked in Tripoli for a while, but missed my desert home and the nomadic life.'

'I always think I'm descended from gypsies or nomads,' I laughed. 'So perhaps I too have Tuareg blood in my veins!' I felt a special bond with Hussein after this conversation and from then on was treated equally as an honorary male. I usually travel alone for precisely this reason. Observing Hussein's desert savviness during the trip, I found it incredible that he had lived in cold, chaotic Dublin.

We continued bumping along through Wadi al-Hayat which means 'The Valley of Life', somewhat ironic as Mohamed pointed out a nearby mound where Professor Mori an Italian archaeologist, discovered the famous Tashwinat mummy of a small boy in 1958. From 5600 BC, it predated the Egyptian mummies.

Paulo laughed and produced his little tome for the trip, an English translation of Mori's descriptions of the art sites we would visit. He and I would take turns boring Carlos with our litany of facts on ancient rock art and political slogans.

There are multiple descriptions for ice in Arctic regions, and Mohamed proceeded to educate us in the language of the desert. A *Wadi*, like the one we were in, is the dry fertile valley of an old river, where the few inhabitants of desert regions live, cultivating cereals and citrus fruit in the shelter of date palms. Then, there are *Ergs* — seas of sand and dunes — Ubari was on our right and Murzuk on our left, which is nearly as big as Switzerland. And finally, the mountains of basalt and sandstone are called *Msak*, where the ancient artists left their legacy in caves or on rock faces.

We passed many fruit and vegetable stalls by the roadside and purchased a bag of juicy oranges while stretching our legs. The heat was intense. 'There's the Eighth Wonder of the World,' Mohamed exclaimed further on, pointing towards the vast plain to our north. It was Gaddafi's Great Man-Made River, his breathtaking project to supply the thirsty coastal cities with water from the aquifers under the desert, full since the area was lush savannah grasslands millennia ago. Mounds of stony earth, pumping stations and construction work were visible, with many piles of the biggest pipes I'd ever seen.

'Those are the migrant workers' houses,' Mohamed told us, as we passed hundreds of tiny blockhouses. 'There are oil fields in this area too.' The draining of the aquifers was a controversial project as no one knew the impact it would have in the future. The ancient Garamantes' culture of the same region was wiped out in 500 BC by drought, after tapping into this valuable underground water source which eventually dried up. It was a reminder to us that humankind's detrimental impact on the environment has occurred many times in history.

We caught up with Salim and Ahmed at midday, sheltering from the hot sun under a tamarisk tree, a brushwood fire already on the go. The temperature had reached the mid-30s, and I was hallucinating about a cold drink. Ahmed had a minty tasting tea brewing from some thorny bush nearby and claimed it was good for rehydration, informing us that the Tuareg use it as an antibiotic in an area with no doctors. It washed down our canned tuna and bean salad lunch prepared by Salim, but I quietly discarded the strong tea when he wasn't looking. A group of white crows called *geta* hovered above us hoping for pickings but waited in vain.

Mohamed stated there had been a torrential downpour the previous week and showed us the watermark on the acacia tree Salim had trimmed. It wasn't easy to believe looking at the bone-dry landscape around us. There were strange clusters of mud-coloured cannonballs lying scattered about on the cracked earth, begging to be kicked. 'Come! Time for exercise,' Mohamed called out, laughing. A game of melon football ensued with this strange fruit that is bitter and inedible and bursts on impact.

Afterwards, he gave us a briefing on dangerous desert creatures, pointing to a maze of creative tracks near the wadi. 'That's the scorpion,' he said, pointing to a fabulous wavy pattern, 'and this one is the black scarab beetle.' I shuddered, thinking I must take extra care before squatting in the dunes for my nightly pee. 'There are snakes too,' Salim added. 'We call them the "fish of the desert", as they are tasty to eat. My favourite,' he grinned at me, seeing my look of disgust.

In the afternoon, we headed into the barren and inhospitable Wadi Methkandoush, the name sounding positively biblical to me. This area contains one of the richest concentrations of prehistoric rock art in the world, most dating back at least 12,000 years. It was an effort to climb up the steep slope of the massif on our left, and the abominable flies were eating me alive despite my Aussie cork hat. We reached a broad ledge halfway up, and I soon forgot my afflictions when I saw the superb art gallery spread before me on the rock face.

It was a safari-canvas of animals carved into the red sandstone — the whole gamut of giraffe, deer, large horned cows, even a baby crocodile. The details were cleverly delineated in strong strokes, representing what roamed on grassland thousands of years before. It was all the more remarkable looking at the desolate basalt land around us. As we continued around the cliff edge, Mohamed pointed to more hunting scenes hard to spot in crevices, including a group of eight ostriches caught in a circular trap. There were human figures as well, mostly female, with a hole designating their sex. I tried to visualise this diverse wildlife at a time when vast herds roamed the plains, crocodiles lurked in swamps, and the nearby slopes were forested.

Further on, we came to the 'wow factor' of the Methkandoush we were all waiting for. On a cliff face above us, highlighted in the afternoon light, was the famous petroglyph of two large cats on hind legs as if boxing each other. Millennia ago, an unknown talented artist pecked these out using a sharp stone. It was truly spectacular, and I was so happy viewing one of the world's rock art masterpieces that I considered on a par with the Mona Lisa.

It was comforting that the galleries were hard to access and that guides are compulsory on visits. Mohamed told us that in other areas, tourists had thrown water on rock art to get a better photo, chipped off pieces for souvenirs or worse still, graffitied signatures on the original. The cats were the highlight of my day, and Paulo promised to read us Professor Mori's comments on them later around the campfire.

By the time we descended, the sun was low on the horizon, and we drove another 130 kilometres before halting for the night. Everyone was tired, and we quietly absorbed the beauty of twilight orange on the rolling dunes. On arrival, Salim and Ahmed awaited us in a lonely hollow, tents erected and home-fire burning bright. What a welcome sight it was to see Ahmed polishing the glasses for tea squatting on a carpet in his desert kitchen!

Paulo, Carlos and I leapt out like young colts let loose to clamber up the dunes before the daylight disappeared. It was no mean feat reaching the crest, and we walked along the ridge, arms outstretched, balancing as if on a circus tightrope. The Portuguese horseplay commenced, and after a few rolls in the sand, I left them to it, digging a solitary nest for myself to laze in and gaze at the grandeur around me. When the light faded, I strolled back to camp for a quiet chat with Hussein.

There is nothing better than the Tuareg bread *tajeelah*, eaten hot from its sandy bed in the embers and under a canopy of stars. Ahmed flapped it about in the hot coals, shaking sand off it while we watched impatiently with jam ready. We always had this for our first course, followed by plates of spicy vegetable stew where we needed more bread for mopping the sauce. By the trip's end, we were licking our plates unashamedly!

The stories started around the campfire afterwards. Salim had eight children from the ages of three to 29, and none of the older ones married. He owned ten camels. 'I'm saving my wages to buy more,' he told us. 'The bride price for each daughter is nine camels, but I can't find husbands for them,' he laughed. Mohamed spoke of a past life in Manchester and later the thrill of flying, jetting to Nairobi, Casablanca and Egypt. Ahmed and Hussein conversed quietly in Tamashek, the Tuareg tongue.

When the moon rose, we walked up the dunes again for a navigation class with Hussein and were quickly lost. 'There's Orion,' he said, pointing heavenward to some distant twinkling dot, 'and Ursus Minor, and who can spot the North Star? Now — find your way back to camp,' he laughed. It was usual for the nomadic Tuareg to tell the time and find their way using the night sky. On our return, he showed us a particular bush that serves as a desert bed, under which members of his tribe bury themselves in the warm sand, just leaving the face exposed and sleep comfortably under the stars.

I retreated to my tent and fell fast asleep after reading the first page of Gaddafi's *Green Book*.

It was still dark when Hussein woke me, keen to show me sunrise over the dunes. The guys were still sleeping as we both plodded up to the ridge and reverently observed the eastern sky splash awake in a hue of pinks and the orb of a new day appear. We slid down on our backsides laughing, and the aroma of Ahmed's coffee and fresh bread awaited us. I called them 'Laughing Cow' breakfasts, after the awful processed cheese triangles that are so loved in many African countries but taste so bland.

Our second day could have been part of the Dakar rally as Hussein showed off his 4WD skills, dune bashing over the Murzac sand sea. We went off-piste, twisting and turning on the rippling waves, an adrenalin kick that was scary at times. As we crested the dunes, I shouted 'Up we go!' with exuberance, like a child on a swing, and didn't realise until later that Mohamed was recording me. A singsong later commenced in three languages, and we were a happy bunch.

The panorama transitioned to a fantastic sculpture park of fossilised monoliths, high arches in terracotta shades and wavy ice cream mounds of sand. Petrified rock formations looked like the battlements of forts standing guard against invaders. We were now on the edge of the Acacus Mountains, a rugged land of flat tepuis and jagged basalt escarpments, stretching to the Algerian border.

Soon we stopped at the ruins of a 2000-year-old city from the Garamantes era; with remnants of old tombs and shards of pottery scattered about. The sand was of different colours, black, grey, orange, red and white and I tried to collect it in layers in my water bottle while the boys artistically drew long-horned cattle and goats. We were amazed to see stone trees nearby, an old petrified forest of upright stumps, millennia in the making.

The dune bashing got rougher, and I was glad of a tea break at a Tuareg camp, where 14 families still lived traditional lives. Their camels rested nearby, numbers on their faces indicating private ownership. Only I was allowed to visit the women sheltering in the sheepskin tents. They were unveiled and welcoming of a distraction, immediately curious to know my age. I played the game of pretending to be younger, but they were wise to it, one stroking my weather-beaten hiker's face and laughing. In the Sahara, a woman slides downhill at 40.

Relaxing by the fire before dinner, I browsed through the *Green Book* and quoted the Great Leader —

Only in the desert is there true union between me and myself.

'I think that's the only sentence that makes any sense to me,' I said. Gaddafi was a lover of catchphrases. The book was written after a period of reflection in the desert and spelt out his vision for people power. His section on women interested me.

A woman has full rights and need not be coerced to turn into a man and forsake her femininity.

'What about his Amazon bodyguards?' I enquired of Mohamed, having heard of Gaddafi's entourage of beauties who dressed in camouflage uniforms.

'You mean the Revolutionary Nuns?' he chuckled, giving them the Libyan nickname. 'When recruited, they take oaths of virginity. It's a smart strategy because it is difficult for an Arab man to attack a woman.'

His expression then became serious as he spoke of the many rumours of rape and abuse suffered by the women as they were passed around Gaddafi's sons and cadres and then discarded. Silence descended, and I was suddenly aware of my solitary female status.

Paulo changed the subject to Professor Mori and got animated, giving us a preview of our art tour in the Acacus the following day. As he spoke of the Pastoral Period, the Horse Period and the Round Head Period, the waft of Ahmed's tasty camel stew distracted us, and the lecture terminated quickly. Our skilled cook had purchased some fresh camel meat from the nomads earlier in the day, and it tasted delicious.

As it would be our last night in the dune wilderness, I decided to sleep under the stars that night, wanting to feel the solitude. After scrutinising the sand beneath me, I cocooned myself in my sleeping bag and lay hypnotised by the twinkling abyss above. On every *womadic* wandering, I like being in isolated places that make me feel insignificant on the planet, yet where I

Rock art of the Acacus

Sahara sands, Libya

Ahmed baking 'tajeelah'

can feel at one with Nature. It's my spirituality and difficult to experience when not alone.

The next morning we visited the fine art gallery of the Acacus, climbing up to a large rock overhang halfway up yet another steep slope. It was testing in the midday heat but well worth the effort. Under the overhang, there were many hunting scenes, men with spears and shields confronting big-horned cattle, and an ostrich in flight. A large giraffe was dotted creatively in white ochre. Mohamed led us to a cleft in the hillside where we could make out sections of a long snake with speckled banding. The paintings were so skilful in their simplicity, drawn in red ochre with a brush of feathers or animal hair or sometimes only using the artist's fingers.

I was moved especially by the remarkable clarity of a wedding scene, where women were washing each other's hair and trying on dresses in preparation for the big day. Their elegant crouched postures could have been a scene from present times. Similar to the Aboriginal people in Australia, the Tuareg believe the rock art is an educational tool left by their ancestors to demonstrate how they lived and what they saw in their daily surroundings.

I felt sad leaving the wonders of the past and the tranquillity of the desert behind as in a few hours we emerged into a valley of green farmland with irrigated gardens. We hit the main asphalt road once more and reached a small settlement with a police checkpoint and an old Italian fort. Mohamed told us that illegal immigrants heading for Europe travelled this route, as well as drug and alcohol smugglers.

It was all getting too civilised for me as we stopped at a small shop for Snickers bars and cold Coca-Cola. It was a shock having to change gear entering a different world, but my heart retained the magic of the dunes and the memory of the Big Cats of the Sahara sands.

AYAHUASCA AND THE SHAMAN

I've always been interested in natural remedies and what indigenous peoples can forage from the land to alleviate pain and treat ailments. Often, these plants or barks are the origins of today's medicines. On my Amazon trip in 2011, I was lucky to visit a *curandero*, or natural healer, in his leafy laboratory deep in the rainforest.

I first heard of Don Rafaelo through an Italian girl, a herbalist who had spent a few days with him. 'You should visit him,' she suggested. 'With your medical knowledge, he might be happy to learn some anatomical terms in English as he also treats foreigners, and he will be grateful for the dollars. The family is saving for a water tank.' I expressed regret at my poor Spanish but boldly decided to avail of the opportunity and got the details from her.

It was monsoon season in Leticia, Colombia's port on the Amazon and torrential rain had me hammock-bound and reading for the afternoon. Don Rafaelo featured in the ethnobotanical tome I was browsing through, and he had a reputation for collaborating with conventional medical practitioners. The hostel owner Jorge, who was an interesting philosophical character, sat down to chat with me awhile.

'Are you interested in ayahuasca?' he inquired. 'I don't do drugs,' I replied, 'but I've heard that many westerners come here for the experience.' I then told Jorge how I lost one day of my life to a bad magic mushroom trip in Thailand. It had scared the wits out of me, and I swore that I would never experiment with drugs again. 'I'll stick to good red wine,' I laughed, 'at least I know how to deal with the aftermath. I like to be in control, so losing it and being off my head freaks me out.'

'It's a tradition in our culture to take ayahuasca when a family gets together, often at the moon's equinox — both as a sacred ceremony and to commune with nature,' Jorge explained. He told me that his brother had attended Stockholm University and did his PhD on this herbal brew that is both hallucinogenic and therapeutic. Later, he showed me a copy of the research, and it made fascinating reading, especially when scientific trials verified the benefits of ayahuasca in the protection and regeneration of brain cells.

Two days later, I was seated in the overcrowded community *lancha*, taking weekly shoppers back to their riverside settlements upriver. Hessian sacks of store goods surrounded me; mostly canned food, bottles of soft drink and bulky canisters of smelly diesel for boats, which were the main transport between villages on the Amazon. Tired children slept peacefully among the sacks, and a suited man with a good suitcase stood out among the brightly dressed villagers. He was returning from Rio de Janeiro to visit family — the 'big shot' who earned good money in the city.

'Where are you going?' he enquired. 'To Narino, to visit the shaman Don Rafaelo,' I replied. Jose laughed and warned me. 'Be careful of his potions.' The boat pulled in at Nazareth and Santa Sofia, clusters of thatched huts on the riverbank — most with satellite dishes attached and exotic shrubbery in bloom by the doorways. Dozing dogs awoke, and excited children came running to meet the boat — eagerly awaiting treats from town. Young women washing clothes in the river paused to wave.

Wilting in the afternoon heat, I was relieved when we pulled into a boat ramp at a small forest clearing where I had to follow the path. However, word had spread on the bush telegraph, as a spritely little barefooted man in shorts was coming towards me. *Hola!* Don Rafaelo greeted me, and I was christened 'Jo' when he heard my complicated name. I was used to this easy nickname.

His home was nearby, and he introduced me to his wife Juliana, who was busy stirring a black pot on an open fire and had a sleeping baby strapped to her back. A few skinny chickens were pecking about in the dirt. 'Juliana only speaks Ticuna, the local dialect,' Don Rafaelo explained. I admired the beautiful beadwork she was wearing, and she smiled, pleased, signalling that she had made it herself.

I was shown to my hut, containing a rough timber bed under a mosquito net, and a small table with candles and matches. There was no electricity or a generator at the shaman's house. I was pleased to spot the book I had been reading earlier at Jorge's as my curiosity was whetted to study further. A small veranda overlooked the forest, noisy with the constant humming, buzzing, and chirping of frogs, cicadas and birds, and I could hear several monkey howls in the canopy overhead. It would be a night for earplugs!

After a late lunch of rice, beans and yucca juice, Don Rafaelo took me to see his garden, which was a pleasant nature trail through the forest. He harvested what he required fresh in the early dawn, and as we strolled, he drew my attention to particular plants or bushes. He had names for them, but also mimicked their use by rubbing his belly, coughing or touching some body part that they were useful for treating. Using my Spanish/English dictionary, we had a good laugh figuring out the explanations, and I repeated terms in English for him. He was a cheerful character, and I warmed to him immediately.

Naturally, there was an abundance of coca plants scattered about, and he gave me a few leaves to chew as we walked. The locals use them frequently for energy and to settle the stomach. I hoped they might assist my brain with the language difficulties and reflected on how much damage this seemingly innocuous leaf has caused in the Western world.

Colombia is the world's biggest supplier of cocaine, but the processing plants are deep in the jungle. Don Rafaelo informed me that there was a military post sited nearby, and constant patrols were on the lookout for drug smugglers as well as FARC guerillas. Despite my poor Spanish, I was delighted to be getting the gist of his conversation and explanations. Many of the plants he used were rich in nutrients and boosted the immune system, and I found it interesting when he showed me sugar leaves which substitute as a sweetener instead of store sugar. However, I wasn't sure if I understood him correctly when he said he used the leaves of a fig plant mashed with lemon juice and a child's urine in the treatment of fever!

'La purga,' he said, the local name for ayahuasca, at the same time pointing to a dark shrub with glossy leaves growing just off the path. In the PhD study, I had read that the torn leaves and stalks are boiled with a particular vine containing DMT, which is the hallucinogenic component. This makes a potent concentrated liquid which is strained to remove impurities, and the tea is drunk under carefully supervised conditions. I knew from Jorge, and from talking to other travellers, how important it was to fast and cleanse the body for two weeks beforehand, strictly abstaining from caffeine, alcohol, cigarettes, meat or sex. A qualified shaman should lead the ceremony to reassure participants that the drink has been brewed properly, the correct dose administered, and any side effects closely monitored. The whole experience lasts a few hours, and apparently, it's normal to vomit during it.

I must admit I was curious about the ceremony and would have loved the opportunity to witness the proceedings, but I was reluctant to participate in it myself.

On our return, Don Rafaelo showed me his client report book where former patients left comments on their ayahuasca episode, some in English. Many described their euphoria, 'out of body' experiences, as well as auditory and visual hallucinations. But one or two admitted to having a dreadful trip of dark paranoia. I shuddered as I remembered my own crazy experience in Thailand taking magic mushrooms.

The shaman also had a reputation for treating HIV — clients who were desperate to try anything, as there were few conventional drugs available for treatment at that time. The patients stayed with him for a few weeks as the first stage involved a total body cleanse and vegan diet, whilst taking other concoctions to build up the immune system. Several had returned to him for further remedies, claiming it improved their symptoms and wellbeing.

Dark came early in the forest as the cacophony increased at dusk and fierce mosquitoes descended on me in search of fresh blood. I read by torchlight under my net, trying to recognise the plants I'd seen in the wild and translate the Spanish descriptions. I was genuinely very impressed with Don Rafaelo's knowledge and healing powers and felt I would have trusted him had I been seriously ill. He inquired if I had any health complaints and I explained that I was generally in good shape but sometimes suffered bouts of arthritis in the damp Irish winters, but I solved this by travelling to warmer climates.

In the morning, before catching the midday boat back to Leticia, his teenage son Iban, took me for a tour through the flooded undergrowth of narrow water channels in an old dugout. There was a small leak in the boat, so I had to bale regularly with a rusty can, which was worrying as I wondered what lurked in the depths, but it never got serious.

The interspersing light and shade played on tall trunks of ceiba, eucalyptus and balsa wood trees used in boat building. As we approached a stand of broad buttressed fig trees, a family of crabs scurried out from the roots and Iban netted some for fish bait. Afterwards, he took a photo of me clinging to a ropey liana hanging down against the backdrop of giants. He was a reserved boy, and I was appreciative of the silence to take in the ambience of the setting.

The morning heat increased, and a flutter of blue morpho butterflies followed us back into the light. I was sorry to leave the dreamlike state induced by the forest, but it was time to return to Leticia on the community boat.

Saying fond farewells, Don Rafaelo pressed a plastic bottle into my hand. 'For your arthritis,' he mimed with a hobble of his spindly legs. I laughed and thanked him.

Back on the boat, settled among the hessian sacks again, I took the bottle out for a closer inspection and opened the lid. It was a pale yellow colour, and there was a whiff of lemon.

JOURNEY ON THE AMAZON

I sat gazing at the expanse of the Amazon, at Leticia in southern Colombia — a triangle called *Tres Fronteras* bordering Peru and Brazil. The plan was to travel by boat downriver to Manaus, the jungle city of Brazil and I was excited to be making this famous journey at last.

The essential item required for the 1000-kilometre trip was a hammock, cheaply purchased at the night market on the riverbank. This was abuzz with all the commerce of a frontier town, where merchandise of every kind changed hands either legally or surreptitiously. Touts grab any roaming gringos and lure them to a cheap lodging house or shipping agent, or their uncle's shop for souvenirs.

My five-dollar hammock was similar to a cheap umbrella. It was made of thin, lightweight nylon, and sported the green, blue and yellow colours of the Brazilian football team. I thought this would undoubtedly spark conversation with the locals. I had to seek expert advice on the type and length of rope needed for slinging it to the rafters onboard to ensure I wouldn't come a cropper in the middle of a stormy night.

The riverboats left for Manaus every few days at varying times; it took four days if you were lucky. These boats are the principal means of transport for river dwellers going anywhere on the 7000-kilometre stretch of water. Goods of all kinds are offloaded at a few major ports but also get loaded into smaller craft mid-river near villages. The passengers are diverse, from an immigrant in a New York T-shirt arriving home after years abroad, to a portly *senora* and her brood visiting relatives for Easter.

I quickly discovered that the boats are run with the precision of a boarding school, and I soon learned the routine. The lower deck holds the cargo, which is efficiently loaded the day before departure and varies from crops in hessian bags, to cardboard boxes of techno gear from China to crates of smelly fish or squawking hens. Even the latest model Land Rover might get squeezed in for a wealthy plantation owner requiring a bit of status in a remote area.

The middle deck was 'Hammock Hotel' with no first-class en suite or deluxe section. It was the luck of the draw where you ended up, some seeking a spot in which to languish with a water view, but you then risked getting soaked in a sudden storm or a windy swing in a gale. Tarps were lowered down the side of the vessel at night, providing some protection from the elements but making it stuffy with so many slumbering bodies.

The upper deck was a recreational area to seek quiet and catch the breeze or a few rays of sunshine on pale Celtic skin. I was thankful it wasn't too hot, and there were no mosquitoes.

Usually, the few *gringos* congregated together and spoke English as the everyday travellers' language. However, with 300-500 passengers on board, it was the perfect opportunity to connect with local people and learn about their way of life. I was fortunate to undertake my trip before the wide use of social media, and I was practised in the comedy of conversation using facial expressions and waving hands about dramatically. It's much more fun, and the best way to improve elementary Spanish or Portuguese.

The region of Leticia is in the midst of dangerous FARC guerilla territory. Before boarding at the wharf, we entered the immigration hut, where sniffer dogs circled everyone's luggage, on the hunt for large quantities of coca leaves, processed drugs or tobacco. A free-for-all dash then ensued, in the race to grab a good location. I hadn't a clue how to hang my hammock, and was too short anyway, but luckily a tall friendly Peruvian educated me in the art of tying it securely to the rafters. I smiled at my neighbours, all lined up head to toe, perhaps only a ruler's length away, front, back and each side of my spot. It was certainly not the place to be fussy about privacy.

After storing my rucksack neatly underneath my patch, I tried not to make a fool of myself settling in for the first time. The trick was to sit into and lie diagonally across the hammock, getting used to the balancing act of weight distribution. Naturally, I got turfed out multiple times before getting the hang of it and a few people watching my antics, burst into peals of laughter. The cutest thing was to see shy children peer gingerly over the sides of their hammocks, giggling at the clumsy foreigner. Parents urged them to say 'Hello' and ask me my name — a chance to practise their English taught at school.

There were segregated washrooms at either end of the hammock deck, and these were kept spotlessly clean by the boat staff. There was always toilet paper and a constant flow of tepid water in the showers. The mess room was a crucial area for passengers, as mealtimes were eagerly anticipated, just like any posh cruise ship. Meals were eaten at a long table covered with gaudy plastic and served by Maria, the cheerful *senora* at the food hatch. Old calendar scenes of beaches and ski slopes adorned the walls as well as pictures of blonde models. I quickly discovered it a wise move to befriend Maria early on as I'd seen some others do. She might give you forewarning of the bell ringing for meals, in advance of a long queue forming, and there was a good chance those at the first sitting might get a tastier morsel or something extra.

The staff were friendly and helpful and obviously enjoyed their work. The menu was the usual wholesome South American staple of rice, beans and meat or chicken. With the enticing smell of food wafting in the air, no one remained eating longer than necessary, as it would be too unkind to the hungry faces peering in from outside, licking their lips impatiently.

I was grateful not to suffer the 'Amazon belly' on board, as the toilet situation wasn't conducive to dawdling inside with constant knocks on the door. Outside regular mealtimes, big jugs of orange juice or pots of super-sweetened coffee with slabs of cake were plopped randomly on the table.

The open upper deck was where all the action happened. It served as the bar, the nightclub, an impromptu gym and cafe all rolled into one, and provided an ideal viewing platform for birdlife or events on the water. At any time of day or night, the muddy coloured waters were mesmerising in their vastness, and on the distant shore, the dense jungle and undergrowth held a particular mystique. On small islands, fish eagles perched patiently on scraggy bushes ready to pounce on some unwary catch and one afternoon a rare pink dolphin arched to the water's surface, to everyone's delight. The boat mainly motored midstream in the strong current.

On approaching thatched or tin-roofed settlements onshore, small boats would suddenly appear, and a speedy acrobatic operation took place in minutes. Swinging close to the side of the ship, passengers embarked or disembarked swiftly, and assorted luggage or cargo was flung overboard.

On the upper deck, the gregarious barmaid Teresa, endowed with the gift of the gab, was carefully selected to banter with customers and entice as many as possible to buy grog. Yet at no time was there any drunkenness or aggressive behaviour onboard. In the early dusk light, tables and plastic chairs were out, and passengers became acquainted over games of cards and dominoes. Of course, this was mostly men, as the women, generally non-drinkers, minded children below. By the second night, regulars were nodding and chatting amiably like old friends, and there was a convivial atmosphere under the stars.

While there was still light, a wonderful tradition took place that amused everyone and was of particular delight to children living far from sweet shops. The boat schedule was well known to villagers on the riverbank, and youngsters, even mothers with toddlers, rowed out in dugouts to follow in the wake of the boat. Patrons at the bar would purchase crisps, biscuits and chewing gum and package them in plastic bags to throw overboard. There would be a scramble of small canoes all chasing the 'goodie bags' and shouts of joy from whoever retrieved one. I loved seeing the look of happiness on a three-year-old's face if they struck it lucky.

The days blurred into one another with a quiet rhythm, and on the final day, we passed the 'Meeting of the Waters' where the dark Rio Negro converges with the sandy-coloured Amazon. The two different coloured rivers are delineated with a clear line and run parallel for six kilometres without mixing. This extraordinary occurrence is due to differences in the temperature, speed and density of the water and draws many tourists. When the colours eventually merge further on, the central Amazon flow is dark green, depending on the amount of plant matter.

As we approached Manaus, passengers dismantled hammocks, and there was great excitement arriving at the port with the prospect of stretching land legs again. I said goodbyes to my hammock neighbours who had become friends and hugged the children who were no longer shy. Once the boat docked, there would be a mad scramble to disembark.

I'd befriended a fun group of travellers onboard, and we planned to hang out together for a few days in Manaus. On the way to a hostel, our eyes were agog at the sight of Silvia's ice cream stall with its luscious fruity mounds of delight. It was an excellent start to life on land.

After an indulgent hot shower in what we labelled the 'Ritz', it was time to explore the jungle city, and we headed straight for *Praca da Matriz*, one of the most picturesque colonial squares I've ever seen. The famous *Teatro Amazonas* dominated it, and we admired the building whilst sitting under the shade of a cluster of graceful trees, licking Silvia's delectable raspberry ripple. The Opera House is one of the most luxurious and remote in the world with its opulently tiled dome rising above the neoclassical building. We returned later as a rosy sunset softly illuminated the spectacular setting; all enhanced by a pizza dinner in good company and an excellent bottle of Portuguese wine.

On an English-speaking tour of the Opera House the following day, the facts were mind-boggling. It cost five million US dollars to construct between 1885 and 1892 when Manaus was one of the wealthiest cities in the world due to the rubber boom. The design was Renaissance with electric lighting: the roofing tiles came from Alsace, a grand staircase in Carrara marble and 198 chandeliers came from Italy — 38 of these in delicate Murano glass from Venice. All the materials arrived by slow steamship which must have been one of the most remarkable shipping feats of the time.

In the grand theatre, we sat in the polished jacaranda-wood seats from the local rainforest, and I gazed upwards admiring the elaborately painted dome ceiling. The balconies were from the finest Scottish steel, and an enormous Venetian chandelier graced the centre. 'What fun it would be to go on stage and sing,' I joked with the others, but security kept a beady eye on us. In my mind, I conjured up the strings of a long-forgotten orchestra accompanying the high notes of an aria, and the ripple of applause from the audience.

On entering the ballroom, I was amused having to don felt booties to protect the magnificent marquetry floor. It reminded me of my convent school days when the nuns used us as child labour to polish the wooden floors until they were gleaming! A gent's smoking room next door sported several fine ornate spittoons, and the whiff of good tobacco still lingered in the air. Next door, the stylish ladies powder room had Margot Fontaine's ballet shoes on display, worn on her last performance here in 1975.

Emerging into the bustle of the square, I had to shake myself back into the present time, genuinely overwhelmed by the grandeur of the Opera House and its rich history. For a time, I'd completely forgotten my rustic journey through the Amazon jungle to reach here and was temporarily transplanted back to Vienna, Paris and the grand cities of Europe, another world away.

HANGING OUT WITH
TWITCHERS AND COWBOYS

This section of my Amazon trip in 2011 was the wildest and most remote as the majority of travellers continue down the main river from Manaus to Santarem to reach the 330-kilometre wide estuary at Belem. Instead, I detoured north by bus to Lethem, a remote town on the frontier with Guyana and Brazil, in the middle of savannah grasslands.

Guyana is known as the 'Land of Giants' as it has many of the world's largest fauna — alligator, anteater, otter, eagle, rodent, constrictor snake and spider — enough to make the detour worthwhile! Formerly British Guiana, National Geographic documentaries have been filmed there by people such as David Attenborough and Gerald Durrell, and I struck lucky in seeing some of the giant creatures for myself.

I'd been advised to look up Mildred and Tom in Lethem, supposedly the gurus of knowledge in the locality. I quickly discovered that they had split up, but fortunately, Mildred took a liking to me and invited me to sling my hammock up in her kitchen for a few days.

I recognised a strong gutsy 'bush woman' who was eyeing me up as tourist potential, but we clicked immediately. She led a busy life establishing community projects, liaising with NGOs and developing eco-tourism.

As torrential rain poured down all afternoon, many fascinating characters dropped by Mildred's house, and I was party to discussions on frontier matters. Cheap Chinese stores were arriving in neighbouring Venezuela that affected cross-border shopping in Guyana, and global magnates were searching for gold and silver in the hills. The capital Georgetown was on the Caribbean coast nearly 500 kilometres north on a dirt road, and Lethem was primarily left to its own initiative in protecting the environment.

When the downpour eased, I went for a stroll puddle-hopping on the dirt roads. Many of the Indian-owned businesses were closed for the Hindu festival of *Phagwah*. I meandered down a jungle track towards the Amerindian village of St Ignacio to check out a large cashew nut factory that employed many of the locals. Suddenly, I was set upon by a group of children who threw coloured flour at me, which stuck to my damp clothing and had them in peals of laughter. I made to chase them with my umbrella and promptly went plop in the slippery mud, which just brought more loud screeches from the youngsters.

Luckily a woman from a nearby shack beckoned me over and hosed me down, but I was laughing myself now. Gladys gave me a fistful of cashew nuts to munch on, and I decided to abandon my mission for the day as I was now being eaten alive by mosquitoes.

My soggy appearance didn't prevent me from checking out the Takuni Hotel on the way back to Mildred's, where I got chatting to the older barman while sampling the local Banks beer. His singsong Creole accent was a joy to listen to and reminded me of lilting Welsh-valley voices. Maurice used to work in the rubber industry, which went into decline in the 1970s. He'd been a *balata* bleeder, climbing bullet wood trees in stirrups and wire rope to collect the sap from the trunk. He now crafted small carvings of the local wildlife from the latex and sold them as souvenirs — exquisite in detail. I am now the proud owner of an anteater, a harpy eagle, a pink dolphin and one of the rare 'cock of the rock' birds, which I treasure dearly. The advent of synthetics caused a lot of damage to the rubber trade in remote regions such as this.

Back at Mildred's, she treated my swollen bites with crab oil, the local remedy, as the most potent Deet was doing nothing to deter the persistent mosquitoes. To celebrate *Phagwah*, we adjourned to an Indian eatery for hot spicy curries served with cassava bread, and I received an education on the buoyant twitcher tourist industry.

Guyana is a high-end niche market for wildlife enthusiasts, many of them wealthy retired birdwatchers from Canada and the US. One of Mildred's numerous jobs was to ferry them between eco huts in the jungle, and for a contribution towards the diesel, I was invited along for the ride. She laughed when I said I was a child ornithologist aged ten, chasing moorhens on an Irish canal, minus the binoculars.

We headed out at 6 am the following morning in an old Land Rover with a driver called Shamrock, which I thought was a good omen, and the beauty of the savannah soon jolted me awake. In the dawn light, the colours and silhouettes were continually changing as patches of Mauritia palms broke up the flat expanse, and early workers were harvesting the fronds for roofing. The invisible hum of insect activity filled the air, and I was delighted when Mildred pointed out a giant anteater meandering through the long grass, heading for a tall termite mound for breakfast.

Later in dense jungle, Shamrock twisted and turned expertly through a landscape of 'sandpaper' and 'toilet paper' trees. I was amused at these descriptions, but it's true that the rough leaves of one tree polish wood well and the absorbent leaves of the other prove handy in the wilds! At a creek crossing, we got bogged down in the deep mud, and a group of strong Makushi women helped push us clear. They all had wicker panniers slung from their foreheads as they strolled to the cassava fields and their day's toil.

Mid-morning we arrived at Maipire Lodge, a settlement of thatched huts, accessible on raised walkways over the flooded terrain. The smell of rotting vegetation permeated the still hot air. Giant buttressed trees towered over an understorey of moss and lichen and shrill bird calls resounded everywhere. I met with Mel and Fred, two Canadian twitchers who had paid handsomely for a two-week wilderness experience with pit toilets and lots of crawly creatures. Both were kitted out in the ideal camouflage gear to blend into the jungle for stalking birds and carried the appropriate gadgets for the role.

After a brief pitstop, we set out for Caiman House three hours away. I was now perched on the gearstick and wedged between Shamrock and Mildred, leaving the birders plenty of space in the rear to swivel around with binoculars going 'ooh' and 'aah' in ecstasy. I was distracted from my discomfort by an expert lecture on the rare bare-throated bellbird with its metallic 'tonk-tonk-tonk' mating call, the beauty of vermilion flycatchers and the vivid crimson topaz. When sighted, the couple ticked the names off the charts hanging around their necks.

On arrival at Caiman House, Mel and Fred disappeared to their deluxe suite, and I was shown to my hammock suite in the garden, a thatched structure in a tranquil area, perfumed by surrounding bromeliads and pretty orchids.

The main lodge was a field research station for the black caiman, the largest alligator and predator in the Amazon and that night I was invited to join a tagging programme on the Essequibo River. The boats had reinforced hulls for protection against thrashing caimans, and we scoured the undergrowth by flashlight in search of beady eyes. On spotting a caiman, the two trackers, Felix and Fernando, would snare its neck with a hoop, rodeo style — and drag the creature downriver to tire it out, before securing its jaw with duct tape and hauling it onto a sandbank for examination.

We watched spellbound as the trackers took measurements and noted the sex and any scar marks. I even managed to have a close-up photo taken with trussed victim No. 618 — with a somewhat nervous look on my face, awaiting a sudden thrash of the tail. Fernando inserted a microchip in the pelt, and 618 was cut in the cartilage as well for future tracking. All of us stood well clear when he removed the tape and hoops, and the flailing caiman slunk off to freedom in the dark depths.

On our return journey, we detoured to an ox-bow lake where the cacophony of frogs amongst the giant flowering water lilies was as good as any opera house, the ghostlike canopy providing a majestic backdrop. Giant moths shimmied in the light, and a cloud of megabats squeaked into sight as an encore, on their nightly hunt for fish and fruit. I wallowed contentedly in the magnificence of nature, and it made my night to see a sloth sluggishly climbing a tree trunk, its lengthy white claws highlighted in the moonlight.

Back at the lodge, I met my newly arrived hammock mates, the Rupununi cowboys. Justin, Eddie and James were from a cattle ranch in the deep south of Guyana and may have looked like macho gauchos but were the funniest, kindest guys, and shared rum, stories and Glen Hansard music with me into the wee hours. Aged in their mid-20s, they had canoed upriver for two weeks with a young Canadian, Melissa, who was flying out the next day.

Justin came from three generations of European ranchers who had intermarried with the indigenous Guyanese over the years. In earlier times, they drove thousands of cattle to the coast, but that ended with an armed Rupununi uprising in 1969 that shook the country. A few ranchers were killed, and the state took over the plantations. Head full of stories and rum, I was lulled to sleep by the hum of cicadas interspersed with the loud snores of three young cowboys.

By the time I surfaced for breakfast the next morning with a sore head, the passionate twitchers were returning from their dawn stroll, and I left them to their animated chat of thrilling bellbirds and screaming piha. After a few strong coffees, I spent the morning reading to the children in the community library next door, where I was informed only the smartest go to secondary school in Lethem, and very few make it to university.

Near the lodge, Makushi village was very traditional with stacks of clay bricks drying in the sun, women on doorsteps weaving palm fronds for basketry or roofing, and everywhere the labour-intensive production of cassava flour. I shuddered as I remembered how I hated tapioca milk pudding in my childhood and would spit out the slimy bubbles. Now, observing the process from scratch, I quickly developed more respect for the final result.

The stripped root is grated on a rustic homemade grater to speed up the elimination of cyanide and afterwards the ground mix is squeezed through a snake-shaped *matapi* cylinder to remove more poisonous juices. The end product of flour baked in rounds of flatbread is dried and stored on the thatch roofs. Fermenting the cassava makes a drink called *parakiri* which involves 30 stages, but I refrained from tasting this potent concoction.

The cowboys invited me along to see Melissa off, and later they were visiting their auntie Diane McTurk, well-known for her extraordinary life rehabilitating giant river otters to the wild. The mad drive in the open truck was memorable for the blast of Caribbean reggae that shattered the evening peace of several fish eagles snoozing in the savannah palms. The bush airstrip was nothing more than painted stones marking the runway, with a red flag at the end. Melissa hugged the boys farewell and hopped into the waiting six-seater next to the pilot, on her first stage home to Canada.

We arrived at Karanamba Lodge just in time for the night feeding of Philip and Belle, two young rescued otters. River otters are renowned for their pelts, and this slick pair leapt out of their cage in excitement and hopped around the 79-year-old Diane like pet dogs as she led the way to the riverbank. Their vicious teeth eagerly parted as she fed them piranha and ugly catfish for starters before they were encouraged to hunt for themselves in the river. Meanwhile, I was keeping an eye open for lurking caimans while watching the otters frolic in the water.

I envied Diane her life in the wilds pursuing her passion, as I loved animals and once yearned to be a vet. This tough lady features in National Geographic documentaries, and at dinner afterwards, she told me of her earlier life at Oxford and working as the Press Secretary at the Savoy Hotel in London. It all seemed such a contrast to her current lifestyle in the savannah with her beloved otters.

Driving home, as our music competed with a backup chorus of bats, frogs and clicking cicadas emanating from the dark, the world of the Rupununi did indeed seem a lifetime away from the lights of London, and my own urban life.

Next day, I got a ride back to Lethem with cheerful Ricardo, returning to work in the lucrative silver mines of the Kanuka Mountains. He shared the lunch prepared by his wife — cassava bread with delicious homemade peanut butter and spoke proudly of his clever son who wanted to study engineering. The only traffic we met were a few bullock carts of local families who pulled in to let us pass. Back in town, I checked into the shabby Takuni Hotel where the ubiquitous mosquitoes of Lethem were awaiting my return, but I was now well-armed with an ample supply of crab oil.

An eco-tourism meeting was held the following day, and I was lucky to be offered a ride into Iwokrama, a conservation area on my route north to the Caribbean coast. Delayed by endless servings of barbequed chicken and cold beers, it was another night ride in the back of a truck to Annai village. I felt sorry for the driver's wife Veronica being woken at a late hour to show me to my hammock hut, part of a homestay community project under development. I was their first guest, and it was intriguing to learn that the main lodge nearby was being constructed in the shape of a jaguar paw. We were in a big forest clearing, a peaceful spot encircled by the silhouetted jungle canopy.

I woke to the sound of children playing, and two little girls were feeding their pet scarlet macaws with mango pieces on my doorstep, waiting eagerly for the tourist to wake and amuse them.

Hand in hand, we skipped to the kitchen for breakfast through a garden of green vegetables that had me looking forward to dinner that evening.

Veronica was salting hussar fish to dry in the sun, and this ugly, scaly brute was breakfast with freshly baked cassava bread. I paid the price by puking it up in the bushes an hour later. On hearing that I worked in a hospital, the conversation turned to sad tales of losing children young, TB ever rampant in the villages, and complaints of men having a good life while the women did the hard work.

Her humorous husband Manuel then led me off for my private twitcher tour after we had agreed on a fair price for both of us. As we traversed the clearing and entered the dim forest, he explained that there were still a few jaguars in the area that were a threat to livestock. It meant that conservation was a big issue with local farmers concerned with making a living. As we approached the river, we saw a tapir creeping along the bank, a large mammal that looked like a pig with a pointed anteater snout. 'I miss my hunting days sometimes,' Manuel stated regretfully. 'Well, I'm glad you still carry a gun,' I replied.

A barricaded checkpoint to deter poachers marked the entrance to Iwokrama, and we quietly made our way to a rocky area, the breeding ground of the rare 'cock of the rock'. Manuel explained that males of the species congregate in a lek, a place where they perform whacky dance displays as a courting ritual to attract the females. I was fascinated watching this weird male parading his stuff on a large rock. Quite a small, crested bird, sporting brilliant red and orange plumage, it cockily evaded my camera by flitting into the bushes and skittishly teased me with its antics. I played the elusive game for a while, eventually capturing its beady eye peering out at me. Manuel pointed out the bored-looking missus perched on a branch above us, who paid no heed to her mate's larking about. A drab brown colour, she posed perfectly for her portrait.

Thrilled to have seen this rare species and with no bird list to tick off, Manuel and I continued walking on a forest path where armies of leaf-cutter ants were on manoeuvres, scurrying with fodder back to their nest. Suddenly, he stopped me at the base of a giant silk cotton tree and pointed to the high canopy, where it took a while to make out the large stick nest of the harpy eagle. I nudged Manuel in excitement as the cute furry head of a chick stared directly at me for a second, then scanned the treetops hungrily waiting for lunch to arrive. We waited patiently, and sure enough, Papa soared into view with his incredible wingspan, clutching what looked like a small monkey in his rear talons. I felt extremely sorry for the unfortunate victim, as it still squirmed in its death throes.

It was a grand finale to my time in the jungle, and Manuel dropped me off at a muddy crossroads on the main road north to Georgetown. A rough palm shelter protected me from the spattering drops and darkening sky where a storm was brewing. I hugged my youthful David Attenborough goodbye as the bus approached, with few passengers on board. After taking a window seat, I gazed out at the pristine rainforest until the heavens opened and sheet rain rendered all invisible. The dirt road became a muddy mess, and the bus slid about erratically avoiding giant potholes. Soon, we arrived at a section where fibre-optic cables were being laid in deep channels, bringing the internet to the interior. *Nowhere is immune to progress,* I thought to myself and pitied the sodden workers still digging and operating machinery in the deluge.

Later in the evening, we disembarked for dinner before crossing the Essequibo River on a dodgy looking pontoon. The crash of rapids nearby thundered in the fresh night air; the rain had ceased, and a clear sky twinkled with stars. I didn't wish to be anywhere else.

Ravenous after losing my breakfast, I greedily wolfed down the tasty stew served up at the ramshackle Creole roadhouse, until a few bauxite miners told me it consisted of a rodent called *lab* after which I feared for my stomach again.

Before boarding, I dashed off into the bushes by the riverbank for a pee and was admiring the starry abyss above when I heard rustling in the undergrowth. I froze, trying to finish my business quickly and glanced

Diane McTurk and her river otters

Breakfast in the Amazon rainforest

Waiting patiently for 'goodie bags', on the Amazon

Belle goes fishing

about me with my head torch when I suddenly saw it and very nearly screamed.

This gigantic snake was slithering along only a few metres from me, and I knew from its massive green bulk that it was an anaconda, the largest snake in the world and endemic to the area. It didn't help at all that I knew it was non-venomous — a movie shot of one coiling around its prey flashed before my eyes, and I could feel myself suffocating. I so wished to be anywhere else now!

Despite the immediate instinct to rise and flee, I slowly lowered my head, clicked the light off and waited. After a few minutes that felt like a lifetime, I could hear the engine of the bus starting up and fearing I'd be left behind, slowly raised my head and looked about again. It was gone.

As I rose quickly to my feet, I felt the stew heaving.

HAVEN IN HAITI

Our chartered plane descended out of the clouds, exposing a lush hillside, densely covered with shanty-town sprawl sending tentacles in every direction. We were about to land in Port-au-Prince, the capital of Haiti and would spend a week there rebuilding in the aftermath of one of the island's worst natural catastrophes. A devastating earthquake of 7.0 magnitude on the 12th of January 2010 shook this most impoverished country in the Americas to its foundations, socially, economically and politically. It took just 35 seconds for 300,000 people to perish and 2.5 million were left homeless. Drinking water was contaminated and an outbreak of cholera, introduced by UN peacekeepers, followed in dealing the double blow.

I was volunteering with an Irish aid organisation called Haven, who only operate in Haiti, and the goal for our group of 200 was to build 55 houses in a week. Our initial trip was postponed due to the cholera outbreak, and I was relieved to arrive finally in late October 2011. It had been hard work fundraising for the venture, rattling that collection bucket at supermarkets near my home in Ireland and asking businesses, friends and family to donate to the worthy cause. Each volunteer raised five thousand euro, an amount that would build two houses. Now, the real work would commence, and I felt apprehensive, wondering what harrowing scenes we would witness during the week. I also hoped I was up to the task of labouring in the intense heat and could play my part.

It was 3.30 pm local time, and a sheet of hot, humid air hit my pale winter skin as I stepped onto the tarmac. As an NGO, we bypassed the usual airport arrival procedures, and a convoy of five buses with armed security guards pulled up to the plane for our drive to the accommodation camp at Christianville, several hours away.

Haiti is the island that dared 'rise up' in 1791 in a slave rebellion that took 12 years to succeed, creating the world's first black-led republic.

Since that time, a legacy of foreign exploitation and the despotic rule of dictators Papa Doc and Baby Doc Duvalier had pillaged the country. As if that wasn't enough, it had been ravaged many times by natural disasters.

Haiti assaults all the senses, and the route through the squalor of Port-au-Prince was particularly confronting. There were open sewers, where mongrel dogs and scrawny chickens foraged and children played nearby. Piles of rubble from the earthquake lay all about and the buildings still standing were an assortment of corrugated iron or cardboard shacks and lean-tos with families squatting underneath.

It was a Sunday, yet the streets were a chaotic din of humanity, everyone hustling to make a meagre living. What struck me most were the many faces with dull eyes and the whittled-down look of being trodden on one time too many, resilience broken. Groups of youths hung about aimlessly, waiting for anything to happen — or nothing. Women hauled sacks of manioc on the sidewalks or crouched low over charcoal burners making bread and food to sell.

As always, innocent children at play provide scant relief from misery and here was no different. Little groups, spotlessly dressed in donated clothes, jumped up in excitement at the passing bus of foreigners. They must have witnessed many, as Haiti had more aid organisations operating at that time than anywhere else. The need was great as 80% of the schools, half the hospitals, and many government buildings were destroyed. Two cathedrals and the UN building crumbled in the quake.

Leaving the chaos and poverty of downtown behind, we drove past many temporary tent settlements that regularly became permanent. The names of foreign aid agencies were widespread on canvas and corrugated roofs and food containers.

The density eased as we travelled along the coast, with neat plantain plantations on the hillsides, and wooden tables by the roadside sold vegetables and bottled water. Barber stands were doing brisk business as well as pop-up bank kiosks. It never ceases to amaze me how trendy haircuts always prevail in disastrous situations — it must be the psychology of looking one's best regardless. Some areas we passed looked better than others, but there were no expensive yachts under sail in the picturesque bay.

Colourful *tap-taps* or truck buses provided some welcome relief to the eye, with biblical scenes gaudily painted on the bonnet, and sporting religious maxims in carved wood, such as 'MERCI JESUS', 'ACCEPTEZ SAUVEUR' and 'CROYANCE' in large capitals. But the entire bodywork of the vehicles was a mosaic from a comic book, with even the window glass graffitied with fiery dragons and voodoo insignia.

We reached our barbed-wire compound, and I was exhausted after delays departing Dublin added to the direct nine-hour flight. The briefing pack we received on the plane allocated our bus and tent numbers, and our passports were confiscated for the week. Tent number 31, which I shared with four female volunteers, contained the basics; camp beds with sponge mattresses and mosquito nets, and a dim light bulb. We weren't here for the luxuries.

A communal cold water shower block and toilets stood nearby, and shrieks of glee would emanate from it in the evenings, as workers washed off layers of sweat and dust. A leafy courtyard with a bar/cafe served as the entertainment area to unwind in. I observed a few joyful reunions take place, as many volunteers were veterans who knew the ropes, returning to devastated Haiti multiple times.

Our wake-up call was at 5.45 am on Monday, setting the pattern for the week ahead, maximising cooler working hours before the debilitating midday sun. A half-hour was allowed to shower, slurp porridge and strong coffee before boarding the commuter bus to the worksite. Many volunteers resumed dozing or chatted amiably, but I was always rushing for a window seat to see all I could, and not being a morning person, I hoped for a silent companion. With the dire security situation and alarming crime rate in the country, there would be none of my usual independent explorations to get to know the Haitian people and culture through ordinary encounters. As Haven was responsible for our welfare and safety, we were strictly monitored and controlled at all times. Understandably the charities had a job to do and didn't have the resources or time to look after individuals wandering willy nilly.

There was a primary school outside our compound gate, where happy giggling children arrived as we were leaving. Motorbikes pulled up with three or four gleaming faces on the rear, hair plaited in red ribbons and spotless white shirts ironed — a new generation full of hope for a brighter future. They were fun to chat with, and when I shouted *Bonjou*, the Creole for 'Hello', they would yell in English, 'What is your name?' Some of the boys played a marble game in the dirt, flicking stones into a circle.

It was a one-hour bus ride to Leogane, the epicentre of the earthquake and our building site. On the way, I peered through the dirty window at devastated areas, observing cracked and lopsided houses affected by the quake. Nature was already taking over and burying them in tropical foliage.

Armed guards protected the site, and a long queue of Haitians hovered outside the gate in the hope of work. The large building area consisted of long rows of square cement foundations, earthquake proofed, which had already been constructed by another NGO, Habitat for Humanity. Haven would build the wooden upper-halves and roof the houses in corrugated iron.

Back in Ireland, people had volunteered according to their skills. As a useless handywoman, I offered to work as a water carrier — the mule, who carried frozen water bottles to the building teams to keep them hydrated. My years lugging heavy rucksacks as an avid hiker were my best credentials, but my poor basketball skills showed. I would spend the week perfecting my aim to the amusement of the builders on the scaffolding and the children laughing at the fence!

Two building teams were working on each house under the supervision of a foreman/woman, and it was astonishing how rapidly they joined the sheeting, and the structure of a small house took shape. All age groups and both sexes wielded hammers, drills or a paintbrush. Everyone had to wear a hard hat and steel-capped boots while on-site, and the heavy footwear made my sweaty day more tiring — however, the camaraderie and satisfaction of what we were achieving more than compensated for the discomfort.

The houses were partitioned into two or three small rooms and would accommodate a family of six to eight people. Lead flashing was placed around the perimeter to deter termites, and they had a high concrete platform in case of flooding. Haiti experiences hurricanes and earthquakes regularly. 'Why are there two doors for such a small house?' I asked a foreman on the first day. 'It's because of domestic violence,' he replied. 'It's a serious problem here, and a back door provides a quick escape for the women.' It was sad to learn this on top of the multiple problems facing Haitian women.

In African projects, many foreign aid agencies concentrate on empowering women to run a small business, which gives them self-esteem and their own income to feed hungry children. Haven did likewise. The organisation ran literacy programs and an income-generating program for women, in conjunction with training men in construction skills. The goal was to eventually replace foreign volunteers.

I thought it an excellent idea that a member of the recipient family worked with the Irish team on their new home. It made them feel part of the project, and I felt quite emotional seeing various family members visit and do the tour of a humble house as if it was a mansion. Each dwelling was constructed in such a way that the owner could extend it at a later date, thus allowing them to contribute themselves instead of being the beneficiary of charity.

Haitians, like many of African descent, are not an indoors nation, and watching the passing parade from the porch is more important than the sleeping quarters. Growing up in a small Irish bungalow myself, where a private bedroom was unheard of, I understood precisely the benefits of such an arrangement. Being always surrounded by a family unit of varying ages helps develop tolerance, not easily acquired when children isolate in their own 'techno bedrooms'.

Again, with social interaction in mind, communal latrine and shower blocks were built in the vicinity, allowing women to congregate and gossip, similar to the wells and water taps of rural regions. These were valuable traditions to preserve if possible.

My work uniform was a Haven red T-shirt, sporting the logo of a small house and a family within. The red colour was specific to the water teams, and it was usually drenched in sweat by midday. I detoured by the medical tent frequently for doses of Dioralyte to rehydrate, and supplies of salty biscuits and sugary crunch bars kept our stamina boosted. We had a mess tent for meals and breaks, which also acted as a shelter from the sizzling sun. The temperature soared to 40C at midday, by which time I was ready to stick my head in the giant cooler boxes that were the depot for our water bottles!

My aim dramatically improved as the week progressed, and as I got to know the various teams, it was rewarding to be yelled out to by name when someone needed a cold bottle of water. I quickly befriended the children who stood outside the wire enclosure all day long, continually shouting for water or goodies. In the beginning, it was 'Hey you!' but by the end of the week, many yelled out 'Gardette' or 'Jo' or 'George', and we all had a good laugh.

I threw over bottles of water that were half-used, discarded by the builders when too warm, and the odd cold one when no one was looking. These would often be sold on, as purchasing water was expensive for Haitians. The cute kids who put on a dance or a show became my favourites, and I gave them sweets and biscuits that were often viciously fought over.

I became friendly with a few of the Haitian women hanging about, particularly Esther and Rosaline. This pair used to help me collect empties between checking on the progress of their new homes. It was a shame about the plastic waste, as the streets and countryside were already awash with plastic and I only hoped that a recycling program existed to deal with it.

Our second day was the 1st of November and All Souls Day, a big festival in the Haitian calendar where many wear black and purple, and drums were beating all over the place. It is said that Haiti is 70% Catholic, 30% Protestant and 100% voodoo. The essence of the island has its roots in *vodou*. Initially brought by African slaves and merged with Caribbean beliefs and Catholic saints, the ceremonies take the form of dancing in a writhing snakelike fashion to incessant drumming for hours until the dancers enter a trance-like state.

The spirits, or *Iwas*, are then summoned to 'mount' a follower, who may speak in tongues and make predictions. Pleas are made to a pantheon of gods to intervene with life on earth, and they are pacified with offerings at shrines. The snake god Damballa is the equivalent to the Irish St Patrick, pictured with snakes at his feet, and other gods are equivalent to St James and the Virgin Mary. Haitians bore all those traits I admired about Africans, stoic in tough times yet exhibiting an exuberance in old traditions only thinly disguised with the blanket of Christianity.

In the evenings, a rotation of different families came into our camp to sell their crafts and artwork, ensuring a fair business system. The primitivist art of Haiti is very distinctive with its voodoo roots and simplistic style, depicting everyday life. Stalls were exhibiting brightly coloured canvases, and tables displayed models of *tap-taps*, hand-painted boxes and placemats, tin geckos, and an assortment of wooden flowers. This artistic craftwork often provided the only income for needy families. For those of us with French, it was an opportunity for a humorous language lesson as the Haitian Creole is very similar, but also confusing.

As the week progressed, it was satisfying to see the houses take shape as windows were inserted and the roofing completed. Everyone had a good laugh when, before being painted, one building sported the Irish tricolour, and the words *Aras an Uachtarain* were written on the wall, the Gaelic for our 'White House'. And a clever prankster stuck a portrait of our president in the window!

As their homes took shape, Esther and Rosaline abandoned me and regularly swept their new porches with great pride. It was a touching sight, and they both told me how thrilled they were to soon move from crowded tents. All the volunteers pared down their luggage, distributing clothes brought out from Ireland and leaving anything behind they could. I donated my stuff to these two fun women I'd shared laughs with, and soon Irish sports jerseys became a common sight on Haitian backs.

I had hoped to visit the local hospital to see what conditions were like, but it proved too difficult to arrange for security reasons. As well as outbreaks of cholera, Aids was a big scourge at the time. Some of us visited a local orphanage one afternoon. A Haitian woman ran it, and the children were well cared for. Cute three-year-old Tungaware developed a fondness for me and wanted to keep wearing my groovy sunglasses. Blowing bubbles was his favourite game, and I took a few photos to show the toyshop owner back in Ireland where his donations ended up. It was heartbreaking when I was leaving as the little boy, with tears in his eyes, kept tugging at my shorts and wouldn't let go. I just wanted to lift him in my arms and take him away with me.

A friend of mine was building schools in Port-au-Prince and lived in the city with his Haitian workers. John visited the compound one evening with this band of strapping, muscular young fellas resembling a football team. Cabriolet, Desole, Gracia and the others were keen to have a cold beer and see how the Irish partied.

I was appalled to learn their salary was only $US2 per day, but John told me this was double the national average. Still today, more than half of Haitians live on less than $US1 a day. I spent the night listening to shocking and fascinating stories of class differences between mulattoes, privileged Blancs, corrupt politicians, gangsters demanding extortion and big drug cartels. It was disturbing to learn that after slavery was abolished, France had the gall to demand reparation for lost slaves to their colonies, and this debt had only been paid off finally in 1947. This burden ensured that Haiti had remained enslaved to poverty, disasters and corruption.

John had armed security and asked permission for me to leave the compound for the night, but sadly it was denied for legitimate insurance and safety reasons. It was disappointing to have my hopes of seeing the outside dashed.

Friday arrived quickly, and we had a handover ceremony at 4 pm when the paint was barely dry on the new homes. Speeches were made and ribbons cut during the emotional ceremony, and both Esther and Rosaline beamed with pride. The 55 completed houses were only a drop in the ocean in coping with homelessness but seeing the happy faces of recipient families was a big deal and a just reward for our week's work.

My fan club of children shouted farewell for the last time as I boarded the bus with a sad heart and Rosaline hugged me wearing a favourite T-shirt of mine and the steel-capped boots!

Since 2009, Hurricane Matthew battered Haiti in 2016, another earthquake occurred in 2018, and ongoing corruption and inept leadership has prevailed.

I learned that the houses we built are still standing and I sincerely hope Rosalie and Esther are happy and content in their new homes.

THE REDLEGS OF BARBADOS

I was ambling down the quiet road in the stifling afternoon humidity when I spotted her and stopped in my tracks. She had to be a Redleg, sitting outside the corrugated iron shack peeling corn, with an emaciated mongrel at her feet. Her features were so Irish — an unhealthy pallor in the tropical heat, and her hair was straw-coloured. Yet, when she glanced up and saw me, her face transformed itself with a radiant toothless smile, and she beckoned me over.

Her name was Mary Fenty, who looked to be in her seventies, and she really could have been one of my country aunties back home, caught unawares by the parish priest without her false teeth.

'Hello,' I said. 'I'm Gerdette from Ireland, am I right thinking you might have a bit of Irish blood in you too?' She laughed, and her blue eyes sparkled. I couldn't understand her thick brogue, but that was a good sign, as there are a few regions in Ireland where the speech is rapid incomprehensible garble to outsiders.

Mary reached for a plastic bottle next to her, poured some concoction into an old tumbler and offered it to me. I was hesitant to taste the stuff but sipped it out of politeness. It was sweet with an immediate strong bitter aftertaste that made me wince, and I suspected it was the homemade mauby I'd been warned about, brewed from boiling a native bark with lots of sugar, various spices and well fermented. We shared the tumbler agreeably, and I recognised a cue for comfortable silence. That's how it is sometimes on the road — let the encounter be without words and questions. After a time, I continued downhill to the sea with a new warmth within that wasn't just the mauby.

It was 2013, and I was travelling from Trinidad hoping to reach Montserrat for the St Patrick's week festival in March. I was researching the Irish diaspora who had been living in the Caribbean for centuries. Here in Barbados, they were called Redlegs, and lived in the northeast of the island, on unproductive land fit only for growing sugar cane. Fronted by the wild Atlantic, the terrain was not unlike what they'd left behind on the other side of the world.

In a book titled *To Hell or Barbados: The Ethnic Cleansing of Ireland*, I'd read that the Redlegs were the descendants of Irish rebels and undesirables, shipped by Oliver Cromwell to the Caribbean colonies in the 17th century. When he invaded Ireland, the impoverished Irish were evicted from the fertile land in the east of the country and driven to poor bogland on the western Atlantic seashore.

It was later regarded as a better alternative to ship these destitutes to the sunnier climes of Barbados to work as indentured servants, but virtually slaves, on the tobacco and sugar cane plantations. This practice was a lucrative business for the British Empire, and an Irish white slave could be sold in Barbados for as little as ten pounds at the time.

Unused to back-breaking fieldwork in the tropical sun, the pale-skinned Irish burnt badly, hence one theory for the name Redlegs. By the mid-1700s they were replaced mainly by black African slaves who were more productive in hot climates. The Irish became foremen for absentee landlords, sitting comfortably at home in England waiting on the next consignment of rum. These days, another term *Backra Johnny* — pidgin English for sitting in the back row at church as second class citizens — is used to describe the remaining Irish.

As I continued walking in the afternoon haze, I passed old wooden shacks shaded by breadfruit and banana groves and only scrawny hens braved the heat, pecking about in the dirt. A few children played in the shadows of a cluster of boxy concrete bungalows and stopped to stare as I passed by. I soon reached Martin's Bay and a pleasant sandy beach, and I collapsed in the Bay Bar Hotel to await Raymond James, my host for the night and I washed the bitterness of the mauby down with a cold Banks beer.

It was my first time travelling as a couchsurfer, and the experience had been a good one so far. With the Caribbean renowned as an expensive cruise destination and no known hostels, I'd signed up to the website and had been pleasantly surprised to discover I wasn't over the hill yet in my 50s! The system offers travellers a free bed provided by a local person in exchange for cultural interaction, and it works well for those unable to travel, as a method of learning about other traditions and making strangers friends. I had enjoyed being a host in Ireland for a time. No money changes hands, but of course, it's only fair to be generous and contribute in some way.

Raymond and I talked, getting to know each other, and he insisted on ordering the house speciality for me to sample — a 'flying fish' sandwich. Barbados is renowned for its fish fries.

He was a tall, reserved man in his 50s, a native of Trinidad and the former CEO of a company in Barbados. He enjoyed hosting couchsurfers for the easy company and confessed that he didn't have much in common with his Redleg neighbours.

The area we were in was called Scotland because of its similarity to the landscape of real Scotland with its craggy limestone hills, and the small population of Irish descent lived in the Zores district adjacent. On learning of my research, Raymond generously offered to give me a lift to the historic area of St John's Parish the following day as public transport was scant in the region.

Replenished by the tasty fish sandwich, we drove up into the hills to Raymond's home in the overseer's former residence, on an old cane plantation. The surrounds were a museum of rusty scraps of machinery from a bygone era — a cane harvester, an old weighbridge and a collection of broken carts. Raymond gave me a quick rundown on the process of harvesting sugarcane, but of course, in slave times it was hand cut with machetes, and the slaves sweated 24-hour days in the boiler house. I learned that there were only two factories left in Barbados producing sugar, molasses and rum when there were 24 in 1964. The fine old 'Big House' in the vicinity needed restoration, and a lawyer from the capital Bridgetown had just purchased it.

Wandering through the cane fields later that evening, I remembered movies I'd watched, set in the Deep South and depicting the horrors of slavery. The rustle of the wind through the cane was unsettling. The area seemed lonely and abandoned by a world that had moved on, and I sensed the pain and suffering of the past linger on in the soil. As dusk set in, I hurried back to the house and was glad to see a bottle of rum and two glasses set out on the veranda, and Raymond was raring to chat.

Knowledgeable on the history of Barbados, he explained the unfortunate outcome of the Irish on the island. After seven years' indenture, few received the promised smallholding at the end of their contract, and most became a wretched subclass who were looked down on by both blacks and better-off whites. Over the years, the habit of 'keeping to themselves' resulted in inbreeding. They also experienced a high incidence of diabetes and haemophilia due to poor diet, and the population declined. It was such a tragic history.

In present times, with only a few hundred left, it was heartening to learn that the Redlegs were now 'marrying up' with the blacks, a practice encouraged to improve the gene pool and to raise their social status. I noticed a few white grannies with coloured grandchildren which I found uplifting. It had been a long day travelling from Bridgetown, and a head full of rum and sad facts, I slept and dreamt of negro spirituals mingling with Irish ditties in the cane fields.

The history of segregation all happened on Newcastle Hill, where Raymond dropped me the following morning near the small village of Clifton Hall. In colonial times, the gentry lived at the top of the hill in their stately mansions and lush gardens, taking the air while the blacks and Irish lived at the bottom in squalor, eeking a meagre living from fishing. Back then, improving your social standing involved moving up the hill to a better address, whereas in current times, the sea view address is more desirable.

Fascinated with old headstones, I wandered into the gothic St John's Church, constructed on a clifftop in 1645 with spectacular views across the Atlantic. I came upon some peculiar remains resting amongst the shady fig trees. One grave contained a soldier who asked to be buried standing so he could better enjoy the view! Grand tombs had the names Culpeper, Briggs Maxwell and the triple-barrelled Mayer-Sealy-Goddard. A sundial brightened the cluster of cracked concrete.

One large vault descended to the resting place of Ferdinando Paleologus, a descendant of the last Emperor of Byzantium who died in Barbados in 1678. He lived in one of the 'Great Houses' nearby now owned by the Commissioner to Canada.

It was time to leave the aristocracy in peace, and it started to rain, so I half-ran into St John's village and sheltered in a local drinking shack opposite the school. Ignoring the infamous mauby, I settled for a beer and intrigued the locals by writing up my notes. Curiosity got the better of two men near me, and when they learned I was Irish, they directed me to Mary Gibson in the small store next door. At first reticent and suspicious, Mary soon opened up a little and came out with a great observation on Ireland. 'They don't remember us, so we don't mind them,' she declared. I felt that this statement said it all, as few in Ireland are aware of their kin in Barbados who had largely been forgotten.

When the rain cleared I continued down Newcastle Hill where the houses were an odd assortment, and I noticed a few painted in the Irish colours of green, white and gold. An old restored mill looked charming, and with its trimmed hedges and rose garden, it could have been from picturesque Devon. I took the turnoff to Zores, wondering where such a name originated from and came to a small shop where 'Rastaman' Thomas, a Billy Connolly lookalike with his cap, was cutting cassava sticks and packing them into sacks. I couldn't believe the resemblance, but Thomas had never heard of Billy Connolly!

Rita Gibson was rocking close by in her chair, with warmth for a stranger in her pale blue eyes and started to chat. There was no doubting her ancestry and speaking with a strong accent, but at least coherent, she had nothing good to say about Irish men.

'I bagged myself a bad one who fathered me five children, drank all our money, and ran off with a young black woman,' she laughed. Rita was delighted when her daughter Sarah took up with Thomas, who as a Rasta didn't drink alcohol. I noticed that Thomas soon abandoned the cassava cutting and started rolling his tobacco with ganja for a smoke. The couple had four children, and Rita was determined to keep her grandchildren on the straight and narrow, hoping one clever grand-daughter might stay in education and become a teacher.

Sarah herself appeared from inside the shack to see what the commotion was and remained standoffish for a while sizing me up. As Rita and I chatted on, she soon joined in and was a simple soul but had a kind heart. After a time, she lured me inside to taste some concoction boiling away in an old cast iron pot, telling me it was whelks and catfish in a spicy curry sauce. Fearing the worst for my bowels later, I sampled a little and nodded approval. It had a chewy texture like an octopus.

I felt privileged to be welcomed into their lives for the short while, as I was aware an Irish documentary had been made in the area some years previously, and a few residents had resented the intrusion in their lives. On leaving, I was very touched when Sarah insisted I take a jar of her spicy sauce with me for my family in Ireland.

I walked to the bus stop a few miles away near St Margaret's Anglican Church and had time for another graveyard browse. I am fascinated by old headstones. The contrast with St John's at the top of the hill was noticeable, modest graves with Irish names like Ward, Greaves and Gibson dating back to the late 1800s. Soon after arrival in Barbados, Catholicism was beaten out of the Irish immigrants, and in current times most were Anglican if anything at all.

As the bus changed gear ascending Newcastle Hill on its journey south, I realised how fortunate I was to meet with the last remaining Redlegs of Barbados. I hoped that soon they would be just Bajan, integrated into the rest of the island population and living at the top of the hill!

THE EMERALD ISLE OF
THE CARIBBEAN

As the island of Montserrat came into view, the devastation caused by the eruption of the Soufriere Hills volcano in 1995 was shocking — rivulets of pyroclastic ash leading down to the former capital Plymouth and continuing out to sea like an airport runway. Puffs of steam mingling with the cloud was a good sign of pressure getting released. Soon, the higgledy-piggledy portacabins of the temporary new capital came into view, and we docked in Little Bay.

I was on the banana boat from the island of Dominica, surrounded by sacks of yams, limes and plantains, and after spending a rough night in an airless cabin breathing diesel fumes and sleeping on plastic sheeting that made me sweat, I was beat. As the only passenger on board, I was grateful to get added to the ship's manifest at the last minute — the other transport option entailed a lengthy detour via Antigua. I'd been couchsurfing from Trinidad in the south, and this was to be the highlight of my trip — the week-long St Patrick's festival due to commence on the 13th of March.

In the bay, a large billboard with green shamrocks bid me 'A Hundred Thousand Welcomes to the Emerald Isle of the Caribbean', the English translation for Ireland's *Cead Mile Failte* and the Montserratian national flag was flying over the immigration hut. The island is a British Overseas Territory, but as well as the Union Jack, the blue flag features Erin, a pale-skinned Irish Coleen with red hair clad in a long green dress, holding a cross and Irish harp, signifying the island's Irish heritage.

I certainly didn't receive a warm Irish welcome from my dark kinsman the custom officer. He didn't know how to handle a scruffy looking white woman disembarking from the banana boat with the weekly vegetables. However, on showing my exit flight ticket and money, I was free to find the nearest cold tap for a good wash.

Before finding one, I heard a shout in a loud Cockney accent, and it was Winnie, meeting and greeting me. I was here for the craic of the festival and staying with an ardent Methodist, who didn't drink, hadn't seemed like a good idea when it was suggested by Winnie's friend Sara in Dominica. Liking my independence, I carried a tent intending to camp. Still, too whacked from the boat trip to argue, and always enjoying the interaction with a local, I gratefully accepted Winnie's kind hospitality to stay in her home. We ended up becoming the best of friends.

She lived in the district of Barzays, a few miles inland in a wonderfully cool house she shared with cute seven-year-old Brianna, who was looked after by Winnie. Shy at first, the girl was soon showing me her dolls, and then I crashed after that long-awaited wash. I grew to love these two individuals over the next two weeks as if I'd known them all my life and these chance meetings that evolve into good friendships are one of the many rich rewards of travel.

Born in Montserrat, Winnie had joined a wave of immigrants to the UK in the 1950s and was London's first female bus driver. She and her Jamaican husband saved hard to retire back in Montserrat and bought a beautiful home with lush gardens. Six months later it was flattened by the volcanic eruption of 1995 that rendered the whole southern half of the island uninhabitable. Devastated, Winnie walked away with a plastic bag of quickly-grabbed photos and sought comfort in God and the Methodist faith, founded by Wesley, who had himself been saved from a fire. Sadly, Winnie's husband had passed away, and now in her 60s, she was a pillar of strength in the community and a bundle of energy and positivity in her own right.

During my stay, I was to hear many harrowing tales of islanders' losses and suffering, and the trauma of that time was still palpable on the island. One would often hear the terms 'before' and 'after' used in the context of the eruption. I quickly realised that Montserratians are a reticent people who observe quietly and let you talk to get the measure of you, then they are all smiles and openness. I learned not to ask too many questions. And as I'd experienced on previous occasions, hitching the roads and staying with someone from the community opened doors of friendship and conversation often denied to the regular tourist on their holidays.

Winnie did her power walk on the quiet roads at dawn while I was still asleep. After dropping Brianna at school, I would often accompany her in the community van, as she drove oldies to their medical appointments. They enjoyed being roused from their slumber by a stranger and talked willingly about past times and Irish ancestors. The hospital and clinics were pleasant places decorated with tropical flowers, and the immaculately

146

dressed staff were friendly and cheerful. The formality of introductions was amusing — many people had titles; whether Mister Jonathan, Nurse Sybil, or Dr Clarissa, and Winnie was regularly called Sister Winifred. I was to discover that Montserrat has the most PhDs in the Caribbean and it was a tragic day for the populace when a sea of ash and lava covered the campus of the American University of the Caribbean.

My favourite oldie was Miss Annie, a good friend of Winnie's and a former preacher. This very sprightly 94-year-old tended her vegetable garden of pigeon peas, spinach and ginger plants, and waited for the jingle of the van for her afternoon treat of soursop ice cream. She had an infectious cackle of a laugh and seemed to be always boiling sugar and grating ginger to bake her much-loved sticky ginger bars.

It wasn't long before my head was brimming with stories and facts as Montserrat has a fascinating history on many fronts. As had happened in Barbados, Cromwell dispatched Irish political prisoners as indentured servants to work in the cotton and sugar cane fields in the 17th century. He deported free noblemen as well, and this created a class system. Unlike other Caribbean islands, the Catholic religion was tolerated in Montserrat, and it became a refuge for persecuted Irish Catholics. By 1678, half the population were Irish and the remainder English, Scots and Africans. As the sugar industry expanded and more African slaves arrived, the Irish became foremen and managers for absentee British landlords.

It was a shock discovering the real roots of the St Patrick's festival. It commemorated a failed slave rebellion on the 17th of March 1768 when the black slaves took advantage of their Irish foremen being drunk celebrating the feast day, and the slaves thought it an opportunity to rise up against oppression. Cudjoe, the ringleader, was strung up from the famous silk cotton tree at Cudjoe Head and eight other rebellious slaves were executed.

The skin shades of the people I met resembled a paint colour chart, from albino white through various coffee shades to jet black. Several exhibited latent throwback features of red hair, blue and green eyes that had laid dormant for a few generations. Most families on the island had Irish names — O'Reilly, Allen, Sweeney and Murphy, but it was the origin of the surnames that proved interesting. Many were legitimate descendants of Irishmen who married African freed slaves and often could trace their ancestry back a few hundred years. They were very proud of their Irish heritage, and the island choir had toured Ireland a few years previously and searched graveyards for long lost ancestors.

Others had Irish surnames because it was the custom for African slaves to lose their African names after disembarking the slave ships and they were given the Irish name of the plantation manager, who happened to be a Murphy or Daly. This group had just cause for grievance at losing their African identity and heritage, and a type of Pan-African/Black Consciousness movement had evolved to usurp the Irish-style festival with its shamrocks and leprechauns.

Montserrat's population declined by a third to 5000 residents in the late 1990s, as many who were evacuated initially to Britain decided to remain there. The island is only eleven miles by seven miles wide and the reduced population now lived on the northern section formerly considered poor land. The small communities and parishes of St John's, Look Out, Davey Hill, Salem and Old Town were sited only a few miles apart, and the new interim Government was in Brades.

The fertile volcanic soil of the southern Exclusion Zone was off-limits due to continuous volcanic activity. In a few days, I knew the region as well as my small hometown in Ireland. One night walking home late after a concert, it was comforting when a lone voice echoed from the hill above in the dark — 'Safe home, Mammy.'

Wilson, an electrician, gave me a lift one morning and I ended up accompanying him on his round reading the meters in the area. Chatting away, our views on pretentiousness were similar as he explained that some islanders gave out about others rising in status. Seemingly begrudgery and jealousy caused differences between those who fled after the eruption and those who stayed. He was interested in hearing it had happened in Ireland between those who emigrated to improve their lives and those content to remain behind.

After all our talk on pretentiousness, I wondered what he thought when I hopped into a swanky Geotracker Suzuki beach buggy with two Canadians who were taking me to Air Studios. I didn't wish to be seen in it, but the opportunity to visit the studio on the border of the exclusion zone was too good to refuse.

In 1971, the famous recording studio was built by George Martin, the fifth Beatle, for $US3 million and was one of the most prolific recording studios in music history. Legends, such as The Rolling Stones, Stevie Wonder, Elton John, Michael Jackson and others recorded their albums there. It had a reputation as one of the most sound-proofed studios in the world because of the noise of Concorde flying over. Hurricane Hugo destroyed 90% of it in 1989 and then the volcano finished it off six years later.

I felt sad witnessing the utter dereliction of the building now engulfed in tropical undergrowth, the pool full of sludge and the smell of mildew and decay in the air. Part of the wooden stair collapsed as we were poking at the 'Hall of Fame' floor slabs trying to decipher the celebrity names and handprints. I've heard that the studios are now off-limits and deemed too dangerous to visit and volcanic ash has buried the famous paving. Hearing this, I'm glad I have my three little pilfered souvenir tiles, sadly minus any celebrity handprint!

Families still visited their productive volcanic farmlands in the Exclusion Zone during the day, and the dangers were monitored continuously at an observatory established by the British in 1995. Security guards checked the permits of those allowed through and a constant stream of lorries ferried volcanic soil and lava rock to the north of the island for building purposes and export. This forbidden territory was very alluring, but during my visit, the volcano rumbled regularly, and the region was closed to outsiders. The closest I got was when Rose Farrell and her daughter Julie offered to take me to Garibaldi Hill, a good lookout point onto the devastation beyond in the Exclusion Zone.

Former million-dollar villas lay half-buried under ash on the slopes of the Beverly Hills area nearby. The tops of trees were just visible on the once fashionable golf course, and Rose pointed out the half jetty remaining where cruise ships used to dock. The Old Government House building and the former university peeked out amongst a lunar sea of grey ash and overgrown bushes that stretched to the horizon. It was hard to imagine this eerie landscape as the bustling capital of Plymouth twenty years previously.

On our left, the multiple lava domes of Soufriere dominated the skyline, its cone always increasing. With new green growth on the slopes and puffs of steam merging with the clouds, it was a beautiful looking volcano, and the monster looked too peaceful to be the cause of so much heartache.

The Farrells belonged to one of the prosperous Irish families on the island and traced their ancestry back to a free Irishman. They once owned a guesthouse and a hardware store in Plymouth, and the lava flow decimated both businesses. People had been forewarned of the eruption and evacuated, but nineteen farmers were killed while checking their crops in the Exclusion Zone.

I could sense the two women mourning their former life, and Julie expressed sadness looking at the destruction of her happy, carefree childhood. It hit home to me how suddenly Nature can destroy lives. We soon had enough of the putrid smell of sulphur in the air and headed to a quiet black sand beach where pumice stone was floating in the sea, and a lone seagull keened in the wind.

I wandered around Brades one day, where many of the government offices were operating in portacabins. Shipping containers had been put to good use and converted into small stores. I met Murphy, an old Rastaman wearing a Bob Marley cap, who was selling bush rum and strange medicinal concoctions in one of these containers. There were tubs of homemade hair wax, jars of guava root syrup for stomach ache, mauby bark for lowering blood pressure, and an aphrodisiac potion from the *bois bande* tree he claimed half the island men took. It was a fascinating education. Murphy was trying to resurrect the old African traditions and advised me not to miss the calypso competition at the festival.

I declined his bush rum and settled for an ice-cold ginger beer in the Green Monkey beach bar across the road. A few regulars were playing dominoes, and I chatted to two men setting up geothermal energy infrastructure on the island. They introduced me to one of the vulcanologists working at the observatory, but despite attempts to educate me, the scientific jargon relating to volcanic eruptions was beyond me.

One afternoon, I swung by the school as I'd promised to cheer on Brianna, competing in the festival sports day. She won the 'tie the diaper' competition with nappies that resembled the Irish flag, and a teacher persuaded me into joining the relay race as her auntie. It was a great laugh. One class performed a very interesting little play where in one scene; the little black boy was not allowed to play with the white Irish girl. It harkened back a few hundred years to the realities of segregation, racial and class differences.

The heat and energetic play with the kids soon drove me into the Air Studio Bar for a quiet cold beer. I sat at the long mahogany bar salvaged from the recording studio and studied the plaques and old records of the musicians on the walls. Usually energetic, even I was wilting trying to keep up with the pace of nightly festival events while recording the many stories and events in my diary.

I rose early to have breakfast chats with Winnie, who loved to hear the gossip of the night before and know who was giving me lifts when hitchhiking. We shared many stories about our lives as the friendship deepened and yet I wondered how she tolerated this mad Irishwoman staying with her, coming in at all hours.

Events livened up on the 16th of March, the eve of St Patrick's Day, with The Rude Boys String Band launching a new album at the Desert Storm Bar. It evolved into an impromptu shindig on the street with the island's steel drum band joining in. African beats and rhythm belted out into the sultry night air. Street food stalls served up the national dish 'goat water' which is a tasty goat stew served with crusty bread. Codfish with provisions is another island favourite, provisions being homegrown root vegetables like yam, taro and pumpkin — the stodgy fare that filled a slave's hungry belly in former times.

At the community centre, the Emerald Choir put on a world-class performance. Bedecked in national costume, the women wore flared African skirts in green, white and orangey-brown check with white blouses and African *tignons*. The men sported snow-white shirts with ties of the same check cloth, and I was surprised to see Irish *crios* belts, rarely seen now in Ireland. The tradition of these woollen sashes, woven and worn by fishermen on the Aran Islands, had crossed the Atlantic.

The choir sang ditties my mother used to sing: *I'll tell me Ma when I go home the boys won't leave the girls alone* and the popular *Fields of Athenry*. A traditional band visiting from Dublin came on stage playing the guitar, the uilleann pipes and banjo and then a troupe of young dancers tapped away to Irish jigs and reels. It felt bizarre to be witnessing all this Irish fanfare in the Caribbean.

Remembering Murphy's advice, I walked down the road to a big field where the calypso competition was in full swing. This style of Afro-Caribbean music originated in Trinidad and Tobago. It was used in slavery times to mock the slave masters, keep African traditions alive and communicate news in a secret language. The young performers were jumping about, and it wasn't easy to understand the quick swing of words and jest in the local Creole. A young girl called Cary Irish was the runner up with:

What have we come to?
When you destroy my country — there will be no future for me.
Things have gone cuckoo.
Telling teachers, we shoot them.

The winner was a cool looking dude about eight years old, in white pumps, smart pants with red braces and a dicky bow. He pranced about the stage and had the crowd in an uproar with a song called *Milk*. I missed the words, but the gist was — 'we always need milk' — a rude reference to Montserrat sucking dry the tits of Mother England for aid money. The show ended with the famous hit *Hot, Hot, Hot* by Alphonsus Celestine Edmund Cassell MBE, a well-known Montserratian calypso and soca musician and the island's first superstar. He used the stage name Arrow, and I remembered hearing the hit on *Top of the Pops* in the 1980s.

On the morning of St Patrick's Day, I attended Mass at St John's Church said by Father George from County Kerry in Ireland. He warned Irish visitors that the Mass wouldn't be the quickie we were accustomed to, and sure enough, it lasted a lengthy two hours!

Lava flows of Montserrat

Winnie picking flowers for church!

I was mesmerised by the display of green finery among the congregation, and I was glad I'd borrowed a flowery green dress off Winnie for the day. Everyone sang the hymns and as Father George called out birthdays, wedding anniversaries and other celebrations the congregation clapped. It went on and on. At the finish, everyone wished each other 'Happy St Patrick's Day', and I taught a few Montserratians how to say *La Fheile Padraig faoi shona dhuit,* the greeting in Gaelic.

In the afternoon, the razzmatazz extravaganza of the parade was a vibrant contrast to the commercial St Patrick's Day parades of New York or Dublin. There were no advertising or company floats, just an assortment of people in outlandish costumes. Drummers in Guinness top hats wore green T-shirts with the logo 'Kiss Me I'm Irish' — others were wearing the map of Africa and voodoo costumes. A group dressed like slaves walked in irons and musicians played calabash instruments and steel drums. All ages were out to have a good time dressed in their best Irish-Caribbean finery.

American and Canadian holidaymakers drove about in beach buggies ornamented in greenery and shamrocks and the 'Paddywhackery Bus', as I called it, ferried people from venue to venue. Celebrating St Patrick's Day can often evolve into a pub crawl, but the tourist revenue was sorely needed in Montserrat to rebuild after the eruption.

When I discovered a stall selling cupcakes with shamrocks on the icing, I bought a couple for Miss Annie, who was quietly observing the fun from her chair whilst selling her sticky ginger bars. She couldn't walk well, so I took her tray and circulated among the spectators, encouraging them to buy. A few went over to chat with her, and the attention and extra money made her day!

The Slave Feast in the evening featured African bands playing Senegalese and Malian music, and the outdoor venue was a sea of sweaty faces and bodies grooving to the beat. Only the haunting sound of the kora quietened the crowd. Although the dress was Irish, there was no doubting the origin of the swaying hips and even young children had an innate sense of rhythm. I met Kate, an American doing a PhD on connections between Irish and African dance, researching the similarities between 'heel and toe' and the 'quadrille' brought to Jamaica from the Congo. Yet another specialist!

There was no idle recovery time the following day. Winnie was determined to clear my head with a walk in the pristine lush forest of the Central Hills district. We were lucky to spot the Montserrat oriole, a black and yellow bird endemic to the island but had no luck seeing the endangered mountain chicken which is a giant frog whose legs were a local delicacy. A few small snakes slithered off at our approach, and I was relieved to learn none were poisonous.

Wielding her machete, Winnie cut a few banana bunches and beautiful red heliconia flowers to decorate the church. The hilly landscape was broken by deep ravines called *ghauts* which transform into fast-flowing water channels in the rainy season. Sitting by a dried-up waterfall, we enjoyed our picnic of Johnny cakes, deep-fried corn balls, washed down with tangy sorrel juice. Small lizards were sunning themselves not far away and looked just as I felt. The peaceful scene was a real tonic after the festivities, and I tried not to dwell on my imminent departure.

The next day was my last, and in the morning, Montserrat radio interviewed me on a programme called *Under the Tamarind Tree* — a cross between *Desert Island Discs* and *This is Your Life*. In African tradition, the tamarind tree's expansive foliage provides shade from the hot sun, and people gather underneath it to chat and tell stories. The presenter Dr Clarissa had me choose my four favourite music pieces and give a rundown of my nomadic life — all rather gruelling as I wondered who on earth would be interested. I selected two Irish songs by Van Morrison and two by the Malian musician Ali Farke Toure to reflect the Irish/African mix I'd witnessed all week.

The nervousness of being on the radio distracted from the sadness I felt leaving Montserrat and parting from new dear friends. It was heart-wrenching saying goodbye to Winnie and Brianna before taking the evening ferry to Antigua. Since my visit in 2013, we've kept in touch and remember to chat around St Patrick's Day, reminiscing on our good times together.

One of the sadder aspects of travel is the constant 'hellos' and 'goodbyes' to those met on the way. It is a reminder of the transience of everything and how the present should always be treasured.

Many places I've visited have touched my heart, but a large chunk remains in the Emerald Isle of the Caribbean.

SHAMED IN RWANDA

I was on the Jaguar night bus to the Uganda/Rwanda border in 2014, and I felt uneasy about my visit to Rwanda. I'd just visited the museum at Idi Amin's torture chambers in Kampala a few days previously. Like in Cambodia or Auschwitz, there's a sense of foreboding at witnessing the awfulness of genocide. Having no guidebook for Rwanda to consult, I knew little about the politics of what happened in 1994, but I had watched the brutal events in the movie *Hotel Rwanda* and was aware of the UN's failure to act.

The bus was full of slumbering passengers, and I was the only *myzungu* on board, seated next to an older man who kept to himself. There was little curiosity about me at the late meal stop when everyone was too concerned to fill hungry bellies and queue for toilets in the dim light. In this area of the mountainous west, locals were used to tourists arriving to experience their *Gorillas in the Mist* adventure. I wasn't hungry; however, I felt irritated at the driver leaving the engine running, belching out its thick exhaust pollution in the direction of the food stands close by.

It was 3 am as we approached the border post at Gatuna, with its military presence, and money changers besieged the bus. An official boarded to check passports, and as the only foreigner, he directed me to a nearby hut where another official insisted that I did indeed need a visa with an Irish passport — and I argued that I didn't as I had checked online. A senior officer was summoned, and a discussion ensued on whether to allow me to proceed. Meanwhile, the bus driver was honking the horn, and he sent a passenger to hurry me up. Eventually, the debacle resolved when I parted with a few more US dollars on top of the official visa charge. Such are the vagaries of border crossings!

Two officials accompanied me back to the bus and instructed me to empty the contents of my rucksack onto a nearby table. My fellow passengers stared impatiently from the window, and the driver was huffing and puffing with annoyance. They had been searched already and were ready to move on. Assuming it was a drug search, I complied with a smile which soon turned to shocked surprise on being told that plastic bags were banned in Rwanda. The officer pointed to a sign in the background I hadn't seen:

'Use of non-biodegradable polythene bags prohibited'.

Five or six bags lay on the table and the officer roughly emptied the contents. The first plastic bag held my dirty underwear and socks; the next — sticky shampoo containers, followed by one with squishy bananas and mangoes for the journey and lastly the most valued — my emergency muesli supply from home. The official promptly produced a wad of brown paper bags.

'*C'est cinq francs pour les sacs en papier, Madame*', he demanded, which involved another transaction swapping dollar bills for the local currency Rwandan francs. The exasperated officer explained in French that they were letting me off the hefty penalty this one time.

Face beetroot with mortification, I stuffed everything into the paper bags, repacked my rucksack and scurried back on the bus, apologising to my fellow passengers, some of whom now gave me sympathetic smiles and looks of pity. They were familiar with the rules. I felt utterly shamed coming from a first world country that should know better, but I was still in shock — *this was Africa after all,* and in my experience, the continent was littered with plastic and rubbish.

We continued into the streaky hues of early dawn and too annoyed to sleep, I gazed out the window at an astonishing landscape of terraced hills and lush tea plantations that reminded me of India. Everywhere was green and beautiful, and there was no rubbish to be seen! The small villages we passed through sported tidy brick houses with colourful well-tended gardens; very French chic. My bus companions were animated and friendly now in the light of day. A kind lady gave me a few coins at the toilet stop, which, to my surprise, had toilet paper, soap and towels.

I arrived at the central bus station in the capital Kigali at 6 am, and a motorbike taxi took me to a cheap recommended hotel, the Gloria. As it was too early to check in, the receptionist disappeared to the kitchen and rustled up a *cafe creme* and a French baguette to fortify me while I waited for places to open. She informed me in French that the Genocide Museum nearby acted in lieu of a tourist bureau and would open at 8 am.

It wasn't the cheeriest start to the day. The museum was excellent for its detailed explanations in English, outlining the history of Rwanda under Belgian colonisation and how their rulership exacerbated the racial tension between the Hutus and Tutsi. It was that common practice of keeping people divided so that they don't unite and rise up. The Tutsi, for many centuries, had been the elite minority caste descended from royalty, and the majority Hutu agriculturalists were treated like serfs in a feudal land system that simmered to a boil under colonialism. There had been a previous massacre in 1957 when 100,000 Tutsi were butchered, and many fled, leaving the Hutu in power. These Tutsi returned under the control of Paul Kagame to regain their lands, and all hell broke loose during the 100 days of mass slaughter in 1994 when 800,000 people died. The international response was shameful.

The graphic pictures detailing women being raped and given HIV, people set alight with kerosene and children macheted to death were genuinely horrific, and the fact that it happened so recently during my lifetime had a significant impact on me. The intimate details of children's lives and their favourite toys were particularly heartrending, and a dimly lit cabinet of skulls and clothing said it all. I felt ashamed to be human. When I read the list of the many genocides of the 20th century, beginning with the Germans in Namibia in 1904, then Armenia, the Jews, Pol Pot, and the Balkans; I genuinely despaired at lessons never learned.

Shocked and numbed with the horror of it all, I went for coffee in a nearby cafe, and as I watched passersby, I wondered what their memories were of those years and what scars they bore. *Was that man a perpetrator or a victim?* I found myself asking as I noticed many people with mutilations and injuries.

I felt sensitive about asking questions, but the girl in the archives office was happy to talk.

'You do not ask what anyone is anymore,' she said, 'as no one wants to remember that time,' and her face saddened. 'If you're Tutsi, your people have died in the most terrible circumstances, and if you're Hutu, you suffer the trauma that your people did the unthinkable. Now everyone is just Rwandan.'

It was also interesting to hear that the movie *Hotel Rwanda* was banned in the country as they deemed it an inaccurate portrayal of events and the film was shot in South Africa.

The museum didn't charge an entrance fee, but donations were encouraged, and I placed a rose on the mass graves in the dignified garden adjacent, where the remains of 250,000 victims lay interred. It suddenly struck me that such events were still happening in parts of the world and were just a brief broadcast on the evening news.

Back at my hotel, I couldn't nap, and unsettled from what I'd seen, I freshened up and cleaned out my rucksack, folding the paper bags carefully. It was a luxury to have my own room after the shared travellers' dorms in Uganda. Venturing out later, I asked for directions to the Hotel Mille Collines, wanting to see the original setting where many Tutsis sought refuge from the atrocities. I headed for the skyscrapers that indicated downtown and passed numerous roundabouts with colourful flowers and manicured shrubs as centrepieces. It was as if I was in a small European city set in Africa, and as smiling people went about their business, it struck me how quickly history moves on from tragedies.

The hotel belonged to the Kempinski group, with a plush lobby leading through to tropical gardens surrounding an enticing pool in the late afternoon heat. I decided to have my first local Mutzig beer at the crowded bar in the hope of a chance chat with anyone, as my head was muddled with unanswered questions. I was fortunate to meet Hans, a German volunteer with an environmental agency, and the perfect person to ask about the plastic bag ban.

'You're lucky you didn't get fined,' he said after hearing my story. 'Sometimes Rwandans are imprisoned if they're caught smuggling plastic bags into the country, or they're forced to make public confessions. Women often hide a bundle in their bras. There are vigilante checks in stores, and if found, the business is immediately closed.'

The enforcement seemed particularly severe to me, but Hans explained that Rwanda was lauded as a green example in Africa and had won awards for its efforts. After the genocide, President Paul Kagame, the former Tutsi rebel, had introduced a National Development Plan called 'Vision 2020' that would take Rwanda from an impoverished nation to a sustainable middle-income green economy. Despite some controversy over his continued leadership, the policies had succeeded in uniting the people and improving GDP dramatically.

'Rwanda puts Europe to shame,' Hans continued. 'They have been planting trees in denuded areas affected by the war, building hydroelectric power stations in the mountains and improving the national parks to boost tourism. The gorillas bring in huge revenue.' I told him of my hopes to see these astonishing primates shortly.

Fading fast after my lack of sleep and exhausted mentally, I had to go, but Hans' parting words were 'I hope you are here Saturday — you need to see *Umuganda*.'

Two days later, on Saturday morning, the first thing I noticed was the silence, and I could hear birdsong, a rarity in an African capital. On other mornings, I had awoken to the din of traffic and the early shouts of traders heading to a busy vegetable market near the hotel. Curious, and thinking it a festival, I had inquired about *Umuganda* the previous day, only to learn it means — *coming together in common purpose to achieve an outcome* and is the monthly community clean-up day.

All traffic stops between 8 and 11 am, and businesses close as it is mandatory for citizens aged 18 to 65 to take part. As I strolled around the city, I witnessed women sweeping public spaces with palm brooms and men trimming bushes or scything grass around monuments. In the absence of garbage bags, the rubbish was collected in sacks made from banana leaves, cloth or papyrus. I helped a woman in a park pick up cigarette butts as she hummed quietly about her work. Elsewhere, I later learned about other *Umuganda* activities such as building houses for the poor and providing transport for the elderly.

The community spirit I witnessed that Saturday morning was incredible and lifted my spirits as I left for the mountains with a lighter heart.

As I write this in the year of Paul Kagame's 2020 Vision, Rwanda is still a success story aided by the UN and foreign investment. It is the world's largest exporter of coltan used in electronics.

However, it is the green policies, and community concern for the environment reflected in *Umuganda* that could be an example to us all.

GORILLAS IN THE MIST

It was early evening in Kinig village on the edge of Virunga National Park in Rwanda, and the mist lay low on the forested slopes, just revealing the jagged peaks of four of the seven volcanoes. Somewhere up there, I reflected, is the world's only population of mountain gorillas and my memories of Dian Fossey's life with them flooded back. Due to her protection, their number increased from 240 worldwide in the late 1960s to the current population of nearly 1000 in 2014. Sadly, she paid the ultimate price by being macheted to death by a poacher in 1985. At the time, eating ape meat was prestigious among the wealthy elite; the heads were displayed as a trophy or disgustingly, the paw used as an ashtray.

The park borders the three countries of Uganda, the Democratic Republic of Congo and Rwanda; however, the gorillas, recognising no frontiers, wander freely in their groups between all three.

It is the ultimate adrenaline experience to spend a precious hour with these primates in the wild. I was scheduled to see them across the border in Uganda the following week and was only planning to hike to Dian Fossey's grave on the high slopes in this region, and then cross the Ugandan border.

I had just arrived at my (for me) upmarket guesthouse and felt like a true British madam from colonial days re-living *Out of Africa*. The massive queen-sized bed in my room was strewn with rose petals and hibiscus flowers with a big 'WELCOME' outlined in yellow blossom, and I regretted not having a silky negligee to wallow in the crisp sheets. Throwing my muddy rucksack in the corner, I appreciated the vista from my terrace before the light disappeared altogether — the majestic alluring peaks where I would hopefully venture on the morrow.

The dinner menu was English style; chops, potatoes adorned with a sprig of parsley, mushy carrots and cooling gravy already skinning over. Michael, the tuxedoed waiter, stood to attention at the table, white napkin draped over his arm and keen to practise his English skills. Hot coals were placed in a clay pot and warmed my feet under the table. Trophies from former hunting days decorated the walls, and the beady eyes of an antelope head put me off my chops.

I was the only guest and did wonder where the high-end gorilla enthusiasts were lodging; only realising the following day, I was in the shabby category of accommodation for a price well exceeding my budget. A group of village men were chatting in Kinyarwanda, the local dialect, around a brazier fire in the back yard. I joined them later, hoping for information on visiting the park. Initially wary of the *myzungu* they smiled as I squatted on the grass and introduced myself. When I inquired about transport to the park office, the competition for my dollars commenced and a young guy, Gilbert, offered to take me there on his motorbike at 7 am for the tour briefing.

I slept well in my perfumed boudoir, and in the morning, the crisp mountain air was refreshing after the blistering heat of the plains. It was eight kilometres to the park office on a rutted dirt road — zigzagging between youths on bicycles piled high with sacks of potatoes for the market and stately women balancing firewood on their heads. The fertile terraced landscape was lush and green, broken by large fields of *ptetirus* flowers looking like a bedspread of white daisies and used in the making of insecticide.

Karisoke Research Centre was a bustle of activity with a large group of camera-toting Americans shouting at each other. Quickly adjusting to the sudden onslaught of mass tourism, I made my way gingerly to the reception desk. The ranger kindly explained in good English that there was no transport to the starting point for the hike to Fossey's grave, but I might have luck catching a ride with the American group. He pointed out their leader Jake, a friendly Liverpudlian operating a wildlife agency in Florida.

'Of course, we can give you a lift,' Jake smiled. 'Help yourself to some coffee and biscuits while you're waiting. We're leaving shortly.'

Gratefully sipping my first proper coffee in days, I was just about to buy my ticket for the hike, when Jake approached me, a big smile on his face.

'I'm going to make your day,' he whispered. 'We have a spare slot on our tour. Would you like to see the gorillas? No charge but say nothing, just pretend you booked locally.' I was ecstatic and nearly hugged him. It *was* my lucky day!

I learned that the Americans were on a global wildlife tour for 18 days and had already seen the giant pandas in China, polar bears in the Arctic, whales in the Maldives, and lions in Kruger National Park in South Africa. Some of them couldn't recall where they'd been two days before.

'And where have you sprung from?' one inquired, curious about my travelling solo. Not wanting to go into detail, I was relieved when the briefing commenced, and we were divided into groups of eight people, each tracking a different gorilla group.

I was assigned to track the Isimba group, seven in number and led by a young silverback called Mutu, as the previous male leader had died of pneumonia a few months previously. Because of his youth and inexperience, Mutu was helped by Poppy, the grand matriarch of all the gorilla groups at 41 years old, and one of Dian Fossey's little darlings. Poppy and Mutu had a baby together, and I laughed at the idea of this gorilla cougar.

'Good for her,' I commented to a tourist next to me as we learned that the mountain gorillas' lifespan in the wild is between 30 and 40 years and their gestation period is similar to humans at eight and a half months, with the birth of one or two babies.

After a jeep ride to the edge of the bamboo forest, we commenced our steep hike, led by the principal guide Jonathan, and two scouts carrying AK-47s, one walking in front of the group and the other behind. Jonathan told us there could be wild elephants or an angry unhabituated silverback to contend with. In Virunga, only about 14 gorilla groups were used to human sightseers, and the rest ran freely in the wild. There was no proper path, and as our guide hacked the way forward with his machete, I was glad of my long pants and sleeves protecting me from thorny shrubs and stinging nettles.

The torrential rain of recent days had cleared, and we were fortunate to have blue skies and sunshine until the forest closed in around us. Several sections were so steep we had to cling onto branches and roots to haul ourselves upwards, and it would have been treacherous in wet weather. Many of the Americans had hired porters to carry their daypacks, and a few unfit looking types struggled with the climb.

Each gorilla group has two trackers who go up the mountain each morning and use GPS to locate where their particular group was last sighted, then communicate with the guide. The primates live above 1000 metres and have been driven higher and higher due to civil unrest in the Congo and tree felling encroaching on their habitat.

It was unpredictable how long or what altitude we would ascend to before sighting the gorillas. It can vary from 30 minutes to five hours, but seldom are tourists disappointed. I became breathless trying to keep close to Jonathan in front, and between gasps for air managed to ask him the odd question. He told me he was an ex-poacher, but his income as a guide was sufficient to feed his large family, and he now understood better the conservation issue.

After two hours of hard slog, he received a call on his radio from the trackers and slowed up, pressing a finger to his lips to indicate silence, not that many of us had the breath to speak. By now the sunny clearings and bamboo stands had given way to the dense rainforest with old man's beard and lichens giving the tall trees an eerie prehistoric feel. I could imagine a brontosaurus emerging from the undergrowth but swept my eyes about in anticipation of a giant hairy gorilla.

Jonathan raised his hand for us to stop, and suddenly I spotted them — two adult females preoccupied with grooming each other. One sifted the thick fur of her companion's neck with meticulous attention, and her deep-set brown eyes had the intense look of a manicurist in a beauty parlour. Behind them sat a third bigger female with an infant clutched to her and its little arms wrapped around her. It was a touching scene and very human. Jonathan mimed that this mother was Poppy and I felt so happy and emotional to be observing this grand dame who was a famous film star, so well-studied in both youth and old age.

Jonathan motioned for us to sit quietly at about ten feet distant, and he slowly pulled some fronds and branches back for better viewing, then glanced at his watch and nodded. The clock had started ticking for our precious hour. He then pointed upwards to low hanging branches on our left and there sat two juveniles, swiping at each other in play. One of them swung into acrobatic manoeuvres as if to perform for our benefit — with chuckles and hooting noises and even sticking a tongue out in our direction. I had to stifle my laughter at the circus performance.

The cameras were clicking steadily, including my own, but after some time, as advised at the briefing, I laid it aside and just watched fascinated. I was shocked before, hearing that some tourists were bored after twenty minutes taking photos and asked 'What's next?' utterly unappreciative of the joy of observation.

I watched captivated as Poppy held her infant close and stroked it from time to time, unperturbed by our presence. The grooming pair had parted with grunting noises as if satisfied, and one approached us, eyes alive with curiosity to check us out. She had such a graceful, peaceful stride of dignity, and as I stared into her eyes, I could really believe this creature being our nearest relative, looking and acting as we do. She swerved sideways then, to scrabble in some bushes, looking for a snack. Jonathan had told us their diet consisted of shoots, fruit and tree bark.

Poppy and her baby – Rwanda

All the while, we could hear some distant roars and thuds in the forest, and after half an hour, we were gathered together and asked who wanted to proceed to track the missing silverback. Most of our group were happy to remain with the female gorillas, but I, along with two fit men, agreed to climb further with Jonathan, accompanied by one of the armed guards. I didn't want to miss any opportunity to see the big boss Mutu.

As we continued further into the undergrowth, the screeching and thumping got louder and closer. Suddenly from a wide ravine, a giant roar preceded a large silverback being chased by the vast bulk of Mutu himself — a gigantic angry male ape thumping his chest in rage with teeth bared. Their speed was phenomenal breaking from the bush, and we dived for cover. I was petrified of being attacked but also overrun with adrenalin watching the conflict.

Thankfully the younger male conceded defeat, disappearing into the undergrowth with a series of grunts. Mutu stood still a moment victorious and also aware of our presence. I peered out cautiously to get a good look at the trademark silver saddle on his back. We'd been advised how important it was to stand our ground with the more aggressive silverbacks, avoiding sudden movement and direct eye contact, which they take as a challenge; all difficult when the immediate impulse is to flee as fast as you can. The five of us cowered, heads lowered, and I noticed the guard raise his rifle but having no fight with us, the giant primate bounded back to the ravine with a final roar.

We looked at each other in relief and amazement, pleased to have witnessed the scene only embedded in memories. There had been no time for cameras. Jonathan explained that Mutu had exclusive breeding rights with the females in his group and that the solitary rival could have been poaching his harem.

Our hour was up, and the mist was starting to swirl in around us on the easier descent.

Jonathan looked very relieved to have us down safely, and I wondered if we'd been in danger.

'That was a fantastic experience, Jonathan, thank you so much,' I said with a grin.

That night, in deep slumber on my perfumed throne, I dreamt of the dark forest, not of the fight, but Poppy's infant unfurling a small hairy arm, outstretched towards me looking for an embrace.

NO MAN'S LAND

There are countries in the world that don't officially exist — with weird unpronounceable names like Transnistria, the Republic of South Ossetia, Puntland and Nagorno-Karabakh. They are not easily located on a map and are not a 'where to go' in search of white-sand beaches and a relaxing holiday. Most are born of strife and conflict, and you need all your wits about you if you are visiting them.

Here I am in 2019 in one of those unknown countries, the Republic of Somaliland, a breakaway semi-desert territory on the coast of the Gulf of Aden. It was created after the overthrow of the Somali military dictator Siad Barre in 1991 but internationally is still considered part of Somalia, a former British colony.

The entire region is a dodgy, unstable region of Africa. Still, I'm always taking risks, and as a rock art nerd, I wanted to visit the Neolithic site of Laas Geel, which was a few hours' drive outside the capital of Hargeisa. When I entered the Oriental Hotel, I was recovering from a fracas with a taxi driver who demanded $US70 instead of the agreed $US7 for the shared fare from the border. At one point, he suggested I squash into the back with the luggage and give up my seat to a woman of extraordinary proportions. The screaming scene at the hotel entrance was not pleasant, and I'm fortunate the hotel management gave me a room in my maddened state.

Good-looking Tarek was very kind and calmed me down with a cold juice before showing me to my deluxe room. I was figuring out how to go downstairs and complain that the toilet didn't flush, the TV didn't work and I suspected the bed linen hadn't been changed in a while — all first world problems! I took a deep breath and returned to reception where Tarek promised to notify a plumber about the toilet.

I had been hoping to find a fellow traveller interested in sharing a taxi to visit the rock art, and I had a peep in the bar. A lone Japanese businessman sipping tea whilst on a conference call didn't look like a hopeful candidate. He spoke no English and seemed confused when I babbled on about Neolithic carvings. Tarek helpfully explained that I should visit the Department of Tourism nearby in the morning and make enquiries there.

I returned to my suite, leaving the door ajar for the promised plumber. It was then that I saw her — this tiny, nimble woman springing along with a small backpack and wearing an unusual khaki flak jacket with bulging pockets. With cropped hair and a tanned face, she had that look of an intrepid traveller, and sure enough, she was one.

Caroline and I adjourned to the bar to drink it dry of orange juice and talked non-stop for five hours. What I'd have given for a cold beer but Somaliland is a strict Muslim country where alcohol is forbidden. I learned about Caroline's membership of the TCC, or Travel Century Club, which you're eligible to join when you've visited 100 countries. I'd heard of it before but didn't know the finer details. Living in California, she was approaching her 83rd birthday and intended celebrating it in the Comoros and Mayotte, which would be her final country on the long checklist of 322 TCC countries. The ruthless club included all those dependencies, overseas territories, French departments and hanger-on lumps of rock like Gibraltar, not cleanly severed from colonial powers. According to the UN, there are 195 countries, all sovereign nations and I didn't ever hold aspirations of visiting them all.

'Have you been to Tristan da Cunha?' I asked her, thinking of this remote island that had plagued me since school days — on a par with Timbuktu.

'Yes, I went there on the supply ship that sails every six months,' Caroline answered. I listened, fascinated as she explained that the wealthy chartered private yachts to tick off remote islands, and the less well-off shared online tips on how to reach far-flung destinations on a shoestring. She had just arrived from Brazzaville in the Congo and explained that while in transit at Mogadishu, where she couldn't get a visa, she had pleaded with the airline staff to allow her to descend the ramp and put her feet on the tarmac! I did my best to refrain from pursing my lips with disapproval at this bizarre attitude to travel.

'What else would I be doing with my life?' Caroline continued. 'I certainly don't want to be a babysitting granny or sit knitting in an armchair.' I took her point and perhaps would feel more sympathetic and do likewise if I were 83.

I asked Caroline if she was interested in visiting Laas Geel with me the following day, but she wanted to rest before flying out at midday. I thought it very sad that anyone would reach such a blasé dulled state where any curiosity for a new place or people gets stifled. Even the twitchers I met, who ticked off lists, were passionate about their feathered pursuits. I changed the subject to my nosiness about her flak jacket. 'I sleep in it, and only take it off to shower,' Caroline boasted proudly. She proceeded to show me her bank cards, passport and money, all neatly and safely inserted in hidden inner pockets, and notebook, pen, torch and other sundries in compartments on the outside. *Such an organised traveller!* Exhausted from my geography lesson, I retired to bed — noticing a bucket of water by the toilet door.

After my very British breakfast of cornflakes, tea and toast the following morning, I ventured down to the Department of Tourism and drank spicy-sweet Somali tea with Mr Shabele. There was no cajoling him into allowing me to visit Laas Geel independently. An armed guard escort was required for security reasons as there was always the risk of foreigners getting kidnapped. Mentally calculating my budget blow-out, I reluctantly agreed, and Mr Shabele made a few phone calls to arrange my transport for the next morning.

Returning to the hotel in the hope of a flushing toilet, I passed a group of men relaxing in the shade, rolling prayer beads and drinking chai. '*Habo!*' one yelled, a generic Somali term for aunty, and beckoned me over. '*Yalla Habibi*, have some tea with us. Where are you from?'

Abdi, who looked about 40, seemed happy to banter in English. He was interested in my views on Somaliland and national identity in general and appeared a learned man. His neighbour, perhaps twice his age, interrupted with queries in Somali and Abdi laughed heartily. 'My uncle here is asking your bride price in cows,' he said. 'His second wife is getting tired, and he wants a fresh one.'

'*Alhamdulillah,*' I answered jovially — 'praise be to God he will find one.' The men guffawed in unison, and as the call to noon prayers sounded from the mosque nearby, the group scattered, leaving me unattached for another while.

Next morning my taxi arrived promptly at 7.30 am, and the driver spoke a little English. We halted at a livestock market on the outskirts of town to check on camel and goat prices for his brother. There was a big difference in cost, and I thought it must all be in the hump — a camel valued at $US800 and a goat a mere $US8. A few streets away, we picked up my SPU, or military escort, an officious young guy in fatigues and carrying a Kalashnikov.

On the 70-kilometre drive from Hargeisa, the two men conversed quietly and shared smokes while I covered up from the fine dust and searing heat. We drove through a scorched eroded plain, broken by a few rocky outcrops and acacia trees and passed a few villages, where the inhabitants sheltered from the sun in dark doorways. The road gradually deteriorated, the last section a rough corrugated track that led to a massive granite outcrop rising from the plateau at the confluence of two dried river beds or *wadis*. Laas Geel means the 'The Camels' Well', but there wasn't a beast to be seen. This region once renowned as the earliest site of pastoralism in the Horn of Africa, transformed over millennia into a barren desert landscape.

The only animals I would see were the strange colourful cows on the rock face above and I was excited to have arrived at this famous rock art gallery. A band of local children came running, and it was nice to see my driver Ali distribute sweets and goodies among them. A local guide at an old tin shack collected my fee, and we then scrambled up the scree slope together to a series of large rock shelters and overhangs that looked like caves. I wandered bewitched past the numerous painted panels on the rock and in hidden crevices. They were in excellent condition as the site was so sheltered and rarely visited. The famous bovines, called aurochs, lacked the hump that has been bred in over intervening millennia and had large curved white horns with reddish tips and very marked udders.

But it was their distinctive wide rectangular necks that stood out — with striped bangles in vivid reds, violet and browns, thought to be ceremonial ornamentation. There were milking scenes with trousered men pulling on the cow's udder. On one panel, a large group of human figures, some with a halo of ochre dashes, had arms stretched upwards revering these beasts who gave them sustenance. Cow worship is common in many cultures, including Celtic mythology, and I was intrigued by these beautiful specimens that were so different from anything I'd seen elsewhere. The few foreigners' comments in the visitor's book were a stark reminder of the remote area I was in, and I was a satisfied woman returning to Hargeisa with some great photos of the paintings.

All travel has its good and bad days — and the following day transpired to be one of those nightmare events dubbed an adventure years later, and a good story to relate! Happy with my Laas Geel visit I returned to the Ethiopian border in good spirits, despite being squashed in the rear of the taxi, with a wandering hand next to me I had to slap away. The young guy just grinned.

At the border hut, the guard stamped my exit visa and waved me on into No Man's Land, towards the Ethiopian immigration post a kilometre away. I remembered this particularly grim stretch of land from my entry a few days previously. As I followed a line of locals laden down with sacks of goods, I zig-zagged frequently to avoid the scavenging mongrels pulling at piles of rubbish and rotting waste. One or two bared sharp teeth at me as I approached and I collected a few stones just in case. I've had a few scary encounters with vicious dogs enough to make me nervous. I hurried along skirting around the piles of dog shit that lay about.

'Salaam,' I said, delighted to reach the Ethiopian hut with clean footwear. The officer nodded and looked at my foreign passport. 'You cannot enter here,' he said, dismissing me with his hand. 'But I have a visa,' I argued, showing him my multi-entry visa from the Ethiopian Embassy in London.

'No good, go back,' he replied and waved at the next person in line. I stood there, tears, anger and frustration all welling up at the same time. 'Please sir, it is a valid visa,' I pleaded desperately. 'Only good for flying,' he shouted, 'not this land border. You must go back to Somaliland and fly to Ethiopia.'

I stood there alone in the heat and dust, the tears rolling down now as the unsympathetic officer disappeared inside. The entry fence was just there, metres away, and it was one of those moments from the movies where I just wanted to make a run for it — but I turned on my heel to cross the hellish No Man's Land once more. I felt utterly dejected and fed up trudging back to the Somaliland side, and wasn't as careful as before where I walked. It was the final straw to step in dog shit, and I growled at a nearby mongrel in frustration.

'Salaam,' I greeted the same Somali officer, this time with a tear-stained face and trepidation in my voice. He looked surprised to see me again. 'I need to return to Hargeisa for a visa,' I said. 'Not possible, you have exit stamp, no return now.' I couldn't believe my ears — this just couldn't be happening to me, and I was near breaking point.

'Please sir, they won't allow me into Ethiopia by land.' He looked harshly at me, no bending in his steely eyes or voice. 'No good, you cannot come back here. Need new visa.' He too disappeared inside.

I slumped onto my rucksack in the dust feeling at an all-time low and let loose, quietly sobbing. Usually resilient, I don't often feel at the end of my tether, but here I was sitting in a shitty No Man's Land with mad dogs, unable to go forward or back. I nearly laughed then — it was so ludicrous.

OK, calm down, I persuaded myself. *This will get you nowhere.*

I gathered myself together and was gearing up for another pleading session with immigration when a well-dressed man approached and asked me if anything was the matter. I described my predicament, getting upset again. Mohamed introduced himself and offered to speak to the border guard on my behalf.

Whatever he said or did, it worked, and they cancelled my exit stamp, leaving me free to return to Hargeisa. I couldn't thank Mohamed enough for his intervention and badly wanted to hug him in defiance of Muslim custom.

'Don't worry,' he said kindly. 'I want you to have good memories of my country Somaliland.'

'*Inshallah,*' I responded, — 'if Allah wills it,' — and he laughed.

Rock art nerd at Laas Geel, Somaliland

THE OMO VALLEY

The Omo Valley in southern Ethiopia is home to some of Africa's most fascinating ethnic groups, whose way of life and cultural practices tested my acceptance of 'otherness'. I was fortunate to visit this unique area in 2014 when it was changing fast. The need for local labour to build roads was a threat to the traditional cattle-herding structure of the villages and mining exploration was opening up the district to outside influences.

The region was difficult to access, involving a flight south from the capital Addis Ababa to Arba Minch near the South Sudanese border, and then travelling for hours on dusty 4WD tracks. I was pleased to find that community tourism was well organised and I was linked up with two Germans, and Tsege, our local driver who understood some of the Omo Valley languages. He would introduce us to the various communities and explain the traditions.

I found it interesting that the visitors' fee was given to a matriarch in each tribe, who then divided it up amongst the families, ensuring grain or necessary goods would be purchased and not alcohol. The charge included a small fee for taking photos, which worked well for both parties. It saved any disputes or haggling, and also discouraged children from begging.

The varied landscapes were breathtaking as we trundled south through dry open savannah on a dirt road, that would soon wind upwards to forested hills of pine and eucalyptus, then descend to lush green pasturelands. African roads are never quiet or dull, and people appeared out of nowhere. Groups of smiling youngsters ran to the roadside waggling hips to entertain us, or if further away, would wave and jump up in the air. It was mainly children who tended the herds of goats or Zebu cattle with their distinctive hump. Gaily-clad women headed for distant wells and hamlets, elegantly balancing water containers or sacks of goods on their heads.

We visited the village of Dorze, famous for its weaving of colourful textiles, done by the men in a little cooperative factory set up by NGOs (non-governmental organisations). Rustic wooden looms were scattered about a shed floor bedded with banana fronds, and I noticed a little boy of about ten skillfully weaving in the corner, too preoccupied to glance up. The use of child labour is commonplace in many African countries and will be slow to change in villages where few children can be freed to attend school.

In the open, I observed two women spin wool, so deft and nimble and all the while scolding toddlers who played with the fluffy pile nearby. One woman signalled to me to have a go, but I couldn't even hold the spinning top properly, never mind twirl it quickly, and both of them burst into peals of laughter. They looked happy in their work.

However, it was the houses that flabbergasted me. I'd seen nothing like them before. They had the appearance of large towering baskets, some on two levels, woven from sturdy bamboo canes and thatched with leaves from the 'false banana' plant called *enset*. There were slatted vents in the bamboo roof to release smoke from the stone hearth that was central on the immaculately swept dirt floor. The creatively plaited walls had hanging gourds and cooking calabashes, or strips of drying animal skin, and a bamboo bench circled the perimeter. Many dwellings had partitions where animals slept to keep the place warm. I was surprised to see no item from our modern world or any canned goods from a store. Despite the smoke being a deterrent, the houses eventually get overrun by termites, and the problem is quickly resolved by chopping off the bottom and lifting it to a new location!

We learned from our local guide Jonah that the *enset* plants growing everywhere as a lush backdrop to the village have multiple uses. The roots make a porridge called *bullo,* which nourishes pregnant women. The fibrous leaves are scraped and the green mush fermented for six months until it turns white, then this is mixed with water and kneaded into flatbread. We passed a group of women cooking this bread on an open fire between two banana leaves, and they gave us some to taste dipped in a thick paste that had me quickly grabbing my water bottle. Ethiopians love their hot spices that include chillies and garlic, and I should have been more careful.

A few men arrived, and the scene quickly turned into a comedy show when the local hooch *araki,* was passed around in a calabash gourd to shouts of *Yoho, Yoho!,* the toasting chant. This sorghum drink also contained onion and garlic, and I politely pretended to sip, while Hans the German seemed to relish the stuff. The villagers were a fun lot and enjoyed these interactions, not just as a source of income, but to proudly demonstrate their sustainable lifestyle.

The entire region was animist, and as cattle herders Jonah informed us that the tribes congregate in September for a mass slaughter of their beasts, to feast on raw beef and arrange marriage alliances.

Although exposed to many different customs when travelling, it was often challenging for me not to judge other traditions. I was aware that Ethiopia had a very high rate of female genital circumcision (FGM), despite it being declared illegal by the Government in 2004. I had visited a medical facility in Addis Ababa, dealing with the horrific ongoing medical complications of this cruel practice that is bluntly a cultural effort to control female sexuality. FGM is recognised globally as a human rights violation, but it takes a long time to undo the tradition of centuries. The practice is still widespread in the Omo Valley, and unless a young girl is circumcised, generally around the age of ten or twelve, she can't marry, and her father won't receive her bride price.

Driving further south, we entered Mogo National Park for a short while, but sadly most of the game in this area had been poached out, and we just spotted a lonely jackal slinking away in the distance. I loved it when we had to brake suddenly in the middle of nowhere and allow a plodding turtle to cross the road.

On reaching the Omo River, the local wooden canoes for ferrying passengers across were a peculiar sight. They resembled curvy peanut shells split in half, each manned by a teenage boy in a generic uniform of brightly coloured T-shirt and board shorts, and bearing a long pole for the crossing. The boys were from the Dassenach tribe who practise flood retreat cultivation by the riverbank, growing sorghum after the rains. Jonah told us that trendy youth are abandoning traditional dress for Western-style clothing.

It was a striking contrast to our arrival at the Mursi settlement nearby where life is all about cattle. A small group of men strode towards our jeep, immediately striking in their tall stature with clay-painted torsos and faces. They wore blankets, and one or two had an AK47 slung over his shoulder while the others held long polished sticks.

However, it was the young women to their left towards which my eyes gravitated. I only briefly noted the colourful dress and adornment, but my gaze froze in horror at the sight of their lip plates. Despite having seen photos previously in a cultural magazine, I found the reality grotesque. As I stared, one girl noticed and proceeded to remove her plate, leaving her lip swinging in a pendulous flap of flesh below the jawline. She laughed then, showing a mouth with some missing teeth.

Tsege, the driver, introduced us to the Chief, who informed us that he had five wives and 35 children. The proud man grinned broadly, stretching the pattern of scar marks around his temples. These were a mark of his royal lineage, but we learned that scarification was common in both sexes, the men having it done on their shoulders only after demonstrating their hunting skill.

In females, the knobbly scars were mostly on the chest and considered sensuous and desirable to the men. I cringed on hearing how it's performed with a knife or razor blade, and afterwards, hot ash is applied to the cuts to infect the wound and promote scar tissue deliberately.

The Chief's son Kebe spoke a little English and led us to a simple beehive hut, with no openings other than a low door. We squatted in the clearing outside, and naked children came running excitedly in a cloud of dust to check out the visitors. The faces on the motley crew around us lacked the warmth and humour of the Dorze, but Tsege had warned us that the Mursi was an aggressive and hostile tribe — the men famous for fierce stick fighting that was now illegal but still happened. We'd been advised to visit the settlement early in the day before the drinking started and conflicts began.

'What is the tradition of the lip plates?' I asked. 'Is it for decoration purposes only?' Kebe replied that the lip is cut in young girls around the age of ten, and stretched over time until a clay plate of 12 centimetres can be inserted. Bigger ones attract a higher bride price in cattle. At the same time, four lower teeth get extracted, and some girls choose to have their earlobes extended. I later researched the origin of the lip plates, and one theory is that in the past, the disfigurement discouraged slave raiders.

The Mursi women mostly wore a strip of coloured cloth tied on one shoulder, and a few were bare-breasted wearing goatskins around the waist. They adorned themselves with an array of beaded or metal bands on both arms and legs, and all had shaved patterned hairstyles.

However, it was the headgear that was a work of art worthy of awards. One young mother who carried a baby sported two warthog tusks arising from a bird's nest of twigs on the crown of her head and had two painted gourds weighing it down on either side like massive earrings. It was extraordinary. Another young teen modelled a bonnet of what looked like shrivelled pomegranates or other fruit, bound under the chin with multiple straps of plastic beads. It seemed to me that it was carnival time with the Mursi ladies all year round!

We were free to wander about, and an older wrinkled woman beckoned me over. She was wearing one goatskin as a skirt and wore another draped over her shoulders, bound in front with a decorated leather strap. She

The Omo Valley, Ethiopia

sported a fine feather plume in her hair, fastened to a shell headband. Her demeanour was confident and proud as she signalled to me to enter her hut nearby. It was completely bare, with only a few black cooking pots around the embers of a fire.

The adornment of the person took precedence over the home. The Mursi are considered one of the wealthiest tribes in the area, but it is not money that is of value to them but cattle and female offspring, whose bridewealth will purchase more cattle. We sat for a few moments on the dirt floor, two women of similar age, yet worlds apart and each took the measure of the other in silence. It was a poignant moment.

Our group were silent on the journey back to our accommodation, each one reflecting on the diversity of the day. I found myself questioning progress and development using western models. How can conditions be improved without destroying traditional cultural practices and sustainable ways of living, without allowing greed and exploitation to take over?

And the role of the traveller? Perhaps to observe, accept and not judge.

ST PATRICK'S DAY IN A BROTHEL

The 17th March is probably the only day in the year when I will wear green and go in search of some 'Irishness' as an opportunity to take pride in my nationality and celebrate the national holiday. Of course, this usually involves raising the glass and imbibing a touch of the dark stuff if you're a Guinness lover. Irish bars are widespread, although few are authentic — and over the years I've donned a ridiculous leprechaun hat in Beijing, Sydney, Dubai and many other places.

However, the situation wasn't looking good in 2017 as I journeyed through the depths of the West African rainforest in the highlands of Fouta Djalon, en route to Conakry, the capital of French-speaking Guinea. The day commenced before dawn in the wild north, where I was the last touted passenger to squeeze into the rear of a *sept place,* a battered communal taxi with its particular etiquette. No foreigner ever gets to sit in the prized front seat, reserved for some chatty Big Shot male willing to pay the extra for leg comfort and keep the driver amused.

The next choice seats are by the window, to avail of fresh air and a view, but usually, slim, wiry men get these spots. A Muslim country, the women are squeezed in together and in Africa are not wiry but generally well endowed — often with a baby on the lap, lots of bags and perhaps a chicken somewhere. I was seated next to two colourful Fula mamas, one breastfeeding a baby, a cute toddler crouched on the floor and the sorry chickens on the roof.

Except for Big Shot and the driver chatting up front, there was silence in the rear until my companions became acquainted. We had ample time as it was a 14-hour journey to Conakry. Towards dawn, we pulled off the road, and everyone disembarked for morning prayers in the direction of Mecca. While they prostrated on prayer mats, I watched a dusty sunrise over the distant hills. The heat was getting up, and I already felt gritty as sweat mixed with red dust. I would soon feel embarrassed looking so scruffy, as Africans always look fresh and relaxed in sweltering temperatures, dressed in immaculate neatly-pressed clothing.

We made frequent stops for a group male pee and smokes by the roadside — the blessings of a thick sarong handy for females, as scrubby bushes were thin on the ground to shelter behind. This scenario had to be the most blessed case of camaraderie amongst women that you wouldn't see in the west — a group of females on their hunkers doing their business chatting away regardless.

We pulled in at small roadside stands, where plastic sachets of water, chewing gum for the three-year-old and disposable nappies for junior were purchased. Sadly, at one stop, I noticed that the trussed chickens were now deceased, hanging limply from the roof rack.

Nearing a town or village the road was bitumen for a short distance but it was mostly a potholed dirt track, and the driver frequently swerved all over the place. There were many heavy oil tankers and lorries on the route, and with the windows not closing properly, a layer of red dust soon settled over us.

Passing through tidy palm-thatched villages; women swept dirt yards diligently, and threadbare clothing was drying in the heat. We made two pit stops during the day for goat stew or broiled chicken bones with little meat, but I stuck with my hard-boiled eggs, avocados and the excellent baguettes that are France's best legacy to their former colonies. It was not the time or place to risk getting the runs.

Before arriving in the big smoke, the other passengers wanted to stock up on country produce, and we regularly pulled in at piles of pineapples or cabbages by the roadside. More sacks were shoved into the already overflowing boot or tied up top with the dead chickens. I wondered when I would ever arrive.

Big Shot was a businessman who spoke good French and a little English. Curious, he interrogated me on the reason for my journey and wanted to know where I lived. Then he asked that problematic question I generally get asked. 'Why would a solo white woman travel in such a basic manner when I was rich and should be flying or hire a private taxi?' And finally, why didn't I have children and at least four grandchildren at my age, and where was my husband or son? Sometimes I invented a husband, but usually, I was honest and stated that I liked my independence. This statement quickly had the women nodding and grinning jubilantly, while the men scowled. A rebel in the ranks was contaminating their subversive women with western ways!

However, the banter with a foreign weirdo broke the monotony, and the wary strangers quickly became friendly companions sharing tidbits and stories as the hours passed. The little girl on the floor received her Grade 1 English lesson of 'Hello!', 'Thank you' and 'My name is Sarah' by the end of the day, and I mastered some culinary Fulani.

Once it was dark, I dozed off often to the soft humming conversation of the two women, and only the honking horns of heavy traffic woke me on the outskirts of Conakry. I started to get worried about my unknown bed for the night. Gradually, the others disembarked in the suburbs, where family members met them, and there was a loneliness about the dark after all jumped ship. I was left with the driver who spoke little French and no English. Before leaving, Big Shot explained to him that I wanted to be dropped at a cheap hotel, anywhere where I could put my head down for the night.

Of course, much gets lost in translation, and I got the impression that the driver was a country bumpkin, unfamiliar with the city suburbs or what I wanted. The streets narrowed and got darker and dodgier as we detoured off a side road into a dimly lit hotel compound.

The patron approached the taxi and offered to show me the rooms, as a group of men in the courtyard eyed me up carefully. Inside it was a dingy joint with curtained alcoves off a central area, and I suddenly realised that I was in a brothel, as a few moans emerged from a dark corner. I sensed that the two men were negotiating a cunning deal and that the driver was expecting to share a room with me for the night! He probably usually slept in his taxi and picked up a fresh passenger load in the early morning, so a comfortable bed with an 'auld one', and maybe something extra, would be a vast improvement!

I gestured to the driver that the place wasn't suitable and I insisted on going elsewhere, bidding *adieu* to the disappointed patron. I was nearly prepared at this stage to use my credit card at the Hilton!

We drove back to a better lit area and of course now, the rejected driver was ready to dump me anywhere. Catching sight of a woman at a corner, I asked him to stop, and she pointed us to a cheap hotel down the street. Hotel Marise, advertised as *toute confortable — avec discretion* said it all, but it looked a whole lot better than the doss house we had just left. The Madam scrutinised me carefully and explained in French that the room rates were by the hour. I was now desperate and close to tears, so after some wrangling and pleading, we agreed on an extortionate rate on the condition that I check out by 7 am in time for the cleaners.

She passed me over to a security man, who led me down a dingy corridor where loud TVs resounded from the rooms, typical of course, as I had ended up in a few brothels before on my journeys. It drowns out the erotic sounds of the night and keeps both the disappointed and satisfied clients entertained.

Room 5, in the middle of the corridor, was my lot for the night. I immediately checked the bed linen, but I always carry a lightweight silk liner for just such occasions. I also noticed that the TV didn't work, but I was too tired to be fussed, and asked Francois, a friendly young guy at the front desk if he could fetch me a cold beer.

He kept calling me 'Mammy' and probably equated me with his grandmother, but I was delighted when he returned in ten minutes with an icy cold bottle of Skol. There was no key to my room, so I bolted the door after him and cast my eye about at the shabby un-chic wallpaper, tested the bed which creaked — but that wouldn't be bothering me. A wad of old purple chewing gum stuck to the bedpost, and two condoms sat on the locker next to the bed.

It was 11 pm on St Patrick's night, and as I took a deep swig of the beer, I thought —

Well, Slainte and Happy St Patrick's Day Gerdette! This is unique — there will never be one like this again, but at least it makes a good story!

And the concert soon started through the thin wall on both sides, the rhythmic creaks ever quickening and the moans reaching a crescendo of lust in unison.

Hail, glorious St Patrick, dear saint of our isle, On us thy poor children bestow a sweet smile.

THE DOOR OF NO RETURN

In the course of researching the Irish indentured servants deported to the sugar and tobacco plantations of the West Indies, I became curious about the slave trade, and its origins in West Africa. This cruel practice lasting for centuries helped build fortunes for many white colonists in the cities of Europe, and also contributed to the building of America.

Slavery had existed worldwide from ancient times, and was common in the Sahara region and along the Nile, often due to warfare and poverty. However, the triangular transatlantic slave trade begun by the Europeans to achieve maximum profit from the new colonies, significantly differed in that it was racialised. The ships sailed from ports in Europe — the labour was loaded in West Africa, offloaded in the West Indies, and spices, coffee and sugar were shipped back for the grand parlours of Europe. This horrific journey for many taken from their homelands in Africa was called the Middle Passage. It is hard to imagine that everyday items like pepper and coffee we take for granted today, were once luxury items, produced on the back of slave labour.

West Africans had a centuries-old thriving trade in salt and cotton with Arab and Berber merchants, and their skill in gold and metalwork was renowned and spread to Europe. The Portuguese arrived first in 1471 during the reign of Henry the Navigator, in search of gold and ivory. They built the castle of St George on a rocky outcrop near Elmina, on the coast of what is now Ghana in West Africa, initially as a trading post.

They bribed local chiefs, wary of permanent European settlement, with gifts of beads, alcohol and guns and struck deals with false promises. The construction of Elmina Castle displaced local villagers, and a revered animist site dedicated to a river god was destroyed. A familiar tale!

Within 50 years, there was a string of Elminas stretching along the new Gold Coast, 40 in Ghana alone, all similar in Crusader castle style. They were separated from local villages by a dry moat, and a strong bastion faced inland as a defence against invading tribes while cannon stood ready on the ramparts to attack pirate ships.

The French, English, Dutch and Spanish all gained a foothold in the greedy race for gold and these places had names like Fort James, Fort William, Fort Amsterdam, Fort Patience, and ironically, The Fort of Good Hope. Soon gold and ivory were forgotten as free labour was needed for the sugar cane, coffee and tobacco plantations of the Americas, the West Indies and the Caribbean. The forts became holding stations for thousands of Africans enslaved in abject misery — a new commodity labelled 'Black Ivory'.

My visit to Cape Coast Castle near Elmina, in 2017, left a profound sobering impression on me. The beautiful white-washed castle of towers and parapets sited on the pretty rocky coast with crashing waves below was beguiling. It was hard to believe that it once held such horror and unfathomable human suffering within its walls.

At the entrance, a guide told me how Africans were first kidnapped by slave merchants in villages sometimes hundreds of miles inland, and forcibly marched to the coast bound with ropes or chained to wooden yokes. Starved and abused on these gruelling journeys, any dignity remaining was taken from them on arrival at the forts. They were sold to the Europeans for guns, cheap goods and sometimes mere trifles and baubles. In Benin later, I learned of a case where two fit male slaves were the equivalent of a Dutch clay pipe.

While listening to the guide, it struck me that the kidnapped were treated like animals yet were husbands, mothers, and children with names. They belonged to the Yoruba, Igbo, and Akan tribes and in their home villages worked as farmers, shopkeepers, goldsmiths and musicians. They lived ordinary family lives that were suddenly ripped cruelly from under them.

Inside the fort, I descended underground into three vast dungeons, where older and younger men were separated, and the third contained the women and children. My eyes welled up as I looked at the line on the wall two feet up, which marked the level of the floor before they started digging during restoration. This line represented the layer of dried and hardened excrement that had built up on the ground over the years. It was horrendous to hear that up to a thousand slaves ate, slept and survived in their urine and faeces, often for months on end before boarding the slave ship. You could see scratch marks clearly on the walls from the desperate dying or those getting crushed in the horde.

I felt suddenly disgusted and ashamed to be a white person, unbelieving that any human could inflict this on another. Yet this happened, and what must it have been like for those enduring such a hell? What went through their minds as they wallowed here in filth for months, not knowing what the future held for them or where they were going?

I walked along a dank, musty corridor to another grim feature in the fort, the 'Door of No Return'. Along the entire coastline, there were many of these doors fronting the open sea through which the slaves walked their final steps on African soil, boarding the ships for a life of servitude in an alien land, from where they would never return.

The slave ships were adapted from former merchant vessels and had broad decks with large kettles for cooking, as space below was maximised to contain as many slaves as possible. Often 500-600 bodies were crammed into an area so low they sat between each other's legs, and couldn't change position either day or night. Before being loaded, the slaves were stripped, heads shaved, and examined from head to toe by the captain or surgeon, then segregated according to gender and age. Sometimes their bodies were branded like sheep, burnt with a red hot iron under the breasts or on the arm or buttocks. The men were packed together like sardines unable to move independently, secured with leg or neck irons to a neighbour and chained in pairs to plank beds.

On several ships, male slaves were laid on their stomachs and the females on their backs. These positions facilitated the sailors raping them on the voyage, and when the women fell pregnant, it was of commercial benefit that two slaves would be had for the price of one. As dehydration, dysentery, smallpox and scurvy spread rapidly in the airless unhygienic conditions without sanitation, it must have been pure hell for these pregnant women. Seasickness was common, and in the oppressive heat, suffocating men were desperate to extricate themselves from whoever they were shackled to and often killed each other fighting for more air. The dead were collected and thrown overboard.

A meagre diet of rice, beans, yams or palm oil was dished out to the slaves — just sufficient to ensure their survival for the markets of the New World, but sometimes the slaves starved, as feeding the sailors was always a priority. Those who went on hunger strike hoping to die were force-fed with an instrument called a *speculum oris* which kept the mouth open. Occasionally, the slaves were allowed sporadic exercise periods on deck but also forced to sing and dance to entertain the sailors. Any thought of jumping overboard to end it all was thwarted by netting along the side of the deck.

Merciless jailors kept order at all times and frequently flogged offenders with the twisted thongs or unravelled ropes called the 'cat o' nine tails',

The Door of No Return

Cape Coast Castle, Ghana

drawing blood after only a few lashes and causing infections in the steamy conditions below deck.

Depending on winds and conditions at sea, the Middle Passage often lasted as long as three months. It was appalling to learn that for each slave shipment arriving in the New World, only two-thirds of the captives survived. A third died on the march to the coast, imprisoned in the forts or on the ship itself.

On arrival in Virginia, Jamaica or Barbados, the emaciated slaves lost their identities. With their African names too difficult to pronounce, they were given the surnames of European foremen or plantation owners. Having met the descendants of slaves in Montserrat, I felt despondent now witnessing what their ancestors had endured and lost.

Leaving the horror of the fort, imagine the contrast of the governor's house standing regally in the hinterland, with its original manicured gardens and elegant sea-facing verandas. I shuddered at the fine dining and balls that would have taken place here, whilst the miserable hordes in captivity nearby fought over scraps of food, water and air. The slave rations were often only a slice of bread daily. Those who died were thrown into the moat to be eaten by crocodiles. Next to the grand colonial buildings stood a church where the Europeans professed to be Christian. Reared a strict Catholic, I found such hypocrisy of the established church appalling, yet it was commonplace.

I felt a sudden urge to escape the sickening horror of what I'd seen and learnt at the old slavery fort and walked quickly back to the village. It left me reflecting on the chance of birth and white privilege. Despite the initial abolition of slavery in 1807, yet not enforced until many years later, true equality among the races has never been achieved.

Millions of black people today still suffer the yoke of subjugation and oppression borne of white-perceived supremacy.

TRASHY BAGS AND
FANTASY COFFINS

It was a joy to return to Accra after the gruesome visit to the slave forts of the Cape Coast. The memory of the dark dungeons and tortured lives haunted me. Now I was back in this crazy city that never sleeps, and staying at the Sleepy Hippo hostel, near the infamous Nkrumah Circle.

This sprawling transport hub is one of those spaghetti junctions that drive you mad and negotiating the warren of overpasses, underground tunnels and multiple exits ate into the day's sightseeing. I walked around in circles many times, getting more hot and bothered only to end up back where I'd started.

I frequently floundered in the narrow laneways, bursting with traders and a go-ahead stream of humanity, yet I found favourite quiet spots to sit with a cold juice and take stock. Happy Ghanaian women sat stirring black cooking pots from which delicious smells emanated, and many knowingly smiled as I passed them for the umpteenth time. It was always a relief to get back to Tip Toe alley, a familiar landmark close to my hostel. In the early evening, I would sit and chat with Alyssa, a friendly street vendor who made delicious fresh juices and inquired about my wanderings.

The street level at Nkrumah was mayhem, and I was easy prey for the neurotic touts putting bums on seats in the hundreds of overcrowded *trotros*. These 'fill-up-and-go' minivans were cramped sweat boxes dispersing human ants to the suburbs, and I studied the essential intricate sign language carefully. Jabbing an index finger in the air meant you were travelling far, pointing it downwards indicated a short trip and the thumb demonstrated the direction! The inside language was just as amusing; the knock on the van frame a signal to stop; the driver's mate clinking coins a sign to pay up; and the constant snake-like hisses from commuters the way to attract the driver's attention.

Ghana, with its relatively safe reputation and English-speaking appeal, has the most NGO (non-governmental organisation) projects of any West African country. The Sleepy Hippo was full of enthusiastic young British volunteers on a gap year, working in schools and orphanages in disadvantaged regions. I spent a day at one such laudable project called 'Porridge and Pens' which fed and provided an education to street kids. It was distressing to discover how many disabled children were abandoned by their families and ended up in orphanages.

However, another project also grabbed my attention. One morning at the hostel reception, I noticed plastic shoulder bags displayed in the corner, and I recognised the standard patterned plastic water sachets used everywhere. I recalled seeing an older man collecting plastic waste from the gutter the previous day and had wondered what he was doing. I inspected the satchel, noticing the beautiful lining with the colourful waxed *kente* cloth worn by many women in Ghana. In bold colours and wild geometric designs, this cloth is symbolic of the royal Ashanti tribe, and I was fascinated by its creative blending with the plastic.

'Where are these made, Kwabela?' I inquired of the young manager. 'They're from the Trashy Bag factory here in Accra. Quirky, yes?' he replied. I agreed wholeheartedly and asked if there was a retail store I could visit, but he told me the small factory was in a private house. 'It's so clever and creative,' I said while admiring the neat stitching and design and was delighted when Kwabela looked up the address for me.

I headed out early the following morning for my daily battle with Nkrumah Circle, and two *trotros* later arrived at Santana Road in the north of the city. It took a while to find this ordinary house, identifiable by the mountain of dirty plastic bags lying in the yard and cleaned ones spread on the concrete drying in the sun.

When I entered, I found a group of four women chatting happily in the sunshine, all the while pedalling away on manual sewing machines. The industrious whirr and talk ceased as they looked in my direction.

'Hi, I'm sorry to intrude, but I've seen your bags at my hostel, and I'm really interested in your recycling project. It's amazing.' They all smiled, and one woman rose to greet me. 'Hi, I'm Esi. Welcome! I'll introduce you to the manager.'

She led me inside to a treasure trove of recycled plastic products where I met Kobe, busy discussing designs and fabrics with an elegant lady swathed in rust and orange kente cloth. She looked dressed for the catwalk. While waiting for them to finish, I browsed through the unique assortment of laptop bags, cosmetic bags, wallets, backpacks and other innovative items.

I particularly admired a laptop bag where the printing on the plastic surface had the logos *Holy Touch* and *Cascade Mineral Water* strategically placed to catch the eye. It was foam-padded, and the snappy check-fabric lining had the usual pocket inserts, a few with velcro. Everything was so professionally assembled.

'Can I help you?' Kobe smiled, aware he had an enthusiastic customer, and he continued to explain that the UK/Ghana venture had been operating for nine years already and gave me a leaflet outlining the goals and objectives. 'We had to do something about the plastic crisis,' he said. 'It was choking the city drains and causing flooding and the spread of disease.'

The non-biodegradable plastic sachets were cheaper than plastic water bottles and typically dumped or burned when used. Kobe explained that they also recycled thicker plastic ice-cream and juice sachets and made sturdier shopping bags from these. 'You can put bricks in this,' he laughed, lifting one off a stand nearby. 'You should have seen our fashion show *Fantastic in Plastic*. It was a riot.'

Seemingly for the show, a wedding couple were kitted out entirely in recycled plastic; the groom was wearing an evening suit, complete with tails and a top hat, groovy sunglasses and even plastic footwear. The bride modelled a fitted dress with a train, and the veil was adorned with pink bows, all made from plastic. I tried to imagine how quirky and elaborate this would have looked!

'That wedding ensemble would be popular in Ireland,' I said. 'You could just wipe the wine spills off with a dishcloth!' Kobe burst into peals of laughter. 'Perhaps that's why a few American celebrities have purchased the outfits,' he retorted. The Ghanaian people have a great sense of humour and fun, and I found it inspiring that their innovation combined with a passion for keeping their city streets free of litter.

I learned that this eco-friendly social enterprise employed 40 people; street collectors, those who washed the bags, the stitchers, and admin and design staff in the background. The collectors used recycled fertiliser bags which were donated by agricultural suppliers. Each sack held 20 kilograms in weight, and the collectors were paid by the kilo. It was often their only source of income, and several earned $US70 a week in a country where the monthly average was $US100. Now I understood why the older man was collecting plastic from the gutters.

The filled sacks were delivered to the factory daily, and quality control took place in the yard — dirty and torn sachets discarded and the others manually washed in basins of soap and water, then dried in the sun. The company also recycled old billboards, which dominate the skyline in Accra and are frequently changed.

When dry, the sewing groups stitched the sheets of plastic together, even making shower curtains. I was astonished to hear they also manufactured plastic baby carriers, which allowed young mothers to work and mind their babies at the same time.

It was so difficult choosing which of the many cool items to purchase. I left the Trashy Bag Factory feeling uplifted by this sustainable project that should be a model worldwide.

My beautiful satchel, made from dirty street trash, now holds my most valuable possessions such as my passport and important documents and is my 'ready-to-run' bag in an emergency.

***

On the afternoon of the trashy bag discovery, I continued my creative tour of Accra by heading out to Teshie, a small fishing village on the coast — in search of coffins! It would prove to be a far from morbid experience and was more the equivalent of visiting an art exhibition.

Funerals are big business in Ghana, frequently lasting for days, and are an extravagant celebration of food, entertainment and ceremony that can cost a year's salary. The deceased's social status is represented in the size of the funeral and the elaborateness of the coffin. I'd seen two of these fantastic coffins exhibited in the British Museum and had always wondered at the origins of such unique artworks.

Ghana is one of the most religious countries in the world and is the only country in West Africa, where Christians outnumber Muslims. In addition to the usual denominations introduced by European colonialists and missionaries, it was awash with American evangelical churches. People seemed compelled to demonstrate their faith in everyday life, and the eccentric custom of naming businesses after religious sayings was widespread.

When the *trotro* was delayed in traffic jams on the road to Teshie, this unintentional humorous practice entertained me. I passed the *Talk to Jesus Phone Shop,* then *The God Blessing School* and I desperately tried to get a photo of the *Virgin Conception of Mary Bar*, to name but a few. It was easy to become desensitised after a time and recoil at the plainness of *Joe's Fried Chicken Joint.*

I played a game with myself, inventing witty names for the coffin shops. Perhaps, *Coffins to Die For, Forever after Caskets,* or *Jesus Loves your Taste?*

The Teshie community are mostly from the Ga tribe. They believe that the spirits of the dead roam for a certain period after death, before joining the ancestral spirits in the sky. These restless spirits have to be appeased; otherwise they cause misfortune or death. Hence the tradition to send the deceased off in style to the afterlife. Ga chiefs used to be buried in decorated

The Rocket!

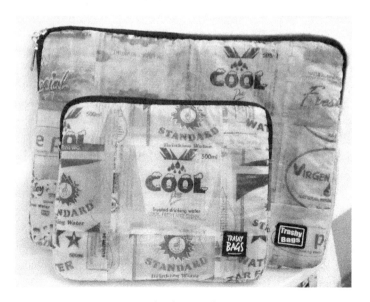

Trashy bag, Ghana

palanquins, and this evolved into a trend for fantasy coffins in the 1950s when a particular artist called Paa Joe became more creative.

It was hot and humid when I arrived in Teshie, and it took a while to find the coffin workshop. Just like the trashy bag factory, it was located in the backyard of an ordinary two-storey house. When I walked in, a young guy in shorts and a Dallas Cowboys T-shirt approached me.

'What can I do for you, Mam? You want to buy a coffin?' he inquired. I laughed, thinking perhaps it could go in the oversize-luggage section on the plane and make an excellent storage trunk until the grim reaper came for me.

Ebo was the son of the owner and explained that coffin making had been in his family for three generations. They used to be fishermen, but the coffin industry proved much more lucrative. We walked over to where a youth was carving out a slender slab of wood, and it looked like very painstaking labour. His companion lay stretched across the coffin dozing!

'It's going to be a rocket,' Ebo told me. I chuckled at this and said I knew someone in Australia who had their ashes rocketed into the sky in a firework, with the Elton John hit *Rocket Man* blasting out during the firework display. Ebo had a good guffaw at this.

'This rocket will be buried, and last a little longer,' he replied. I was astonished to learn that the coffin cost $US700, nearly a year's wages. He brought me upstairs to the showroom, and I ogled at the eccentricity of it all. A giant red casket sat there in the shape of a red chilli pepper.

'Haha, someone must like curry,' I laughed. Another Corona bottle coffin was newly painted, while a Canon camera coffin gathered dust in the corner. An assortment of tropical fish caskets painted in vibrant colours lay about, and apparently, these were very popular with the local fisherfolk. It was positively a fantasy collection and much cheerier than the dull, ordinary wooden boxes I was familiar with at home.

Ebo explained that in the Ashanti language, fantasy coffins are called *abebuu adekau,* and many Ghanaians living overseas ordered them. Foreigners and a few celebrities who'd seen them at exhibitions also commissioned their favourite style. Both President Jimmy Carter and Kofi Annan had succumbed to the eccentric tradition. I was fascinated to hear that sometimes only coffins in the design of the Bible were allowed in the Christian churches in Accra. Ebo was a mine of information, very entertaining and clearly loved his trade.

I left Teshie bemused, and it set me pondering on my eventual demise. What symbolic coffin could represent my earthly existence and see me off to the next life in style?

Would it be a toss-up between a bottle of good Bordeaux wine and a Toblerone bar?

HITCHING THE PAMIRS

The bus dropped me in the village of Baetor, the end of the road. It was little more than a hamlet, and not much was stirring except the odd cart on the way to cornfields. The curious drivers bade me *'Salaam'* with a nod. The long straight road stretched to the horizon lacking any shade, so I squatted under the last tree in the village, knowing the sun would soon beat relentlessly down. I was on the edge of the Pamirs in Kyrgyzstan, hoping to cross the mountains to the Fergana valley by a short route, and visit the last authentic silk factory in operation.

I hadn't hitched in a while but always felt safe in a Muslim country, where age is respected. I would just be another granny needing to get somewhere. It was a region where women are old at 45. And if nothing came in a while, I could always return on the next bus. The route was one of the many branches of the ancient Silk Road, where in times past, the traveller kept pace with the camel. I too was in no hurry.

One or two dilapidated cars slowed, the drivers signalling that they were only going a few kilometres down the road to their homesteads. I didn't want to get stuck in the middle of nowhere, so I declined politely. Then a sizeable canvas-backed truck pulled in with what looked like grandparents and a child in it. 'Kazerman?' I inquired, and the driver nodded while rubbing his fingers together, an international language I understood. 'Dollars?' and we agreed on a fuel contribution. His spritely wife hopped into the back with the boy, and the trio inquisitively sized me up.

'Jo,' I introduced myself and smiled. 'From Ireland' — which usually gets the conversation going although people seldom know where it is. The young boy looked to be 10 or 11, old enough to have some amusement with so I took my phone out and went into 'Google translate', my new toy on this trip. Russian is the common lingua franca other than local Kyrgyz dialects, but these days English has replaced it at school for the younger generation.

Young Amir rose to the occasion much to his grandmother's delight at the unexpected English lesson. 'Your grandparents?' I inquired. He blushed, embarrassed. 'No, my parents.' His mother got the gist and chuckled, indicating Amir was the runt of the litter or a late mistake.

I soon established that the mother Rayana was a doctor, who worked in a busy clinic in the north practising respiratory medicine. I had misjudged her age before as she was probably only in her early 50s, her face unlined with striking Mongol eyes and she wore a stylish floral green *shalwar kameez* with matching headscarf. The boy sported the white Muslim skull cap, and his father Ali had the look of a fierce Pathan fighter with a hennaed beard and a *keffiyeh* scarf topping his traditional baggy tunic. It was a surprise to learn he was a bee-keeper, and with the help of Google, he told me they were fetching new hives from the southern mountain slopes where different herbs grew.

We'd only driven ten minutes when we detoured onto a rough gravel track, and the father Ali mimed that he needed to pray. All became clear as we stopped at a war memorial. 'My father and uncles killed,' he declared sorrowfully. The place was the site of a major armed clash between Islamic Uzbek forces and the Kyrgyz military during border disputes. The family stood silently, and I paid my respects with them — an opportunity in such a lonely outpost to reflect on my deceased ancestors.

After our respite, the road climbed slowly through a desolate grey landscape, and later descended to the Naryn River, meandering gracefully through a peaceful valley. Poplar and willow trees lined the banks, and Ali parked under the welcome shade. I gathered that it was lunchtime as Rayana fetched a few baskets from the back and young Amir grinned at me. 'Eat, eat,' he gestured with his hands. I indicated that I had some snacks with me, but they would have none of it — hospitality to strangers being paramount.

We washed our hands in the river, and Rayana spread a checkered cloth on a grassy patch, laying out a spread of garden produce with sharp knives to help ourselves. It was reminiscent of an organic market stall; a bunch of shallots, large juicy tomatoes, gnarled cucumbers, a bowl of olives and a slab of smelly goat's cheese. Finally, a cut of fatty meat appeared, usually not eaten until evening time, but offered to a guest. Before she sliced the tastiest morsel of fat for me, I made my usual apologies for being a vegetarian, not wanting to offend. Amir poured orange soda into plastic cups for everyone, and it was a contented pastoral scene worthy of a landscape artist.

After lunch, the route ascended rapidly, and the ridge of jagged peaks loomed closer, patches of snow in the ravines. Everywhere was green now with vegetation and as Ali slowed to manoeuvre the many hairpin bends, I caught the waft of wild herbs perfuming the air.

In the early afternoon, our driver indicated he was tired, miming that it was nap time. I was beginning to despair of ever reaching Kazerman before dark but smiled pleasantly and nodded agreeably. We had only passed one other lorry on the road, so I had few choices. Rayana, Amir and I leapt out to stretch our legs while Ali spread himself out in the back and was soon fast asleep.

Nearby, a rocky stream gushed down from the mountainside and Rayana filled the empty drink bottles from its icy depths. The air smelt of wild garlic and sage — both common in these parts.

'Come, Jo,' Amir beckoned and started climbing up a narrow goat path. I was his best buddy by now. Rayana stretched out on the grass to rest, but I clambered after the young boy, and he triumphantly grinned when he won the race to the top. We both sat companionably staring across to the high Pamirs, and a string of turquoise lakes broke up the deep valley below. There wasn't a human settlement in sight. We both took selfies and photos of each other and descended back down a different rocky path. When I inquired if he could sing Amir broke into an Asian ditty while I hummed an Irish tune.

Mother was in slumber in the sage, and loud snoring echoed from the truck, so it looked like we were going nowhere fast. The boy and I built a stone dam in the stream and picked bunches of wild celery growing near to munch on as the afternoon heat waned.

In a while, we trundled slowly onwards on the deteriorating road, and it was scary looking at the steep drop on my side. I was pleased that Ali seemed refreshed after his siesta and was paying attention.

We were now in proper *jailoo* terrain, where the herders decamp to summer pastures with their families. Approaching a cluster of yurts, Ali pulled in once more, pointed towards them and twiddled the fingers at me again. I got the message loud and clear — the tab was on me for afternoon tea!

The family *salaamed* us politely, delighted at the custom, and welcoming to a foreigner. They invited us into their yurt, the walls decorated with red latticework and sporting Alpine scenes from an old calendar. The customary spread lay on a low table, bowls of thick fresh cream and small dishes of apricot and mulberry conserve, with a platter of plump bread not long off the fire. The daughter rekindled the dung fire outside for *chay* which takes time to brew at altitude. Meanwhile, it was

Life in the Pamirs

Ladies of the Pamirs, Kyrgyzstan

the custom to hand round bowls of *kumis*, fermented mare's milk, as we settled ourselves comfortably on the carpet. This *kumis* was particularly sour, and I struggled not to grimace, but knowing it was excellent for my health, I sipped it slowly while nodding in appreciation.

Small talk ensued in Kyrgyz on the purpose of the 'townies' journey, on bees, and the stranger from Ireland. Granny in the corner stared at me as if I was an alien — she was washing bunches of mountain greenery for the pot, and I noticed a dead marmot lying on the floor near her. Amir and I filled the gaps and answered queries with Google assistance. The sweet black tea arrived, and silence prevailed as we devoured the best afternoon tea I've ever had.

I settled the bill in local *somona* notes, adding a few. Rayana filled soft drink bottles with *kumis* to take home. On the hillside, a group of yaks and horses grazed contentedly beside roughly fenced animal pens, and I learned that the family would remain in the *jailoo* for some months yet. The herders owned two sturdy Kyrgyz horses, and on leaving, persuaded Amir and I to mount them, me somewhat wary with my new hip. Still, I was eager to have a photo taken and smiled, suddenly noticing the fast-fading daylight.

It was pitch black when we arrived in Kazerman two hours later although it was only 7 pm. I had dozed off after the rich feed in the yurt. By now, the family and I were firm friends, and they insisted on finding me safe lodgings before parting. Faces appeared in the dark, and figures emerged from nowhere, local curiosity stirred. We were given directions to a shabby looking hotel, and it was time for farewells.

Ali reluctantly took my dollars and wouldn't allow me to give Amir extra for sweets. The boy and I looked at each other sorrowfully, having formed a unique Google friendship. We hugged close, and the bee-keeper's truck then disappeared into the night.

I later found a small jar of honey shoved into the pocket of my rucksack.

THE MAGIC OF VENICE

The Venice Arts Biennale in 2019 had the title *May we Live in Interesting Times*. This phrase has long been cited as an ancient Chinese curse that invokes periods of uncertainty, crisis and turmoil — 'interesting times', exactly as the ones we live in today.

I was lucky to attend the 58th Biennale in this iconic city. It was my third visit to Venice, and as I wandered dreamily along its narrow paved streets and canals, I felt its allure envelop me as on previous occasions. The architectural smorgasbord was as magnificent as ever and free of traffic — the screech of gulls and church bells filled the air. I continually got lost in the labyrinth, but did it matter with a gelateria on each corner or a cosy bar to sip a prosecco and rest my weary feet?

The small hostel I was staying in further enhanced the magic of my stay. I breakfasted each morning outdoors in the autumnal freshness, fighting with a fat cat for the sunniest nook in the courtyard that fronted onto a tiny canal. Terracotta pots of overflowing geraniums and minty herbs adorned the ancient stone slabs, and the owners' boat was moored ready for a trip to the shops. Fortified by a good espresso, crusty rolls thickly spread with Nutella, and a backdrop of family banter in Veneziano, I was happily launched for a busy day at the Biennale.

Venice mesmerises visitors in normal times, however during the Biennale, 90 countries had national pavilions exhibiting contemporary art, and many decadent decaying palazzos opened their doors to reveal the splendour of former times. It was a delight to stumble on small parks and open spaces transformed into a visual paradise of lurid chromatic sculptures, elegant ballerinas and big-footed giants to amuse children.

The canal city is one of the most vulnerable places in the world, and much of the art on display was related to climate change with the goal that artists need to create on the same scale that society can destroy. The plight of refugees and the condition of indigenous peoples were dominant subjects. Typically one whose eyes glaze over after an hour in an art gallery, fueled by regular coffees, I hung in there totally absorbed for two whole days.

I was astonished at the diverse talent exhibited in innovative ways, and the enormous effort of the participating countries. Many exhibits were digital and interactive. Greta Thunberg's face was highly visible, and her alarming warning scrawled on billboards, 'I want you to behave like our house is on fire. Because it is'. How prophetic this was a short time later as Australia burned and images of scorched koalas and fleeing wildlife accosted us daily on television screens.

The Biennale highlighted the fragility of the world's ecosystems and prodded the global conscience to wake up fast. An Inuit production represented Canada, expressing their concerns for the expansion of mining in the Arctic Circle impacting on the environment and the Inuit lifestyle. New Zealand's audio exhibit was frightening as it consisted of three cell-phone towers resembling trees which broadcast 260 lengthy tables of what has vanished and is absent from our world. It played eight hours a day for six months without repeat, and after listening to a list for half an hour, I moved on with a feeling of despair.

As I rested by the waterside, a rusted old boat nearby caught my eye. I was horrified reading the plaque to learn it was a salvaged fishing vessel that had left Libya in 2015 carrying African refugees, who hoped for a better life in Europe. Over 800 people trapped in the ship's hold drowned in the worst maritime disaster in recent European history.

Seeing it right before me, brought the images from the television screen gruesomely to life, and I felt the loss and pain of those individuals who had dreams dashed. Although the other exhibits were thought-provoking, this one particularly goaded my conscience. I felt worn out but woken up to the plight of millions of refugees.

Near the vast Arsenale where the Biennale took place, a massive shining steel cruise ship was docked in the heart of the city and jolted my eye in the same way it does in Circular Quay, Sydney, blocking the magnificent vista of the Opera House. This apparition was like an artwork in itself, disgorging its scuttling horde of camera-toting visitors. Tourism was choking the city daily, and I heard that a tourist tax was about to be implemented.

I discovered a little *bacaro,* or stand up bar in a quiet piazza where locals communed after the tour groups had departed and I retreated there most evenings. Sipping a spritzer or introduced to a tart *bianco della casa,* the bustling signora circulated with a tray of *cicchetto,* a much more romantic name than my 'fish on toast'. Succulent morsels of squid, octopus and sardines were served on small slabs of polenta and tasted delicious. I soaked up the ambience from my quiet corner and was in my element. Sometimes the highs of a Vivaldi violin concerto drifting from the Museum of Music nearby broke the thread of conversation as all paused to listen.

How could anyone foretell that in November of the same year, Venice would experience its worst flooding since 1966, with massive waves from rising tides crashing into the city? Piazza San Marco was under water, and the bulk of businesses brought to their knees. By Christmas, the waters receded, and the aftermath of damaged buildings and mountains of trash was a nightmare to behold. When the tourists fled, the piazzas were eerily quiet and basilica doors closed. The gondoliers idled their days indoors, and Murano glass and lace shops pulled the shutters down.

After long protests against mass tourism and the offloading of cruise ships, the Venetians had their city to themselves to enjoy for a time. This loss of income must have been a double-edged sword for its inhabitants. In Venice, normally every twist of the gondolier's hips is captured on camera as he approaches the bridges, and the residents have little privacy to live their everyday lives.

However bad things are in troubled times, there are always positive events to balance the cup half empty to half full. In the absence of motorised transport churning up mud from the bottom of the canal, Venice's normally murky waters cleared and Nature took control, enjoying a breather from human impact. I heard reports that plant life blossomed, and shoals of small fish and scurrying crabs could be seen on the sandy seabed. For the first time in years, seaweed reappeared, and seabirds swooped for a feed of fish without the disturbance of chugging *vaporetti*. Ducks nested on paths once trodden by tourists' feet, and a warning sign appeared for pedestrians, 'Don't tread on the duck eggs!'.

Yet, as many times before, resilient Venetians emerged from their watery hibernation and cleaned up their beloved city. Vibrant Venice was back in business and all eagerly awaited the star event of the year — the Carnival in February, hoping for a turn in the tide of tourist dollars. This dazzling extravaganza featured revellers in painted masks and ball gowns entertaining the tourist hordes cruising the Grand Canal, and laughter and dance resonated in the historic piazzas.

Unfortunately, the festivities ended two days early as Italy's Covid-19 nightmare began. The real-life fear of this new pandemic replaced Thomas Mann's fictional 'Death in Venice' when a cholera epidemic raged through the city. The word quarantine is derived from the Italian *quaranta giorni*, meaning 40 days. In times of pestilence, ships arriving into Venice from infected ports were forced to sit at anchor for 40 days before offloading.

This remarkable city, once a major trading post at the western end of the Silk Road for centuries has a long history of overcoming pestilence and natural disasters. It has lived through many 'interesting times', and Venetians are always resilient in turning back the sweeping tides.

I know I will be enticed to succumb to the magic of Venice one more time.

Acknowledgements

My life as a writer began with a stranger called Lawrence buying my African masks on Gumtree and introducing me to SSOA — the Sydney School of Arts and Humanities. I am indebted to its Director, Dr Christine Williams, who encouraged me to write and make this book a reality. Over the course of mere months, she patiently mentored and smartened up a slovenly novice writer. I hope she will forgive me for retaining a few of my casual Irish mannerisms in the style that I feel give the stories authenticity. Thank you so much Christine, Lawrence and the other weekly SSOA members who kindly critiqued my writing.

Two of the stories were previously published in SSOA's Impressions magazine — 'A Hard Border' and 'First Encounters'. 'Kicking with Both Feet in Ulster' was published in the Irish Mountain Log, in Ireland.

Thank you to Tony Wheeler for reading my manuscript and kindly writing the Foreword to this book. It is much appreciated, and I owe him a cold beer!

Heartfelt thanks go to John Wedlick, whose support and help was unfailing, and for listening to my doubts and angst over small stuff. His fastidiousness and sharp eye were much appreciated fine-tuning my photographs.

To my younger trio of computer gurus, Andrew, Matthew and my cousin Sinead, thank you for keeping me sane and setting me on the right path after numerous tizzies on commas, em-dashes, paragraph breaks and the like. You opened up a whole new world of jargon that will prove invaluable for my next book — that hopefully will begin more ordered and structured.

I was fortunate to have a vast army of beavers worldwide who read chunks of the many versions of this book to offer advice and critiques. You know who you are, but I'd like to mention you all, and I apologise if I've left anyone out unintentionally. Thank you, Walter, Niamh, Padraig, Anne Clerkin, Dawn, Jayavati, Edel, Hugh, Carol, Ciaran, Maureen and Tony in Ireland; Liz and Dave, Phil and Frankie and Hazel in the UK; the Lewis family in New Zealand and here in Australia — Nita, Bronwyn, Tony, Eoin, Ann and Ciaran Cassidy, Marie, Jenny, Ruth and Michael, Anne Barclay, April, Roger and Leonie. Thank you, everyone, for your valued friendship, your support and the big nudge to put pen to paper at last.

The best souvenir from a life travelling has been the extraordinary people I've met along the way and the close friendships that continued long after, on Skype and WhatsApp when face-to-face reunions couldn't happen: Winnie and Brianna in Montserrat, Sylvia and Pam in Nova Scotia, my dear 'Mossad' friends Paulo, Carlos and Vitor in Lisbon, met on a broken-down bus on Ruta 40 in Argentina, Frankie and Phil who met me in a brothel hostel in Madagascar, Paul and Greti in Thailand, John in Ushuaia, Kathryn in Johannesburg and Janet and David in San Francisco.

To these and other dear friends who've been there forever, asking 'Where are you going next?' or 'How long are you around for?' and 'When are you off again?' — totally accepting of the transience of a mad 'womadic' friend. Thank you for always being there during the good and bad times, providing impromptu beds and lifts to and from airports, a glass of wine and a ready ear for the tales — for lasting the pace or even just keeping up with it!

Amongst these, I need to pay tribute to a very dear soulmate Catrina, who is sadly no longer with me, taken too early only months ago and how I miss her presence in my life. Always optimistic and encouraging, with a 'Go for it!' and 'Well done!' on her lips — I hope she's at peace and remembers the stories.

And of course, thank you to my family — the Rooneys and Reids everywhere and particularly, Hannah, Dara, Matthew and Andy who inspired this work and listened avidly to my travel stories over the years. It's now time to find your own, and I will reciprocate!

Go, lads and lassies — and see the world!

List of Colour Photographs

Front Cover

Sahara Dunes in Libya

Fatima selling kola nuts in Timbuktu, Mali

Back Cover
Left to Right, Top to Bottom

Hamer girl, Ethiopia

Young boy on the Amazon

Brianna, St Patrick's Day, Montserrat

Omo Valley girl, Ethiopia

King Penguin, Antarctica

Goat herder, Omo Valley, Ethiopia

Saddam Hussein, Iraq

Poppy the Gorilla, Rwanda

Muammar Gaddafi, Libya

Harpy Eagle, Guyana

Tungaware at Haiti orphanage

Mursi girl, Ethiopia

Cuddling a sloth, Guyana

The 'Cock-of-the-rock', Guyana

Lightning Source UK Ltd.
Milton Keynes UK
UKHW022319160621
385627UK00007B/211